THE NEMESIS OF POWER

GLOBALITIES
Series editor: Jeremy Black

GLOBALITIES is a series which reinterprets world history in a
concise yet thoughtful way, looking at major issues over large
time-spans and political spaces; such issues can be political,
ecological, scientific, technological or intellectual. Rather than
adopting a narrow chronological or geographical approach,
books in the series are conceptual in focus yet present an array of
historical data to justify their arguments. They often involve a
multi-disciplinary approach, juxtaposing different subject-areas
such as economics and religion or literature and politics.

In the same series

Why Wars Happen
Jeremy Black

A History of Language
Steven Roger Fischer

The Nemesis of Power

A History of International Relations Theories

HARALD KLEINSCHMIDT

REAKTION BOOKS

Published by Reaktion Books Ltd
79 Farringdon Road, London ECIM 3JU, UK
www.reaktionbooks.co.uk

First published 2000
Copyright © Harald Kleinschmidt 2000

Printed and bound in Great Britain by
St Edmundsbury Press Ltd, Bury St Edmunds, Suffolk

British Library Cataloguing in Publication Data:

Kleinschmidt, Harald
   The nemesis of power : a history of international relations
   theories. – (Globalities)
   1. International relations 2. International relations –
   History 3. International relations – Philosophy
   I. Title
   327.09

ISBN 1 86189 058 3

Contents

Preface

We live in a paradoxical world. We describe it as a world of states. But relations among these states are called international relations. How can relations among states be relations among nations? Since when has this been assumed to be the case? How do we have to define states and nations in order to be able to identify the one with the other? Since when have states existed? Since when have we organized nations?

These are problems which have a bearing on international theories, that is, the study of the ways we perceive, conceptualize and debate international relations. International relations are not identified everywhere in the world as relations among states. For example, for the one and a half billion or so people in East and Southeast Asia who use Chinese characters for communication, the graphemes for the equivalents of the English word 'international' (and its like in other European languages) do not refer to relations among nations but to relations 'across the edge of the country'. Thus, whereas the European tradition of international theories has evolved into a complex of thought which makes explicit relations among groups, people in East and Southeast Asia have tended to emphasize the spatial dimension of relations with other parts of the world. Hence international theories are not absolute but have developed historically; they constitute ever-changing patterns of thought of culturally specific origins. Therefore, answering questions about the nature of international relations demands a historical approach. The history of international theories addresses these questions in their temporal dimension. By using chronology as its guideline, it emphasizes change.

Unless we trace the processes that have brought about the current paradoxical terminology, we will be at a loss to understand the subject matter of international relations. This is also the case because the paradox that international relations are described in the West as relations among states is not confined to words. It also impinges upon the subject matter itself. The largest and most comprehensive international organization at present is the United Nations Organization (UNO). It unites nations, but it does so as an organization of states. It is committed to the preservation of peace among the peoples of the world but it is powerless in the face of wilful aggression emerging from, and with the support of, the governments of states. The UNO thus epitomizes a core problem of international relations and the theories about them: how can we organize a sustainable world in peace, with justice and equality? Who sets the criteria for sustainability? Who determines justice? Who assesses equality? There are few who do not see the urgent necessity for humankind to unite. But there are many who disagree about the principles according to which the unification should take place.

'Anarchical society' is the paradoxical expression which makes this dilemma explicit. It has been in use throughout much of the twentieth century and has denoted the clash between, on the one hand, the felt necessity of accepting general norms and rules valid everywhere in the world and, on the other, the recognition of the difficulty in establishing agreement about such norms and rules. We will hardly be able to solve this paradox unless we understand the conditions under which this clash has come into existence between the goal of constituting the unity of humankind and the difficult choice of means to implement it.

Placing theories under the rule of change seems to lead to another paradox. International theories, like all theories, purport to be true, and truth does not change. Indeed, the history of international theories relativizes, and it does so by revealing the unintended transience of theories. But this paradox is an apparent one because historicizing theories does not reduce their value. Instead, international theories remain important as means by which people in their own time reflected on the world at large and did so in efforts to approach the truth.

Like the history of international relations at large, the history of international theories has received scant scholarly attention during much of the twentieth century. Much of the work has had a teleological approach. Scholars working in the field have thus looked back on the past from the present trying to trace the roots of current international theories. The opposite strategy is also possible, namely to take a starting point in the past and to study the critical situations at which crucial decisions were made that have led to the present situation.

I have opted for the latter strategy, hoping that the account presented in this book will make clear the changes that have affected the making and communication of international theories. I have concentrated on European theories, keeping in mind that formulating and communicating international theories have never been the sole reserve of European culture. In attempting to contextualize European international theories, I have greatly benefited from the work of other scholars, most notably Jeremy Black of Exeter, and from the questions and comments of my students at the University of Tsukuba and the Tokyo University of Foreign Studies.

Introduction

No small praise should be attributed to the industry and skill
of Lorenzo de' Medici, so eminent amongst the ordinary citizens in the city of Florence that the affairs of that republic
were governed according to his counsels . . . Realizing that it
would be most dangerous to the Florentine Republic and to
himself if any of the major rulers should extend their area of
dominion, he carefully saw to it that the matters of Italy
should be maintained in a state of balance, not leaning more
toward one side than the other.[1]

Francesco Guicciardini (1483–1540), first a Florentine diplomat, then a papal administrator and finally the author of a
widely read *History of Italy*, began his work with this praise of
Lorenzo de' Medici (1448–1492), the powerful statesman of his
home city of Florence. In Guicciardini's account, Lorenzo
appears as a leader who never held high offices of state in his city
or elsewhere and whose power consisted in the balancing of the
powers of other rulers in order to preserve peace and stability in
Italy. Lorenzo received much credit for his power balancing as a
personal capability in which, in Guicciardini's view, he excelled
because it was somehow new and rare among his contemporaries and an ability that his successors did not share. To
Guicciardini, then, the power of a statesman acting in international relations was a personal gift rather than an institutional
capability, and its use was praiseworthy if it contributed to the
maintenance of some balance in a given area.

Since Guicciardini, Lorenzo's balancing capability has
received much attention. Alberico Gentili (1552–1608), a
Protestant Italian jurist who taught at the University of Oxford,
commented in 1598:

The maintenance of union among the atoms is dependent upon their equal distribution; and on the fact that one molecule is not surpassed in any respect by another. This it is which was the constant care of Lorenzo de' Medici, that wise man, friend of peace and father of peace, namely, that the balance of power should be maintained among the rulers of Italy. This he believed would give peace to Italy as indeed it did so long as he lived and preserved that state of affairs. Both the peace and the balance of power ended with him, great scion of the Medici and mighty bulwark of his native city and the rest of Italy. Is not this even to-day our concern that one man may not have supreme power and that all Europe may not submit to the rule of a single man?[2]

Gentili's account is based on Guicciardini's. Lorenzo appears as the master of balancing power in Italy, which breaks down with his death. But Gentili, the jurist, had more a principled interest in Lorenzo's politics than Guicciardini, the chronicler. Where Guicciardini was concerned with Italy, Gentili focused on Europe; where Guicciardini ascribed the maintenance of balance among rulers to Lorenzo's personal capability which could not be transferred to others, Gentili was certain that the balance of power, which he compares to the distribution of molecules in a given object, could in principle be maintained by anyone in a given area. At the turn of the seventeenth century, the use of power to maintain a balance in Europe could thus be associated with institutional capacities rather than with personal capabilities. To Gentili the institutional capacities of balancing power could and, of right, ought to have a constraining impact on the actions of rulers.

In the eighteenth century, Guicciardini's view continued to have influence but was appreciated in different ways. Among others, Ludwig Martin Kahle (1712–1775), Professor of Philosophy at the University of Göttingen, discussed the balance of power in a treatise which was first published in Latin in 1744 and which provoked much debate in the second half of the century. Kahle quoted Guicciardini's statement on Lorenzo and concluded:

It should indeed be considered as a complete nuisance to observe in quietude one ruler using his forces and all of his power to impose the yoke of servitude upon all others. It is the highest purpose of all empires to prevent damage. This is just like in ill bodies from which the well selected medicines extract with care all that might be harmful.[3]

Lorenzo was thus neither a singularly gifted statesman nor the prophet of a better age. Instead, he represented for Kahle empirical proof that the balance of power existed and enforced certain rules for the conduct of international relations. Kahle categorized these rules as rational ones and insisted that they needed to be observed if disorder was to be avoided. The general principles of reason appeared to command the use of power to maintain a balance in Europe.

Such certainty was lost in the course of the nineteenth and twentieth centuries. A scepticism took its place which informed doubts about whether the balance should or could be maintained and which instruments should be chosen to do so. During the 1930s and at the time of World War II, several scholars devoted themselves to the study of the balance of power. One of them was Georg Schwarzenberger (1908–), a jurist and political scientist at the University of London. He published an influential book on *Power Politics* in which he discussed Gentili. Taking up Gentili's comparison of the balance of power with the equal distribution of molecules, Schwarzenberger commented:

> The growth of nationalism, however, increasingly forbids such an approach. The soil and population of a nation is sacred and not a question of bargaining. The nation is a living and organic unit, parts of which cannot be severed without endangering the existence of the whole. Thus, nationalism and the principle of national self-determination cut across the rationalist idea of the balance of power.[4]

Here, the balance of power stands for lack of mobility and an arbitrariness of the distribution of power. Moreover, according to Schwarzenberger, the power of the states has been checked by a more powerful force which is vested in the nation. Schwarzenberger did not confine the truth of his statement to Europe but credited it with general validity and insisted that, everywhere in the world, determining the balance of power is a matter of life or death for the nation. Power has thus become inept as a means of preserving order and stability and, instead, has been associated with the goal of overcoming resistance in struggles between contending parties.

There are no quantitative measurements for power.[5] It needs to be assessed rather than defined, and these assessments can vary, as these cases show. This book puts into their own historical contexts varying assessments of the power of those persons and institutions that regarded themselves or were accepted by others as international actors. There are in principle two groups of people who can assess the power of international actors: practitioners who are involved in the conduct of international relations as foreign policy decision-makers, diplomats, traders or people promoting cultural exchange; and theorists, some of whom, to use Stanley Hoffmann's phrase, regard themselves as standing, as it were, on tiptoe behind the practitioners and having a somewhat longer perspective on things than them. The two groups are not clearly divided. Some theorists have acted as practitioners, and some practitioners have been engaged in theory-making. But it is assumed for the purposes of this book that practitioners in, as well as theorists of, international relations have their own international theories, although their ways of making these theories explicit differ. Whereas practitioners will seek to display their theories through manifest action in international relations, theorists will prefer to write about them. This is neither to say that practitioners have never written about international theory nor to exclude the idea that theorists may wish to implement in practical conduct what they have laid down in writing. Nevertheless, with the assumption that there are different ways of expanding international theories, there are the merits of allowing comparisons among theorists' and practitioners' international theories. Such comparisons are important because they shed light on the interactions between practitioners in and theorists of international relations.

Theories are complex speculative statements about how the world or some of its parts or aspects may or should be.[6] They are therefore descriptive or normative. In either case, the speculative element in theories follows from partial assumptions on which theories rest and which they make more or less explicit. These assumptions are frequently related to beliefs or convictions specific to certain times, places and groups. The relativity of their underlying assumptions turns these theories into the cultural property of the groups from which they emerge. Nevertheless, international theories contain statements about the rightful use and the illegitimate abuse of power in international relations and these statements may acquire general validity. International theories can neither enforce the rightful use of power nor prevent the illegitimate abuse of power in international relations, but they can determine the conditions under which each takes place. In any case, there is a potential for clashes between the claimed or purported general validity of a theory and the degree of its global enforceability.

For the purposes of this book, international relations are defined as interactions among groups with a recognizable political tradition whose members regard each other mutually as outsiders. Hence theorists of and practitioners in international relations deal with or conduct interactions among groups across boundaries. This definition is wider than what is now commonly accepted among students of international relations, many of whom understand international relations as relations among (bureaucratic) states.[7] But this book covers a long timespan which extends from the Middle Ages to the modern period and thus backwards beyond the periods in which polities that can be called bureaucratic states were in existence. Therefore, the term international relations must be allowed to cover interactions among non-state polities and among actors who neither could nor would avail themselves of the bureaucratic institutions of statehood. This wider timeframe can make explicit the theoretical factors through which bureaucratic states emerged as international actors.

This book puts international theories as assessments of power in international relations into a historical context. It does so in order to describe the change in international theories. Change in international theories is understood to affect the criteria by which power, its rightful use and its illegitimate abuse in international relations have been assessed. Five such criteria will be taken into consideration: the sources of power, the relationship of power and groups, the relationship of power and space, the relationship of power and time, and the goals of the use of power. The first criterion makes explicit whether power is seen to emerge primarily from a personal or from an institutional actor or, in other words, whether it is assumed by practitioners in and theorists of international relations that the use of power is made possible through personal capabilities or rather through institutional capacities. The second, third and fourth criteria display the conceptual context in which the use of power is considered to take place. The group and the spatial dimensions affect the pictures of the world as well as the perceptions of boundaries and, consequently, the distinctions between what is inside and what is outside in international relations; and the temporal dimension relates to the historical institutional bases by means of which actors can use power legitimately.[8] The fifth criterion specifies the expectations for the accomplishment of which international actors can use power. Goals can oscillate between reaction and pro-action. Actors can thus expect that their conduct in international relations contributes to the maintenance or restoration of order in the world, but they can also take the view that their use of power promotes change in international relations. The sum of these criteria defines the cultural background as the context against which international theories shall be read.

The international theories discussed in this book are mainly of medieval and modern European origin. This is not to imply that there are or were no international theories elsewhere. As the departments of or programmes in international relations of many universities in many parts of the world nowadays indicate, international theories are now almost everywhere but their cultural backgrounds hardly differ. For example, international theories exist in Africa as part of an international body of knowledge that is being communicated through such media as satellite television and the Internet as well as through more conventional ways of classroom teaching and academic publication. But there is hardly any genuinely African international theory in the sense that it is drawn on a specifically African cultural background. Universality and globality are different concepts. While globality is absolute in the sense that it applies to what is planetary and pertains to or covers the globe as a whole, universality may but does not have to overlap with globality. Instead, what is termed universal claims to be the case in the world at large but may be tied to a picture of the world which includes only a part of the globe. Indeed, the demand that universality should mean the same thing as globality has only arisen relatively late in the course of the history of international theories. For example, the statesmen and diplomats of Ming and Qing China (1368–1911) insisted that China occupied the highest rank among the polities of the world and that China should assert this position wherever possible through the expansion of Chinese rule by the use of military force. This international theory claimed to be universal in validity but it did not engulf the entire globe. It was Sinocentric to the same extent as contemporary European international theory was Eurocentric. However, for most of this period, both universal international theories and the world pictures that informed them did not clash because their reach was less than global.

Not all international theories, therefore, have to be informed by world pictures which display the world as the globe in the way we see it today. In fact, few ever did so in the past. Medieval European world maps were accepted as pictures of the world although they did not cover the globe as a whole. The same was the case for world maps influenced by Buddhism in South, Southeast and East Asia up to the eighteenth century, although global world maps already existed in East Asia in the sixteenth century. In Africa, prior to the imposition of European colonial rule, various world pictures existed which covered only parts of the continent. It was only in the course of the nineteenth century that these less-than-global world pictures began to clash with the images conveyed through European geographical and historical world maps[9] and were absorbed, if not destroyed, by them. This book focuses on the processes which have contributed to the globalization of international theories in the context of the morally difficult legacy of the Europeanization of the world's world pictures.

PART I

Justifying World Rule

Universalism is an international theory which maintains that whatever is perceived as the world is or should be regarded as a single integrated entity. Universalism may or may not be manifest in secular or religious institutions. But it must in any case be constituted as a framework of norms, rules and values which claims to be applicable to all humankind. In the first part of this book, I intend to follow the process which globalized the European universal world picture and forced theorists of international relations to consider the variety of heterogeneous economic, political, social, religious and cultural units on the globe.

Universalism is a time-honoured international theory. Within the Roman Empire of antiquity, universalism was related to a world picture that displayed the world as a tricontinental *ecumene* which consisted of Africa, Asia and Europe. It was unequivocally vested in the rule of the Roman Emperor to whose control the *ecumene* was to be subjected, despite the manifest though changing boundaries within which the empire existed. But with the decline and fall of imperial administration in the city of Rome, there arose the necessity to ask the theoretical questions of where universalism was going to be anchored and who, if anyone, was going to be in charge of moulding the framework for universal norms, rules and values. In the Occident, the question became an urgent one when the city of Rome ceased to be an imperial residence in 476 and the Roman Empire began to compete with a motley group of loosely interconnected local polities. In the Orient, Byzantium continued as the centre in which the Roman Emperors continued to wield the traditional claims to universal rule. But the relationships between the emperors in

Byzantium and the rulers in the Occident remained controversial. While the emperors in Byzantium insisted that the East and the West continued to be integral parts of the one, single universal Roman Empire and that no international relations were possible inside the empire, the several rulers in the Occident claimed various degrees of autonomy for themselves and conducted their relations with the emperors as international relations.

Consequently, whether institutions of universal rule were necessary and, if so, who should represent them constituted the problem around which international relations theory evolved during the period which we can define as the Middle Ages between the fifth and the sixteenth centuries. During this period, three successive answers were given. First, there was the early medieval request in the Occident that universalism should essentially be defined in religious terms, that it ought to be vested in Christian church institutions and that rulers should execute the task of protecting the highest church institutions however far the influence of these institutions might extend. Secondly, there was the argument that universal rule should be vested in secular institutions under the control of Christian rulers. This argument was hotly debated in the Occident during the fourteenth century. And, thirdly, there was the demand that universal rule should be defined as secular rule over other rulers. This demand was articulated in the Occident during the fifteenth and sixteenth centuries. All of these debates were informed by a picture of a world which centred on the Mediterranean Sea and extended across the tricontinental *ecumene* of Africa, Asia and Europe. Hence, although the round shape of the world was recognized throughout the Middle Ages, universalism as a theory of international relations did not cover the whole globe. It not only failed to include America, the Pacific and Indian Oceans, but also coexisted with other universalisms in East, Southeast and South Asia as well as in sub-Saharan Africa. The globalization of universalism in the sense of the making of a theory of the world in its global entirety has been enhanced by the interaction among these several universalisms since the sixteenth century.

ONE

Religious Universalism Imposed

As a theory of international relations, religious universalism in the early Middle Ages was informed by a specific concept of space, which drew on the Bible, depicting the world as round as well as permeable and rendering existing administrative boundaries secondary.[1] It was also related to certain experiences of time which, in accordance with the teachings of the Church Fathers, identified time as finite, posited it against eternity and associated it with change as a factor of instability and insecurity.[2] It was applied in different ways by various types of groups which, on the one hand, were subjected to particularistic rules, norms and values while, on the other, they were overarched by the Christian Church as a universal religious institution.[3] This institution could allocate power, convey legitimacy and provide values. All in all, religious universalism supported the perception of the world as divinely willed, assigned to human actors the task to act in accordance with divine commands and limited the belief in the change-provoking capability of human actors.

THE UNIVERSAL WORLD PICTURE OF THE EARLY MIDDLE AGES

The standard occidental medieval world map, the *mappamundi* of Latin sources, was drawn on models of antiquity and presented the world as a tricontinental spherical land mass. The land mass was encircled by a narrow strip of water into which a large number of islands were interspersed. The land mass was commonly referred to as the *ecumene*, and comprised the continents of Africa in the lower right, Europe in the lower left and

Asia in the upper part, the water strip sealing off the *ecumene* against the universe was called the ocean.[4] In this world picture, land *(terra)* and world *(mundus)* were not clearly differentiated as concepts because the largest part of the world's surface was believed to be land. There was only one ocean, as the *ecumene* was considered to be indivisible. Although certain types of maps followed the speculative information provided by geographers of antiquity and displayed a fourth continent in isolation from the other three, this continent was regarded as uninhabitable on theological grounds and thereby did not question the principal postulate that the *ecumene* as the inhabited part of the world formed a single permeable unity (illus. 1).[5]

The religious connotation of this world picture was made explicit in the many maps that presented the *ecumene* above or below symbols or figures of the divine world, usually a figure of the trinity or angels or both. Likewise, many maps featured the terrestrial paradise through either an inscription reading *paradisus* or the pictorial symbols of Adam, Eve and the Tree of Wisdom. Because occidental theological exegesis of the Bible located paradise most frequently in Asia, it made sense to assign paradise to a spot in the uppermost part of the maps, to place Asia in this part and to lay the maps out with the east at the top.[6] Beyond its basic layout this type of *mappamundi* contained many references to the Old Testament. For one, the distribution of land and water was usually arranged in accordance with a phrase in the Book of Esdras (IV, 6, 42) which says that six-sevenths of the earth's surface are (inhabitable) land. This was understood to imply that the inhabitable *ecumene* made up by far the largest part of the earth's surface. Moreover, another Old Testament phrase (Ezekiel 5,5), according to which the divinity had placed Jerusalem in the centre of the world, induced some occidental medieval map makers to lay out their *mappaemundi* as schemes of concentric circles, with the city of Jerusalem as the innermost and the ocean as the outer circle. Finally, it followed from this layout that neither Byzantium nor Rome could possibly be located in the centre of the *ecumene*, but that they featured regularly in its lower parts.

The location of Rome in the bottom zone was suitable because it reflected the doctrine adopted from a prophecy in the

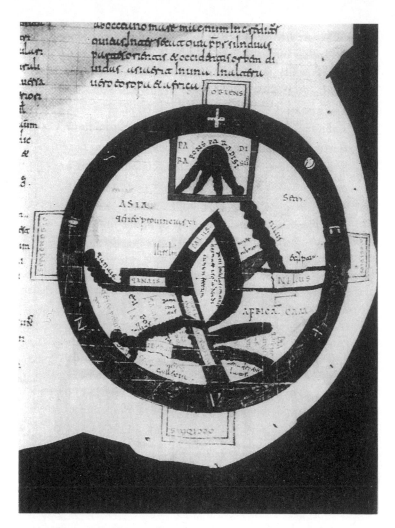

1 Map of the *ecumene*. From Isidore of Seville, *Etymologiae*. San Millán de la Cogolla, AD 946.

Book of Daniel that there were four world empires and that the world would come to its end with the end of the fourth empire. After the acceptance of Christianity as the imperial religion in the Roman Empire of antiquity, the Roman Empire was commonly identified as the last of the world empires. Thus, after the end of imperial administration in the city of Rome, confidence that the world would continue to exist hinged critically on the continuity of the Roman Empire, its 'renovation' by rulers other than the emperors in Rome or its 'translation' on to institutions elsewhere.[7] In summary, the Biblical world picture solicited active support for institutions of universal rule for the purpose of safeguarding the continuing existence of the world as a whole.

EXPERIENCES OF AND ATTITUDES TOWARDS TIME

The finiteness of terrestrial space in a medieval *mappamundi* corresponded thus to the finiteness of time. Nevertheless, counting the years and measuring shorter segments of time presented irritating problems in the early Middle Ages which induced some of the most talented scholars to devote their energy to the study of time measurement. Chronology was an advanced science, although it merged into eschatology.[8] Speculations about the end of the world were possible principally under the assumption that only the interval between the creation and the end of the world was subjected to the rule of time and thus turned time into a finite phenomenon. Nevertheless, it was mandatory to develop methods by which the position of any given present could be determined in relation to the creation and the foreseen end of the world. Biblical exegesis suggested that the world would not last beyond a total of 6,000 years and that this period of time had to be subdivided into six world ages of approximately one thousand years each. In combination with the belief that the Roman Empire was the last of the four world empires, it was initially taken for granted among Christians in antiquity that the beginning of the sixth world age occurred at the time of the foundation of the city of Rome, conventionally dated 753 BC. The fusion of the world age and the world empire chronologies incited speculations among Christians in the Roman Empire of late antiquity and in post-Roman times that the sixth world age was coming to its close and, consequently, stimulated anxieties that the end of the world was near. These anxieties in turn promoted millenarian movements, whose protagonists believed that people should prepare themselves spiritually for the coming of eternity. They usually advocated radical forms of asceticism and defiance against authority. It was the task of Christian chronologers and theologians to stand up against such movements and provide ideologies in support of existing institutions of government. The Christian AD chronology, which originated in the sixth century and spread gradually from the eighth century, was perhaps the most consequential of these efforts. It suggested that the years of the sixth millennium should be counted from the birth of Christ rather than from the (mythical) foundation of the city of Rome and helped extend the amount of years believed to be left until the end of the world.[9]

But counting the years involved a further problem. After the demise of Roman imperial administration in the Occident, there was no longer an agency which could authoritatively impose general standards for the measurement of time through the chronology of its rulers and institutions of government. Hence there was no longer a standard for the beginning of the year, so that regional styles emerged. Likewise, various ways were established according to which the solar and the lunar cycles were to be combined for such purposes as the fixing of the annual Easter date. This was particularly important in Church affairs because the entire ecclesiastical calendar depended on the Easter date. Finally, there was the problem that the measurement of shorter intervals of time, such as the hour, was regarded as depending on the variations of the seasons rather than dividing the day into the same equal portions throughout the year. Instead, the 24 hours of the day were divided into two periods of twelve hours each, of which one was assigned to daylight and the other to darkness. Because, in summer, the period of daylight is longer than the period of darkness, each of the twelve hours of daylight was longer than each of the twelve hours of darkness. In winter, the relationship was reversed.[10] The consequence of this mode of measurement of hours was that the fixing of an hour of the day depended on the season, on the area and even, to a significant extent, to the subjective assessment of the measuring persons. In short, the universalistic belief in the finiteness of time as a whole competed with particularistic attitudes towards the measurement of portions of time.

Particularistic attitudes not only informed methods of time reckoning but also permeated many aspects of social life. Social life was dominated by fears which emanated from the presence of hostile forces in the physical environment, could manifest themselves in awkward climatic conditions, attacks by dangerous animals and the activities of lawless bands of robbers, and could limit the range of human activities.[11] Hence people would, as a rule, seek protection against such evil forces through membership in various types of groups,[12] mainly kin groups, neighbourhood groups, contractual groups such as guilds, warrior bands or religious communities or groups with a common political tradition.[13] Only individuals of outstanding physical strength and intellectual capability, such as rulers and high-ranking Church members, were credited with the ability to overcome the limitations posed by the physical environment.[14] These persons were thus accepted as conveyors of energy to ordinary men and women and as leaders of their groups. There were many of these groups in the early Middle Ages, mostly small bands whose membership hardly exceeded two or three hundred people. Most of these groups were local groups of settlers,[15] but they could also embrace long-distance migrants and unite people of the same kin at a substantive variety of distant places.[16]

Administrative schemes which were intended to overarch or even absorb the plethora of these groups were rare, unstable and thus comparatively weak. They seem to have emerged gradually around AD 500 in continental areas inside the Roman Empire of antiquity. Some of these schemes were referred to in contemporary sources as 'kingdoms' but they did not continue beyond the eighth century, with the notable exception of the Kingdom of the Franks.[17] Frankish kings were thus by far the most powerful and respected rulers in continental Europe during the seventh and eighth centuries. Local groups continued in parts of the continent outside areas under control of the Frankish kings, in Britain up to the end of the seventh century and in most of Scandinavia up to or even beyond the eighth century.

The Roman Empire remained on its ancient foundations in Byzantium, but became positioned against the plethora of particularistic groups. The emperors who continued to use the title of Roman Emperors even in their Byzantine residence upheld their claim to universal rule together with the belief that the Roman Empire was the last of the four world empires. Consequently, they insisted that the particularistic groups were or were eventually to become their subjects, even though, in practice, they had only limited chances of acting in accordance with their claims in the Occident after the sixth century.[18] In place of the Roman Emperors in Byzantium, the popes in Rome as the heads of the Catholic Church emerged as representatives of universalism in the Occident, although mainly in spiritual terms. The contradistinction of the secular universalism upheld by the Roman Emperors in Byzantium and of the spiritual universalism claimed by the popes in Rome was articulated in a letter which Pope Gelasius I (492–496) sent to Emperor Anastasius I (491–518) at the end of the fifth century.[19] In his letter, the pope differentiated the kingly from the priestly power and described their coexistence as a dualism of distinct though interrelated offices.

However, although Pope Gelasius's letter became widely known and was frequently quoted in the early Middle Ages and the subsequent centuries, little was made of the implicit contradistinction between the secular and the sacred or, for that matter, between politics and religion.[20] Instead, universalism remained essentially religious in kind and conditioned the belief, already supported by Gelasius himself, that the secular powers of emperors, kings and other rulers were divinely sanctioned in the same way as the spiritual powers of the pope and the bishops of the Church. Therefore, the word 'church' could be used to describe the community of Christian believers within and beyond the Roman Empire of antiquity as an all-inclusive organization in which secular and ecclesiastical powers converged.

The dualism between universalism and particularism permeated the work of the single most influential Christian author of
late antiquity and in the entire Middle Ages, namely St
Augustine (354–430), Bishop of Hippo Regius in northern
Africa from 395. He subjected the dualism to a rigid order of
values which gave unequivocal preference to universalism over
particularism. He did so by allocating universalism to the divine
world, without limitations of space, without changes brought
about by the progress of time and without the antagonisms of
rival groups, and associated with earthly human particularism
the features of dividing spatial boundaries, the vicissitudes of
time and the rivalries of groups. His purpose for doing so was to
provide an ultimate apology for Christianity as the superior
religion within and beyond the Roman Empire of his own time.

Apology for Christianity was deemed necessary early in the
fifth-century Occident after the sack of Rome by Visigoth
warriors under the leadership of their 'King' Alaric (395–410) in
410. Although the incident was a marginal affair, traditionalists
blamed it widely on the fact that Christianity had been adopted
as the general religion and that all other religious cults had been
prohibited in 391. They appear to have argued that the sack of
Rome was a divine punishment for the suppression of the traditional religions. Moreover, fears and anxieties were not
confined to traditionalists; some Christians also shared them.
This was so because New Testament apocalyptic writings contained eschatological speculations according to which the end
of the world was near when ferocious peoples from the East
spread across the earth (Apocalypse 20, 7–8) and devastated the
Roman Empire as the last of the world empires. The Visigoths
had approached Italy from the east and the sack of Rome could
be understood as the fatal blow to the Roman Empire.

Therefore, Augustine faced the dual task of defending
Christianity against the traditionalists and of assuring Christians
that the world would continue to exist. In order to accomplish
this task, he spent fourteen years from 413 to 426 writing
his work *The City of God*, in which he devoted one book to the

relationship between war and peace. From this book, his theory of international relations emerges. Augustine knew three categories of space: first the private home which he identified as the space of daily experience under the control of kin groups and neighbourhood groups; secondly, the city or the polity which he categorized as the space of regular communication under the control of justice maintained by the ruler and under the regime of morality as the basic agreement among the 'citizens' about their joint objects of love; and, thirdly, the world as a universal space in which the decision on war or peace was to take place. Thus Augustine's principal argument about international relations was that peace and war were universal conditions which pertained to the world as a whole and neither to the particularistic public polities (as the spaces of regular communication) nor to the private houses (as the spaces of daily experience).[21]

Given the apologetic intention behind *The City of God*, it is no surprise that Augustine focused more on peace than on war. He classed peace as a universal phenomenon for two reasons. First, he accepted Aristotle's axiom of the principal sociability of men and women who, he thought, by nature love their kindred and neighbours. Secondly, he relied on the traditions of Roman law and credited men and women with a degree of reasonability sufficient to induce them to obey orders and rules that had been issued by superior agencies, ultimately the divinity. Augustine was certain that rational beings would ultimately abide by government commands and divinely stipulated orders because they would act in order to obtain a beneficial condition for the eternal lives of their souls after death and that such considerations would lead them even to accept earthly sufferings in return for eternal rewards. Augustine then assigned to peace the status of a natural desire of all rational beings who, he thought, were longing for the maintenance of some degree of stability in an ever-changing world and defined peace as a means to make the world more livable as well as the sole earthly condition which mortal human beings could justly enjoy.

Augustine was convinced that divine wisdom and benevolence had installed peace as the final goal of all human activity. He acknowledged that human capability was insufficient to accomplish this goal in a universal scope, but insisted that the attainment of universal peace was impossible because of human sinfulness and, in the last resort, because of the divinely willed transitoriness of the world. In summary, Augustine made no attempt to outline the conditions for perpetual peace as the condition for ever-lasting stability, but maintained that it was the task of human beings and that it fell within human capability to make every effort to render peace ever more stable.[22] Hence, he concluded that a war was admitted solely under the condition that it could establish a platform for a more stable and solid peace.

To Augustine, just war was thus not the opposite of, but an instrument for, the promotion of peace. He identified two reasons for the existence of war.

The first reason emerged from the divisions of the world into a plethora of antagonistic groups whose members adhered to particularistic traditions and experienced their particularisms through the daily use of different languages. He argued that the diversity of languages prevented peaceful interactions beyond one specific space of regular communication and thereby obstructed the sociability of men and women, added to the instability of the world and prevented people from uniting themselves in love.

Augustine's second reason for the existence of war was human unwillingness to obey given general orders as long as they were divided into a plethora of antagonistic groups. Each particularistic group would be committed to its own norms and rules and would oblige its members to be loyal. As a consequence, groups would begin to fight against each other, commit acts of injustice and lead their members into a disturbed state of mind in which they would act against nature as well as divine will and defy given orders. Such things could happen domestically when groups such as robbers, murderers or other unsociable people resorted to force for the accomplishment of their immoral goals.

He justified domestic wars as the means to enforce given orders, subject dissident and sectarian groups to the rule of law and, in this way, to maintain or restore peace. The same was true with respect to the interactions among groups, that is, at the international level. In this respect, his theory of war led Augustine to support the quest for universal rule wielded by the

Roman Emperors because it seemed reasonable to him that peace in the world could become ever more stable if ever more particularistic groups subjected themselves to the rule of the Roman Emperor and could thereby overcome their rivalries and antagonisms.

These moral arguments also allowed Augustine to prove that the Roman Empire was the embodiment of peace in the *ecumene*. He posited the Roman Empire as the embodiment of peace against the particularism of the several local groups creating and defending their own spaces of communication and resisting the universal rule of the Roman Emperors. In the context of Augustine's international theory, then, the Roman Empire was predominantly a moral institution whose main purpose was the safeguarding of peace as the essential condition for the continuity of the human world. He thus juxtaposed the Roman Empire against the several particularistic groups of 'infidels' or otherwise impious people who jeopardized peace by defying the orders issued by the Christian Roman Emperors solely for the benefit of adhering to their own particularistic traditions. His conclusion was that the world would continue to experience instability and suffering as long as dissident or segregationist groups were allowed to defy Roman rule.

Hence, in Augustine's theory, Alaric's Visigoths had inflicted disaster, not because the Roman Empire was a Christian empire, but because this empire, as an earthly institution, had until then failed to establish itself as a truly universal empire. This meant that Christianity should be universalized as a condition for peace in the world, which could be effected most easily within the boundaries of the Roman Empire as a truly universal institution of rule. The universalization of the Roman Empire would thus be the only viable way through which peace was possible as temporary relief from the inescapable progress of time, and this appeared to be so because the divinity was believed to have willed that the universal Roman Empire became the embodiment of Christianity and would therefore not allow the world to end as long as the Roman Empire continued to exist.

Augustine's theory of international relations was tied to the Roman Empire as a Christian institution. Augustine took for granted the secular institutions making up the Roman Empire to which he assigned the status of a universal empire. Yet he was painfully aware of the fact that, as a polity, the Roman Empire was limited in space and had its manifestly existing boundaries. He derived his universalistic principles from religious doctrine which led him to accept the assumption that all human beings (as rational beings) would ultimately accept this doctrine for their own sake. He acknowledged that not everyone in the *ecumene* shared this view but insisted that it was worthwhile to turn the Roman Empire into a manifestly universal empire for the purpose of promoting peace.

War was just if and as long as it was undertaken in order to suppress domestic strife among persons in a disturbed state of mind and to subject 'impious' groups to the rule of the Christian Roman Emperors as the promoters of peace. Augustine's apologetics thus promoted a theory of international relations which, albeit universal in its scope and goals, was biased due to its author's Christian conviction that the *ecumene* was – and by divine law ought to be – subject to the rule of the Roman Emperors. The theory was viable as long as the institutions making up the Roman Empire continued to exist, but if these institutions were fading away or transforming, it had to be adjusted. This was the problem with which a learned monk in the late seventh and early eight century began to struggle.

CHRISTIAN THEOLOGICAL UNIVERSALISM OUTSIDE THE ROMAN EMPIRE

Bede (*c.* 675–735) had already established himself as an expert in chronology and the universal traditions transmitted in the Bible when he set out to produce his own historiographical synthesis from his computational work, his chronicles and insular group-related traditions known to him. He acquired knowledge of the group-bound traditions from written sources, among them papal letters, and also drew on oral material, such as genealogies and information submitted to him by informed clergymen of his own time.

The first synthesis of this kind ever to have been undertaken in Europe was already a masterpiece and has set certain standards for thinking and writing about the past ever since. Remarkably, Bede, who had used the word *chronica* as the title for his previous writings on Biblical traditions, chose the conventional word *historia* for this synthesis, which he concluded in 731. By convention, the Latin word *historia*, in sources known to Bede, had frequently meant a secular account of the past and describing events of the human world as set apart from the divine world.[23] But Bede limited the range of meanings of *historia* by adding two qualifying attributes.

First, his *historia* was to be an ecclesiastical one. This attribute was derived from the precedence of the work of Eusebius of Caesarea (313–339) who had written an ecclesiastical history up to the fourth century. The word *historia* gave expression to Bede's insistence that writing about the past was to be placed in the context of accounting for the universal advancement of Christianity as Orosius[24] had also suggested early in the fifth century along with Augustine's views.[25] But, different from Eusebius and Orosius, Bede added the further specification that his *historia ecclesiastica* was to be partial in dealing with matters related to a group called the *gens Anglorum* only. This group, which has been referred to as the 'English' since the ninth century, was understood to comprise the Christianized group of Germanic settlers in the British Isles which had formerly been part of the Roman Empire but was no longer when the *gens Anglorum* arrived there.

Again, the choice of words reflected a well-considered programmatic intention, namely to display all these immigrant settlers as the members of a single overarching group with joint political traditions and institutions of rule and to refer to this group under the name to be rendered as 'English'.[26] Thus, on the one side, Bede integrated his account of the history of the Church into the universalism represented in the Biblical traditions whereas, on the other side, he separated his account from the universal background into which this history had been placed by such authors as Eusebius and Orosius.

Bede also departed in methodological respects from the previous group-centred oral narratives and their representation in genealogies, although he used them as sources. Whereas the latter had been affirmative in authoritatively stating beliefs about the past, Bede's approach was more critical. Except for the holy scriptures, he consciously tried to relate the evidence which one source preserved to what could be ascertained from other sources. He also tried to weight the relative evidential value of the several sources available to him.

Moreover, whereas the orally transmitted traditions had retained their validity and authenticity without fundamental change by virtue of being handed down from generation to generation, Bede, like the historians of late antiquity, committed himself to writing and publishing a text which was expected to be communicated through reading and copying. Its reception, by virtue of these communicative techniques, was no longer confined to a specific group. Likewise, whereas the oral narratives had been preserved in vernacular languages, Bede used Latin as a *lingua franca* through which matters could be communicated beyond the confines of particularistic groups. Thus Bede imagined a learned general reader who could, in principle, live anywhere.

Finally, where the group-bound traditions had contained particularistic norms and values, Bede's work represented the universal norms and values which were inherent in the spiritual teachings of the Catholic Church and with which the 'English' were shown to have become acquainted through Roman missionary efforts.[27]

Therefore, Bede's main problem in describing the 'Church history of the English' seems to have been one that had been alien to Augustine and the historians of the fourth and fifth centuries. The problem concerned the Roman Empire as the most important administrative entity to be described in an occidental historiographic context at the time. Whereas Eusebius and Orosius had been able to take for granted the existence of institutions making up the Roman Empire and could have described these institutions as universal (though by no means global),[28] Bede had to cope with the fact that, as far as Britain was concerned, the immigrants who were to become Bede's 'English' had destroyed these very institutions. Consequently, universalism, in Bede's own time, could no longer be anchored in manifest institutions of secular rule.

There were two principal ways of solving the difficulty. Universalism could be given up and priority could be awarded to a set of local groups, one of which Bede identified as the 'English'. Or universalism could be vested in the Catholic Church. That is to say, Bede could have confined his *historia* to the particularism of what had happened among the 'English'. In this case, his *historia* would not have been more than a translation of the particularistic oral narratives into the communicative medium of a Latin written text.

The coming of Catholicism to Britain would have appeared as what the local kin and neighbourhood groups in all probability perceived it to be, namely the intrusion of an outside and alien framework of norms and rules, attitudes and perceptions. But, as a clergyman, Bede cannot have had the intention of supporting this image through his *historia*. Therefore, he had to opt for the second choice and traced the process of the coming to Britain of the Catholic Church as the representative of universalism, outside but historically interconnected with the institutions of the Roman Empire. In this way, Bede could describe the Catholic mission as the process of the interaction of the universal Catholic Church with local rulers at a time when institutions of Roman imperial rule were no longer extant in Britain.

But this synthesis had a high price. Bede's *historia* had to include descriptions of institutional changes which annihilated the universal character of the institutions of the Roman Empire. This was so because Bede had to cope with the establishment in Britain of local institutions whose representatives did not regard themselves as affiliated with or subjected to Roman rule. Thus Bede's *historia* came to include accounts of institutional changes which, against St Augustine's intentions, added to the importance of particularism in that it described the successes of local rulers over the Roman Emperors or subsequent representatives of post-Roman institutions of rule.[29]

These changes differed fundamentally from the paradigms which were allowed for in the scriptural traditions of the four world empires, the last of which the Roman Empire was considered to be. In accordance with these traditions, one universal institution would give way to a successor of the same kind, and a universal institution would always exist. But Bede's problem was that the emerging local institutions of the 'English' and other particularistic groups could not be described as successor institutions to those of the Roman Empire. Hence he could not rely exclusively on the universal paradigms provided by the Bible and its exegesis or on the particularistic group-related oral traditions. Bede refused to classify the process he was describing as the destruction of the Roman Empire. He could not do so because that would have meant arguing against the Augustinian belief that the Roman Empire as a Christian empire was not only the last of the world empires before doomsday, but a stable one as long as Christianity persisted. Instead, Bede admitted that institutions of Roman rule had been annihilated in Britain and then insisted that, as far as Britain was concerned, universalism had been vested in the institutions of the Catholic Church.

Nevertheless, Bede's success in describing the transition from Roman universal to local rule in Britain was also due to the continuity into his own time of the Mediterranean world picture which had been associated with Roman imperial rule since antiquity and which continued to serve as the vehicle for the expression of the universality of Roman rule. In other words, universalism, be it associated with the Roman Empire or with the Christian Church, was bound to continue to be defined in the terms which were set by the world picture that had been transmitted in the Roman Empire and displayed the *ecumene* as the permeable domain of universal rule.

In conclusion, Bede's international theory had to solve the problem of blending the universalistic traditions of Christianity with what was made known to him about the particularistic group traditions continuing in the British Isles and in Europe during his lifetime. Bede's solution was to categorize the mission of the Catholic Church as an effort to absorb the multifarious particularistic group traditions into the universalistic norms and rules which were proposed and enforced by the Catholic Church.

VOICES AND IMAGES OF PARTICULARISM

This effort encountered serious resistance during the seventh and eighth centuries from among the representatives of particularistic kin groups. Disagreement over universalistic norms and values emerged when kin members wished to continue transmitting their own group-bound traditions of descent. It seems that specifically aristocratic kin groups resisted the superimposition of universalistic norms and values because their own traditions were transmitted for the purpose of handing on their own norms and values across the generations. Hence these two sets of norms and values clashed. Length of known oral genealogical tradition was moreover a criterion for legitimacy[30] for the exercise of political power and provided a further impetus for the preservation of group-bound traditions so as to ensure the continuity of the kin groups.[31]

In order to preserve these traditions even after conversion to Christianity, aristocratic and specifically royal kin groups penetrated Catholic Church institutions during the seventh and eighth centuries when they acted as founders of proprietary churches and monasteries built on kin land, as supporters of cults of saints of their own kin and as leaders of high Church institutions, notably bishoprics and monasteries. These cults and positions allowed aristocratic kin groups to maintain their own traditions within the institutional framework of the Church.[32] That the maintenance of particularistic traditions and adherence to group-bound norms and values were ubiquitous is on record in a ninth-century educational manual which Dhuoda, a Frankish aristocratic woman, wrote for the instruction of her son William.[33] In her work, she urged her son to respect and revere his father but not to follow the otherwise usual patterns of aristocratic behaviour. She advised him to devote himself to life in accordance with the universalistic ethics of Christianity. This advice implies that the continuous adherence to traditional norms and values was widespread in the Frankish kingdom during the ninth century.

In Britain, similar evidence is provided in a poetic text of perhaps the late seventh century in which Widsith, a professional singer of traditions, is made to recount his experiences.[34] The anonymous poet introduced Widsith as an outstanding traveller of extraordinary powers who managed to traverse not only wide areas, but also the boundaries of time. Widsith is said to have belonged to the aristocratic kin group of the Myrgings of perhaps Saxon origin, visited famous kings and their illustrious entourages, among them Ermanaric, King of the Goths in the fourth century,[35] displayed his knowledge of a large number of groups and their rulers (some of whom were taken from the historiography of antiquity) and recounted the tragic fate of his own group which lost a battle against the continental Angles in Jutland and seems to have then migrated to Britain. The latter can be inferred from the fact that the Widsith poem has been recorded in an Old English manuscript.

If one takes a closer look at the names of the groups which Widsith is made to mention, one can locate at least splinters of some of them in eastern Britain where place-names seem to record settlements which these groups established there after their migrations from the continent. Therefore, the Widsith poem can be used as a record for the appreciation of group traditions during the centuries following the migration. The poem not only introduces a singer of traditions, but also supports the assumption that his audience must have been knowledgeable in these traditions. This assumption is sound because the references to traditions in the poem are usually implicit and come in the form of names with which the audience must have been able to associate appropriate traditions.

The Widsith poet envisaged the relations among groups as emerging from personal communication among their members. The poet allowed neither for institutional constraints nor for the exercise of institutional control. He described the frequency of violent interaction in terms of warfare or other forms of dispute and asserted that defeat in battle was a disaster when it entailed the extinction of group tradition. Otherwise, all appears to have depended upon the communication skills, competence and capabilities of those outstanding individuals who could transgress the otherwise narrow confines of space and time. Thus the conduct of international relations as interactions among groups at distant places bore the hallmark of the unusual or, at minimum, was not an everyday affair.

International relations were understood as taking place in the open space between groups. This open space was a no man's land because the groups usually did not recognize an overarching integrative institutional framework. Relations between the groups could therefore emerge from collective actions by migrants and warriors or from the activities of gifted and daring individuals, or they could cease to exist at all if there was no incentive to maintain them. One might add that, alongside the professional singer of traditions, the long-distance trader or migrant producer was a figure whose task it was to maintain relations between the groups. Traders and migrant producers were important as interconnecting actors as they organized the exchange of goods and techniques of production between the Orient and the Occident, in the Mediterranean as well as in the North Seas and the northern Eurasian river systems.[36] They could act in groups, usually of seafarers,[37] or as individuals, travelling on land and at sea.[38] In any case, traders and migrant producers usually operated at their own risk in what was an administratively unorganized space between groups. In essence, then, the localism of particularistic groups entailed an international theory which stood in direct opposition to the universalism which was associated with the Roman Empire and which continued to be promoted by the Catholic Church.

RESTORATION OF EMPIRE

Charlemagne was King of the Franks (768–814) and King of the Lombards (774–814). In these capacities, he was, first and foremost, representative of particularistic group interests. However, at the turn of the ninth century, the Franks were a group with a special rank in the Occident. At this time, few rulers could claim for themselves a longer tradition of rule than the Frankish kings, and no one could rival them in terms of the numbers of groups and the extension of land which at that time stood under Charlemagne's control.

Throughout the sixth, seventh and eighth centuries, the Kings of the Franks had pushed the boundaries of their kingdom far beyond its nucleus in the north of Roman Gaul southwards to areas south of the Pyrenees, eastwards to the central Alpine regions and northern Italy and into the Danube valley as well as northwards up to the river Elbe. Thus, the Frankish kings, who had initially been rulers of a particularistic kingdom on territory that had been part of the Roman Empire of antiquity, rose to a position of overlordship of large parts of continental Europe and impacted politically even on the British Isles.

Furthermore, in a dramatic move, Pepin III (751–768), Charlemagne's father, had in 751 ousted the ruling kin group of the Merovingians. Having had himself elected King of the Franks, he accepted the pope's sanction in the form of an anointment. In return for papal support, Pepin agreed to act as the defender of the Catholic Church and the protector of the city of Rome with the Vatican as the papal residence. Hence Pepin and his successors in the Frankish Kingdom derived their legitimacy as rulers from two sources, the particularistic traditions of Frankish royal rule on the one side and, on the other, the universalistic traditions administered by the Catholic Church. Whereas the former traditions tied the Frankish kings to their own group, the latter traditions interconnected them with the legacy of the institutions of the Roman Empire.[39]

The norms and values underlying the dualism were mutually incompatible and the resulting obligations for Charlemagne were mutually exclusive. On the one side, he had to defend the universalistic traditions of the Roman Empire as the protector of Rome. On the other side, he had to safeguard the continuity of the Frankish traditions of rule. Charlemagne tried to solve the problem by expanding his rule through the subjection of ever more groups to his control, by absorbing traditions of other groups, such as those of the Lombards, and by taking up relations with rulers outside the Roman Empire of antiquity, namely Khalif Harun al-Rashid of Baghdad (768–809).

In the end, Charlemagne occupied a position equal to that of an emperor. This position placed him in a competition with the Roman Emperors in Byzantium who claimed that they were the only representatives of the Roman Empire. It also prompted opposition from among Frankish traditionalists who appear to have insisted that the Frankish king should not get involved too deeply with imperial affairs. Charlemagne ignored Byzantine resentments and suppressed Frankish criticism against his actions. Taking advantage of a succession crisis in Byzantium and a political crisis in Rome, he argued that the imperial throne was vacant, marched a Frankish army to Rome to protect the city and had himself crowned emperor there by the pope on Christmas Day, 800.

Thus the authority of the Roman Emperors was formally restored in the Occident, but Rome, although it remained under Frankish protection, did not again become the imperial residence, as Charlemagne returned home to the Frankish Kingdom after his coronation. After some hesitation, he began to allow the use of the title Roman Emperor in solemn charters which were issued in his name. However, the Roman Emperors in Byzantium refused to accept the *fait accompli* of Charlemagne's coronation. They denounced him as an insurgent subordinate ruler and went to war. Campaigns were fought without much intensity and, in 812, a compromise was reached according to which Charlemagne recognized the emperors in Byzantium as 'Roman Emperors', and he was recognized by them as 'Emperor'.[40]

The compromise may have also been designed to placate Frankish opposition, for Charlemagne retained the imperial title for himself and his successors without explicit reference to the Roman Empire. Even though Charlemagne's tenth-century and later successors styled themselves Roman Emperors, sought closer affiliation with the city of Rome and made stronger efforts to employ for themselves the institutional legacy of the Roman Empire, the compromise of 812 made it clear that Charlemagne failed in his own time to establish himself at a rank equal to that of the emperors in Byzantium. The latter succeeded, for the time being, in reserving for themselves the guardianship of Roman imperial traditions, whereas Charlemagne was reduced to the bearer of the novel, exotic and, in this sense, meaningless plain title of emperor who, in the eyes of the emperors in Byzantium, could in a sense rule anywhere.

There are several remarkable general features of Frankish international theory at the turn of the ninth century. First and foremost, from the second half of the eighth century, the Frankish kings accepted their subjection to religious universalism by relying on ecclesiastical instruments for the conveyance of legitimacy. They did so in the dual respect of having received the papal unction from 751 as Kings of the Franks and of accepting the papal coronation as emperors in Rome from 800. Although indications for a closer cooperation between bishops of the Catholic Church and various rulers had already been put on record in the late seventh century, specifically in Britain, the acts of 751 and 800 marked a breakthrough in a long-term process by which the principal criteria for the legitimacy of rulers shifted from particularistic group traditions to the universalistic norms and values promoted by the Catholic Church. Rulers who received their legitimacy through Church intervention were therefore no longer controlled solely by group-bound norms and values, but became subject to the universal norms and values supported by the Catholic Church. Although the tension between group-bound and ecclesiastical norms and values disclosed the incompatibility of particularism and universalism as international theories, in the long run, secular particularism gave way to religious universalism as more and more of the ruling kin groups lost control over their traditions after the end of the eighth century.

Secondly, the major reason why particularism waned lay in the prevalence of the eschatological beliefs tied to the Roman Empire. These beliefs stimulated actions in support of the continuity and the strengthening of the Roman Empire at times of supposed or manifest crisis, and they promoted the superimposition of Roman universalism into the particularism of local groups. When the Franks as a particularistic group became the bearers of the Roman imperial tradition through Charlemagne's imperial coronation, the Roman Empire became definable without Rome (or Byzantium) as its centre, and it could be 'transferred' to different particularistic groups. The separation of the Roman imperial tradition from the city of Rome paved the way for subsequent generations up to the early nineteenth century to retain their conviction that the Roman Empire continued to exist beyond even fundamental changes of institutions.

Thirdly, the Frankish–Byzantine disputes over the coronation of Charlemagne disclosed the practical limitations of imperial rule to both the emperors in Byzantium and Charlemagne. Although no one doubted that there was only one Roman Empire, the compromise of 812 did recognize the fact that there were two emperors whose powers were not only legitimized in different ways but also extended over different domains. While the Roman Emperors in Byzantium drew on the traditions of Roman imperial institutions for their legitimacy, Charlemagne used the authority of the Catholic Church. Hence the compromise of 812 prevented Charlemagne from claiming suzerainty over Byzantium no less than it prevented the emperors in Byzantium from claiming some kind of over-rule over Charlemagne's realm. Instead, the compromise advanced the establishment of administrative boundaries even though these were not admitted in theoretical terms. The accommodation between both emperors became possible because both agreed to disagree and promised to refrain from interfering in each other's internal affairs for the time being. That meant that both emperors accepted their mutual relations as international in practice against the constraints of the prevailing theory that the Roman Empire continued as an institution of universal rule.

Religious universalism in the early Middle Ages was thus an international theory which placed the *ecumene* as one single entity under the manifest or potential control of the Roman Emperors as sacred rulers and of the popes. As a theory it stood against the real-world elements and factors which were rooted in secular group-bound particularist traditions. These traditions were irreconcilable with the perception of the *ecumene* as one single entity. Religious universalism was designed and articulated by clergymen, whereas rulers appeared more passively as the defenders of ecclesiastical universalistic norms and values in international relations. Rulers were confined to rather passive roles because they had the primary tasks of acting as the representatives of the particularistic groups under their control and of transmitting group-bound traditions. Consequently, what was regarded as international relations remained contested throughout the period. Universalists insisted that the Roman Empire was a universal empire and that, consequently, relations inside the area once covered by the Roman Empire of antiquity could not possibly be international. By contrast, particularists maintained that international relations were relations among groups. This conflict remained unresolved during this period.

Because international theory was part and parcel of either universalistic thought or of group-bound traditions, it did not appear in a textual genre of its own. Instead, international theory was contained in specialist writings on eschatology or emerged from mainly orally communicated genealogies and other name-lists. The overall goal of universalistic international theory was the defence and continuation of the Roman Empire as an institution which, in the view of the protagonists of this theory, could and of right had to safeguard the world against its destruction. By contrast, it was the major goal of the group-bound international theory to defend and continue particularistic traditions. In any case, early medieval international theories were not concoctions of straightforward *Realpolitik* but drew on moral norms and social values and therefore were rooted in real life. The power used in the conduct of international relations was regarded as a hereditary gift which rulers needed to have in order to be able to be elevated into office and to execute their duties. The interactions between a ruler and the groups entrusted to the ruler's control were close, and it was seen as belonging to the ruler's tasks to shape and protect these groups. Beyond these groups, the goal of enforcing, maintaining or restoring universal rule was a derivative of the current religious dogma.

TWO

Universalism Contested and Secularized

The conflictual relationship between religious universalism and traditional particularism in the early Middle Ages was relatively stable because it was tied to concepts of space, experiences of time and perceptions of groups which continued without fundamental change up to the tenth century. The crisis in this relationship began at the time when some salient aspects of these attitudes and perceptions were called into question. This occurred first with regard to perceptions of groups at the turn of the millennium and subsequently with regard to experiences of time during the twelfth century. By contrast, the world picture as a concept of space remained largely unchanged up to the fifteenth century. This chapter therefore deals with the extent to which international theories were affected by changes of experiences of time and perceptions of groups.

NEW EXPERIENCES OF TIME

Anxieties about the approaching end of the world appear to have increased towards the end of the tenth century, predominantly in Ireland, England, Flanders and France.[1] In one Old English source, a late-tenth-century homily, the end of the world appears to have been envisaged as impending. The homilist wrote:

> The world shall end with the age which is now current. For five of the ages have passed up to this stage. Then shall this earth end [with the end of the current age], and most of this [current] age has passed until this year, which is the year [AD]

45

971. Not all of the world ages had the same length, but the sum of all of them was three thousand years, some were shorter, some were longer.[2]

The homilist who assigned a wrong number of years to the age of the world[3] concluded that one should be prepared for the end, although it was generally agreed that only the divinity could know when precisely the end would come. Nevertheless, the homilist urged the believers to accept it as a well-ascertained fact that the world would soon come to an end. On the European mainland, another tenth-century source had tentatively equated the coming of the Magyars with the apocalyptic prophecy of peoples breaking their walls and used the Magyar conquests as an indication supporting the belief in the impending end of the world.[4]

A number of further references at the turn of the eleventh century seem to confirm that millenarian creeds loomed large in Western Europe at the time. None of these expressions of fearfulness and anxiety was explicit in determining the precise end of the world; such a statement would have raised suspicions of heresy and would then have entailed persecution. Compromises were offered, but they only betrayed the intensity of worries current at the turn of the millennium. For one, Byrhtferth, an eminent English scholar at the turn of the millennium, followed St Augustine and drew on Apocalypse 20,7 for his suggestion that, even after one thousand years had passed, such merely numerical terms might be meaningless in view of Christ's 'presence' *(andweardnysse)* in the world, which would not be countable in cycles of earthly years.[5] Byrhtferth's comment shows that reading the signs of foreshadowed disaster and preparing oneself for the worst could go together with a sense of hope.

This was also the moral which was behind the visions of the early eleventh-century monk and chronicler Ademar of Chabannes (*c.* 988–1034), who seems to have been the first to link millenarian fears together with events in Palestine. One night, Ademar had seen a vision of a bleeding crucifix with a lamenting Christ. Many years afterwards, he sat down to write a chronicle of the world, and inserted a report on the vision into his chronicle. Moreover, in retrospect, he interconnected the vision with events which had occurred in Palestine under the rule of Khalif al-Hakim (996–1021) who had authorized the persecution of Jews and Christians. In the course of these persecutions, the Church of the Holy Sepulchre had been destroyed.[6] Apparently, Ademar had heard of these events through pilgrims' reports, and he understood the news as a sign of the approaching end of the world. And yet, writing several years after the event, Ademar drew comfort from the fact that al-Hakim had been removed from the Khalifate and that peace had been restored in Palestine. The implication is that the millenarian fears may have inspired the spreading in the Occident of rhetoric in favour of the crusades after the middle of the century.[7]

The declining confidence in eschatological speculations unleashed the search for novel experiences of time.[8] Still in the middle of the twelfth century, Bishop Otto of Freising (c. 1111–1158) applied the then conventional concept of time according to which it was regarded as a process which the divinity had willed to be limited to the 'earthly city', and maintained that the 'City of God' was not under the rule of time.[9] In consequence of this concept, time was cosmological as well as historical in kind and, in itself, finite. But this concept of time militated against the Aristotelian definition of time which came to be reintroduced in the Occident through Arab translations of Aristotle's original works in the twelfth and thirteenth centuries. According to the Aristotelian concept, time was experienced as a unilinear infinite process from the former (*prius*) to the latter (*posterius*) and was the prime mover of all things, elevated above all other divine creations.

This concept of time made it impossible to exempt the City of God from the rule of time. In other words, if time was prior to everything else, existence became inconceivable outside or beyond time. But this new concept of astronomical time militated against religious dogma which continued to stimulate speculations about the future in terms of eternity. Astronomical time began to be considered as infinite and beyond human influence, whereas the period during which the world was in existence was constituted as a category of its own and defined as historical time. Historical time continued to be regarded as finite up to the second half of the eighteenth century. It allowed for the counting of years according to a variety of different man-made schemes and cycles, whereas astronomical time had to be measured continuously by standard means, such as mechanical clocks, which could operate regardless of seasons of the year and hours of the day. This differentiation not only conflicted with and called into question eschatological speculations but also opened up the questions of what was the use of the Roman Empire, whether and, if so, how and by whom it was to be safeguarded and, finally, what the relations between the Roman Empire and the rest of the *ecumene* were to be like. In short, the period under review produced much work for international theorists.

NEW PERCEPTIONS OF GROUPS

By the tenth century, Catholicism had transformed kin groups to a degree which rendered the uninterrupted transmission of group-bound traditions difficult. Members of aristocratic kin groups lost important positions in the Church organization, first, after the aristocratic lay clerics who had resided in monasteries and other ecclesiastical institutions were forced out and were replaced by ordained monks; and, secondly, after more aristocratic proprietary Church institutions were placed under the control of bishops.[10] Already at the turn of the eighth century, a process of the redefinition of kinship had begun, through which collateral kinsmen were excluded from kin groups. In consequence, ever more often, kin groups became extinct[11] or began to redefine themselves in terms of their residences rather than in terms of their constitutive traditions of descent.

This process began in the ruling kin groups, rapidly spread into the aristocracy and finally affected motley groups of settlers who began to gather in urban communities of towns and cities at the turn of the millennium.[12] But large parts of the farming population in the rural countryside may have remained unaffected during the Middle Ages and much of the early modern period. Nevertheless, the waning significance of kinship promoted the willingness of residents in hilltop castles and urban communities to define their identities in the spatial terms of their settlements rather than in accordance with group-bound traditions. A process of territorialization was launched in consequence of which groups were identified in terms of the space they occupied with their settlements or in terms of the control exercised by their ruler.[13]

The long-term consequence of the process was nevertheless that settlements and polities as areas under the control of a ruler had to be delineated as territories with ever more precisely drawn boundaries. Groups thus came to be defined more often in terms of space and rule than in terms of descent and by the stipulations of contracts. This process of the territorialization of groups and areas under the control of rulers ushered in the demand that rights to rule over land and people should be defined unequivocally in such a way that the rights of one ruler were exclusive of the rights of all other rulers of the same rank.[14] Where this was not possible because contending claims existed the issue had to be settled through war. Thus the period under review offered ample opportunities to military professionals and kept busy rulers and other practical decision-makers in international relations.

DEFINING CONTRACT OF RULE AND RESTRICTING ACCESS TO INTERNATIONAL RELATIONS

Aristotelian philosophy reshaped not only experiences of time, but also the principles on which later medieval international theory was founded. As a consequence of the territorialization, international relations had to be reconceptualized as being across the boundaries of polities. The model upon which the territorial polities of the thirteenth, fourteenth and fifteenth centuries were drawn was the city. According to Aristotle, a citizen was a resident in the city who had the right to participate in judicial institutions and in government.[15] Twelfth-century statutes of urban communities refined this definition by specifying that citizens acquired the right to take active part in legal and administrative processes through the contract which constituted their urban communities. In this sense, just rule over urban communities was rule by consent.[16] The contract was more than a legal construct. It was the single most important secular instrument which the ruled had in their hands for the legitimization of rulers of urban communities and, at the same time, for the limitation of the rulers' power. Many urban revolts were justified by the claim that rulers of towns or cities had abused their power, and when the revolts were successful charters could be enforced which established more restrictive rules for the exercise of power.[17]

Early in the fourteenth century, theorists began to apply the secular principle that just rule was rule by consent to polities other than urban communities of towns and cities. Again, these theorists drew on Aristotle who had argued that rule over free men and women as autonomous actors was unlawful because only slaves as dependent actors could be commanded by their owners.[18] Fourteenth-century theorists concluded from this phrase that, since the divinity had created all men and women as free persons, rule in all types of polity could only be the result of some voluntary contract which had previously been concluded among the ruled, and they argued that, through such a contract, the inhabitants of a polity had installed a government for their own benefit. These theorists thus took for granted two characteristics of these polities. The first characteristic was that the polities over which government by consent was to be installed through contracts were clearly demarcated by recognizable spatial boundaries. The second characteristic was that those inhabitants who had a say in the legal and government matters of these polities formed a group with a degree of homogeneity sufficient to allow them to act in concert for the establishment of rule by consent.

Although urban communities and territorial polities shared the common platform of contractualism a dualism occurred which set apart both types of polity in the later Middle Ages. The urban communities of towns and cities were constituted on legal bases which differed from those of the territories in the surrounding countryside. Whereas the towns and cities became territorialized as self-governing communities, the rural villages in the countryside were absorbed into polities under the control of territorial rulers. Therefore, in the urban communities, the contract led to lasting participation in government of some inhabitants or their representatives, while in the territorial polities participation of the ruled was understood by most political theorists as being confined to the initial consent to the establishment of the government.

The contractualism of fourteenth-century theorists thus enhanced the integration of urban communities and rural territorial polities. It did so by limiting the contract-making capability to definable groups of residents in given areas at the expense of humankind as a whole. The consequence was that secular contractualist theories could not be employed for the legitimization of institutions representing universalism. Henceforth, urban communities and rural territorial polities could be conceptualized as a category of space of regular communication which was and of right had to be distinguished from institutions representing universal rule. As secular theories of spaces of regular communication, contractualist theories were constituted as political theories whose goal it was to define the rulers of urban communities and rural territorial polities as international actors.

In detail, the several fourteenth-century political theorists proceeded in different ways. There was first and foremost Engelbert of Admont (c. 1250–1332), a Benedictine monk and abbot of the Styrian monastery of Admont. Throughout his life, he was primarily a scholar with an astonishingly wide range of interests.[19] Engelbert was much influenced by Aristotle's works which he seems to have studied carefully. Like many other theorists before him in the thirteenth century and after him in the fifteenth century, Engelbert was concerned about the future of the Roman Empire and about the consequences which the prolonged crisis of imperial institutions might have for the world as a whole. Like many others, he wrote an eschatological treatise on the beginning and the end of the Roman Empire which he completed around 1312.

In this treatise, he proposed two types of legitimization of government. One was based on religious universalism; the other on secular contractualism. Engelbert made no effort to reconcile these two opposing theories. Instead, he reserved the first theory for the Roman Empire while he applied the second one to all urban communities and territorial polities. With regard to the Roman Empire, Engelbert argued that the divinity had willed that this institution should exist as a safeguard against the destruction of the world. He concluded that, because human actors were incapable of overturning divine decisions, they had not been involved in the process of establishing the Roman Empire which could not then be legitimized through any specific human contribution. Consequently, human actors had only one choice, namely to accept the existence of the Roman Empire as an institution of universal rule and to execute the commands issued by the emperors.[20]

With regard to urban communities and territorial polities, Engelbert took the opposing view that their inhabitants had concluded hypothetical contracts for the purpose of installing rulers above themselves. He noticed that each of these contracts was confined to a particular community or polity and insisted that the contracts were irrevocable covenants. That meant that, once the inhabitants had concluded a contract and invested a government, the contract was binding forever and the government so installed had unlimited duration.[21]

Other fourteenth-century theorists who shared Engelbert's convictions did realize the necessity that they should explain why the Roman Empire was not a manifest institution of universal rule in the sense that the emperors were the actual rulers of the *ecumene*. In order to provide this explanation, the Italian jurist Bartolus of Sassoferato (1314–1357), whose works were widely read in the later Middle Ages, devised an elaborate casuistry.[22] He distinguished four types of polities: firstly, peoples of Roman origin living in polities under Roman rule and Roman law; secondly, peoples of Roman origin living in polities under Roman law but not under Roman rule; thirdly, peoples of non-Roman origin living in polities under Roman law but not under Roman rule; and, fourthly, peoples of non-Roman origin living in polities neither under Roman law nor under Roman rule due to some privilege of freedom that had been granted to them previously by Roman Emperors.[23]

The use of these distinctions allowed Bartolus to retain some hypothetical form of universalism which he associated with Roman rule and could trace back to the divine sphere. Bartolus could then admit the manifest coexistence in his own time of peoples of different origin as well as under a variety of rulers and still insist that the Roman Empire was the only original and genuine world empire. He could explain this seeming paradox by arguing that the Roman Emperors had used their own competence to exempt peoples from Roman rule and Roman law. In suggesting this explanation, Bartolus could rank the existence of non-Roman legal systems and polities as the result of secondary human decisions. He could also argue that such diversity was not incompatible with the belief that the Roman Emperors as the guardians of the Roman Empire and of Roman law had been invested with universal rule by the divinity.

But the price for this explanation was dear. Bartolus's logic was one that was totally focused on the past. It suggested factors of the secondary diversification of some original unity with no recognizable concern for the regaining of unity in the future. Hence, Bartolus's casuistry was exclusively secular in kind, as no one could possibly derive from it any hope for the restoration of the Roman Empire as a universal empire.

Like Engelbert's, Bartolus's international theory was thus a means to explain in terms of secular theory the coexistence of a universal empire and many autonomous urban communities and territorial polities. The coexistence was explained in terms of the modalities in which legitimate rule had been established and which defined international actors in terms of the legitimate control over spaces of regular communication. Thus, in terms of international theory, the decision about who was admissible as an international actor was recognized as depending on two factors, a discernible territorial substrate of rule and the ascertainable consent by the ruled to the ruler as the representative of their collective will.

Engelbert's contemporary, the Florentine poet and politician Dante Alighieri (c. 1250–c. 1320), took a different view. Under the impact of an expedition which Emperor Henry VII (1308–1313) was about to carry out to Rome, Dante prepared a treatise on monarchy in 1310 in which he tried to support the emperor's plan to seek coronation in Rome and stabilize the Roman Empire. Dante agreed with Engelbert in the scepticism with which he judged the future of the world. Yet he was more concerned than Engelbert about the pluralism of many coexisting urban communities and territorial polities and deplored the frequency of civil strife and warfare.

Dante then proposed a solution to these problems which stood against Engelbert's convictions. Whereas Engelbert, like Bartolus, admitted the pluralism of heterogeneous urban communities and territorial polities, Dante requested that the Roman Emperors should be restored as the actual and only rulers of the *ecumene*, and, like Augustine, he argued that the pluralism of coexisting rulers contributed much to what he perceived as the evils of his time. He specified competition among rulers who were eager for conquest, and diversity of legal and moral principles which stimulated attitudes of hatred and disrespect.

Under the influence of Aristotelian philosophy,[24] Dante suggested that moderation of desires and the equity of goals were the best means by which peace and stability could be accomplished in the *ecumene*, and he concluded that these means could most appropriately be provided and secured by a universal monarch.[25] Dante's international theory was contrary to Engelbert's because Dante rejected the idea that just rule was rule by consent and because he denied that there was any positive value in the coexistence of many urban communities and territorial polities. Instead, in Dante's view, the *ecumene* was most stable if there were no international relations at all.

Already during his lifetime, Dante's optimism was reduced to mere wishful speculation. Henry VII died on his way to Rome and left all hopes unfulfilled. Moreover, in the 1320s, a radical version of Engelbert's contractualism was proposed which called into question the postulate that adherence to universalism was necessary. Marsilius of Padua (*c.* 1280–1342/3), a scholar of renown and an influential though controversial adviser to Emperor Louis IV (1314–1347), demanded in 1324 that the contract between the ruler and the ruled should be executed in practical politics and that, to that end, rulers should be popularly elected. Marsilius derived his demand from his insistence that there was no reason why the contract between the ruled and the ruler should be irrevocable. Against Engelbert, Marsilius maintained that the right of the ruled to invest the ruler was inalienable and thus remained with the ruled beyond the investiture.[26] Without using the phraseology of contractualism explicitly, Marsilius argued a theory which drew on the voluntary agreement of the ruled to the ruler and posited them as legislators.

A generation later, John Quidort of Paris (*d.* 1360), a scholar at the University of Paris, applied Marsilius's theory to contractualism. His conclusion was that, if the ruled were legitimators, they also had the competence to revoke the contract, to elect a different ruler and even to establish a new form of government at their own discretion. For John, the *ecumene* consisted solely of urban communities and territorial polities and had no place for an institution of universal rule overarching these communities and polities.[27]

The fourteenth-century debate on the salience of universalism came after, and possibly in response to, suggestions which had been made in the thirteenth century by St Thomas Aquinas (*c.* 1225–1274). Aquinas, one of the most influential theologians of the later Middle Ages, made an effort to provide, among many other things, a platform for the derivation of norms and rules which could be regarded as the inalienable property of humankind as a whole. Aquinas identified this platform as natural law, which he considered to have been divinely ordained. Thus, to Aquinas, natural law as divine law was universal law because the divinity had willed it to be applied to all humankind.

First and foremost among the rules and norms making up natural law was the right to live. Taking the right to live to represent the essence of natural law, Aquinas moved on to a discussion of the law of war which he included in natural law. He did so because he understood the law of war to consist of norms and rules which were considered to be valid among contending parties which had abrogated all relations and were determined to resolve their dissent by resort to martial arms. The most difficult theoretical problem with the inclusion of the law of war into natural law was that war was an obvious violation of the right to live. Aquinas's solution to this problem was informed by St Augustine and high medieval decretals, and it demanded that wars should be permitted only if they were just.[28] Aquinas then took the argument a step beyond St Augustine and elaborated the criteria through which the justice of wars could be determined.

He identified three criteria: firstly that wars had to be fought for morally defendable aims; secondly that they had to be conducted by established rulers; and thirdly that they had to be declared. Only war aims that sought to rectify previously committed acts of injustice could be morally defensible. Thus just wars could only be defensive campaigns for the restitution or compensation of previously suffered losses. Only rulers who held their position by legitimate titles, had been installed through due process and could thus act as representatives of the population under their rule could be accepted as established. Declarations of war had to be explicit advance manifestations of the intention of applying physical force and had to be accompanied by the specification of the reasons for the war. These reasons had to follow from the morally defendable war aims. War was thus awarded the status of a legal contest with the divinity as the judge.[29]

Unlike Augustine, Aquinas could not envisage peace as the stable condition of a veritable universal empire. Instead, his exposition of the law of war presupposed the existence of urban communities and territorial polities as spaces of regular communication as well as of rulers who could be identified and acknowledged as the highest representatives of the wills of the ruled in a given urban community or territorial polity. Consequently, Aquinas made no attempt to vest control over natural law into any institution.

Instead, the very essence of his argument on natural law was that, because it was instituted as universal law by divine will, it neither required nor allowed human control or any degree of manipulation by human actors. Therefore, Aquinas advocated a de-institutionalized version of universalism which he set as a legal category and derived directly from the divinity. Under this condition, Aquinas could disregard institutions of universal rule, admit rulers of urban communities and territorial polities as the sole type of international actors and yet retain the conviction that legal instruments for the maintenance of order in the *ecumene* were in operation.

There were few conspicuous figures among the rulers of the
high and late Middle Ages. Of course, emperors such as
Frederick I (1152–1190), Henry VI (1190–1197) and Frederick
II (1197–1250) attracted a great deal of attention among contemporaries as they strove and failed to fend off the
secularization of universalism and to expand the Roman Empire
over the *ecumene*. But none of them could equal Charlemagne,
though Frederick I did his best to advance the cult of
Charlemagne as a saint. Of course, there were also some cru-
saders, among them King Richard the Lionheart of England
(1189–1199) who became notorious for his extravagance and his
daring. But Richard's crusading adventure ended in imperial
custody from which he was only bailed out under humiliating
circumstances. Nevertheless, as in Charlemagne's case, we can
infer rulers' international theories from the principal actions
that are on record. These actions displayed a *faible* for warfare.
Charlemagne had been conspicuous for having himself led
many campaigns over a long period while few other early
medieval rulers had received praise for their eagerness to go to
war. By contrast, in the high and late Middle Ages, the warrior
king was a common figure.

The change of images underlines the waning significance of
religious criteria for the legitimization of rulers. Although
rulers never totally waived them during the Middle Ages they
tended to prefer secular criteria, and these were military
achievements, specifically victory in battles fought by themselves or their appointed generals. The period thus witnessed
increasing sizes of armed forces, the deployment of new and
technologically more sophisticated weapons, increasing numbers of fortifications and armouries, and, as a consequence of all
that, an explosion in military expenses.[30]

Hence rulers seem to have eagerly taken up the challenges
implied in the secularization of universalism. They responded
to this process with strategies for the expansion of territorial
polities and began to commit themselves to actions by which
they could compete among each other for the highest rank, the

most extensive territory, the largest population and the richest resources. In the end, a hierarchy of rulers came into existence at the top of which those rulers were placed who could claim to be in sole control of the largest possible territorial polity.

The territorial rulers met with opposition to their strategies from two sides, namely that of the emperors and that of the urban communities. Up to the middle of the thirteenth century, the occidental emperors tried to defend their position as religiously sanctioned universal rulers. They lost this position with the end of the crusades to Palestine but were able to reform the Empire into the direction of a territorial polity. On the other side, the councils of towns and cities in many parts of Europe strove to have their urban communities recognized as autonomous entities by neighbouring territorial rulers. Among the 4,000 or so urban communities which existed in the later Middle Ages, many of those which were placed under imperial control managed to acquire a degree of autonomy that allowed their councils to act as if they were territorial rulers. Elsewhere, councils remained confined to the self-administration of internal communal affairs. Territorial polities and urban communities were the two most important representations of spaces of regular communication in the high and later Middle Ages.

Although all urban communities were local and confined within narrow walls, universalism took root there in a novel shape, namely in designs for a world system of trade. Professional traders founded companies, established and expanded ever closer networks of trade which interconnected towns and cities in many parts of the *ecumene*. The networks were maintained by companies which established branches in several cities as well as through cooperation with other traders and their companies, specifically at places in North Africa and in West Asia.

The activities of professional traders greatly eased the exchange of goods and techniques of production between Europe, Africa and Asia, advanced a sense of market interdependence and the competitiveness of products and techniques of production throughout the *ecumene*.[31] But, most importantly, they supported the demands that trade should follow its own rules and patterns and should thus be exempted from interventions by rulers. Hence the contractual urban communities became not only a model for the organization of spaces of regular communication but also the centre pieces in a world system of trade which was considered to operate autonomously in accordance with its own rules and patterns. An economic universalism thus came into existence whose proponents were those who were most eager to advance the spatial and legal separation of local urban communities of towns and cities.[32]

Not surprisingly, religious universalism continued to receive support from Church institutions. But, like the emperors, the Church took a new attitude towards universalism, which was devised to advance missionary efforts rather than empire-building. Immediately following the eclipse of the crusades in the middle of the thirteenth century, the popes launched a series of missionary expeditions, initially to Central and East Asia, and later also to East and Southeast Africa. It was the explicit purpose of the missionary expeditions to spread Christianity to the boundaries of the *ecumene*.[33] In this sense, the organizers of the missionary expeditions continued, with different means, the same universalist strategies which the emperors of the twelfth and thirteenth centuries had pursued through military means during the crusades. In this way, the missionaries and the Church organizers who commissioned them disclosed their conviction that Christianity could be regarded as a universal religion only if it was manifestly practised everywhere in the *ecumene*.

The theories underlying the manifest actions of rulers and other actors in international relations were controversial. What were contested, then, not only among the theorists, but also among the practitioners of international relations, were the criteria by which it was to be decided what kind of rulers could be recognized as international actors. Territorial rulers and councils of urban communities agreed that only a legitimate ruler could be an international actor because only a legitimate ruler could represent the ruled living in a given space of regular communication. Consequently, only those territorial rulers or councils of urban communities were admissible as international actors who had the sole right to represent the population under their control and who could legitimately and with justice decide on war and peace.

According to this view, territorial rulers and councils of urban communities occupied the supreme rank in the hierarchy of rulers because they had no one above themselves except, in certain cases, the emperor. In Latin texts, the word *supremus* (supreme) was used to express this status which anticipated what came to be referred to as sovereignty in the sixteenth century.[34] But the emperors and the pope rejected this claim as they assumed that only a universal ruler could occupy the supreme position in the hierarchy of rulers. But, after the end of the crusades, the claims of the emperors and the popes for supreme ranks among rulers counted for little, not only because the crusades had ended in catastrophic defeat but also because the pope and the emperor could not agree which of them was to occupy the highest rank.

During the period, there were five conflicts about the rank of rulers as international actors, and they occurred simultaneously and interdependent with each other. They were (1) the conflict between the emperors and the popes about the legitimacy of the emperor and the emperor's right to protect the Church; (2) the conflict between the emperors on the one side and, on the other, kings and other territorial rulers about the privileges of the emperors; (3) the conflict between territorial rulers and the councils of urban communities about demands for the autonomy of the government of the latter; (4) the conflict between the occidental emperors and the Roman Emperors in Byzantium about their mutual rights and privileges inside the Roman Empire as well as between the Roman Catholic Church and the Greek Orthodox Church about the position in Christendom of the pope in Rome; and (5) the conflict between Christians and Muslims about the control of Palestine.

The problem in the first conflict was that whereas, up to the tenth century, it had not been felt necessary to separate the temporal from the ecclesiastical sphere, clergymen began to claim in the course of the tenth and eleventh centuries that the Church should be governed solely by the clergy and should be exempt from interference by rulers. Specifically, high-ranking Church officials began to support the doctrine that rulers should not be allowed to interfere in the process of admission to high Church offices.

The issue became critical when, in 1046, Emperor Henry III (1039–1056) deposed three rival popes and placed his own candidate on the papal throne. Afterwards, in 1059, a Roman council decreed that popes could only be elected by cardinals. On these grounds, when Pope Gregory VII (1073–1085) was elected, he immediately began to take the view that the emperor's obligation to protect the Church did not involve the right to rule over it and promoted the autonomy of Church institutions against the then ruling emperor, Henry IV (1056–1106). Gregory drew up a radical document probably in 1076 in which he insisted that the pope, as the highest representative of the Church and Christendom, could not be judged by anyone and was the only person to be rightly called the holder of a universal office.[35]

As the emperor refused to accept this doctrine, a conflict arose which, since the twelfth century, has been referred to as the 'Investiture Controversy'. It was explicitly fought over whose right it was to invest bishops. A compromise was accomplished in 1122 by which rulers gave up their privilege of participating in bishops' elections. But at a deeper level, what was contested was whether the pope or the occidental emperor was the highest representative of the Roman Empire as a universal empire. The problem remained unsolved even after the controversy petered out in the twelfth century. Nevertheless, the compromise of 1122 promoted the desacralization of territorial rulers and the partition of the *ecumene* into secular-political and religious-ecclesiastical spheres.

The occidental emperors had to seek to manifest their rule in terms other than those provided by religious universalism and they were obliged to seek demonstrations of the universality of their rule in the manifest terms of control over the entire *ecumene*. However, there arose no feasible opportunities through which the occidental emperors could succeed in demonstrating their capability of ecumenical control and, consequently, they were reduced to being mere secular representatives and protectors of the Roman Empire which, in turn, became itself conceived as sacred and began to be styled as the 'Holy Roman Empire' in 1157.[36]

In the case of the second conflict, the problem was whether or not the occidental emperors had any suzerainty over kings in Europe. The problem became an urgent one when, after the tenth century, the number of rulers who bore royal titles in association with a territory increased. With the exception of the areas which came to be identified as Germany during the eleventh and twelfth centuries and of Bohemia, it was understood that these kingdoms were outside the Roman Empire. While the core parts of Bohemia were regarded as integral parts of the Roman Empire, kings ruling in 'Germany' had taken over the imperial title from the Frankish kings in the course of the tenth century so that, in this case, the royal and the imperial titles were often borne by the same rulers and thus hardly distinguishable.

Hence, while the late medieval emperors could take the view that they were suzerains over the Kings of Bohemia and that the Germans were the 'nation' on to whom the Roman Empire had been 'transferred', the kings outside the Roman Empire rejected any imperial claims towards suzerainty.[37] Therefore the gap between the theoretical claim of the emperors to universal rule clashed with the demand for the recognition that the Roman Empire should have definite external boundaries which marked it off against the territories under the rule of kings. Eventually, the emperors were forced to accept in terms of practical politics that their rule was confined to the Roman Empire within its customary boundaries.

In the third case, the problem was that urban communities of towns and cities were established on the legal basis of contractual agreements among their settlers and were thus legitimized in accordance with a secular theory of politics. Inhabitants of many towns and cities insisted that their settlements were contractual communes for which they sought to obtain recognition as autonomous legal entities by neighbouring territorial rulers. Inside the Roman Empire, these urban communities sought protection from the emperor against rulers in their vicinity and often attained a degree of autonomy by which they could constitute themselves as entities in their own right.[38] This was possible inside the Roman Empire because the privileges of the emperor over these communities were frequently confined to merely formal suzerainty and a limited amount of taxation.[39]

The quest for autonomy of urban communities was enhanced by the fact that the towns and cities became by far the most innovative forces in the high and late Middle Ages and generated a large amount of monetary affluence which could be converted into military strength and political power. Hence the urban communities were controversial precisely because they presented what appeared and appealed to many as a successful alternative to both, the universalism of rule claimed by the emperors and the principles of territorial rule practised by kings and other rulers.

In the fourth case, both emperors at the helm of the Roman Empire came under increasing pressure to delineate their spheres of influence vis-à-vis each other more precisely than in the early Middle Ages. The title 'Roman Emperor' came back into use for the occidental emperor in the 980s, and this usage made explicit the intensifying rivalry between the western and the eastern emperors. Still, Emperor Otto II (973–983), himself married to a Byzantine princess, made plans to marry his son to the daughter of the emperor in Byzantium and, in this way, demonstrated his willingness to restore the unity of imperial rule through hereditary succession.

But his eleventh-century successors did not continue the policy of peaceful accommodation. Emperor Conrad II (1024–1039) even had an imperial bull issued in which he announced that Rome, not Byzantium, was the capital of the *ecumene* and held the reins of power.[40] That meant that the relations between the two emperors were to become increasingly conflictual and hostile while the potential for cooperation towards common goals was declining. The decline was aggravated by a decision by Patriarch Michael I Kerullarios (1043–1058) who, in 1054, decreed that the pope in Rome had no authority over the Orthodox Church and excommunicated the Latin Christians. Henceforth the Catholic and the Orthodox Churches have continued as two separate and independent ecclesiastical organizations. After the end of the eleventh century, the Byzantine–occidental controversy merged with the conflict of the crusades.[41]

In the fifth case, the problem was how the relations between Christians and Muslims were to be conducted in areas under Muslim control. Neither in the Iberian peninsula nor in Lower Italy and Palestine had there been any conspicuous difficulty before the end of the first millennium. At that time, however, Christians began to take hostile attitudes towards Muslims and devised plans for the restoration of Christian control over these Muslim areas. Since the fifteenth century, these wars have been referred to as crusades. In the Iberian peninsula, conquest loomed large in the high Middle Ages after humble beginnings in the eleventh century. In Lower Italy, Emperor Otto II plunged into warfare against the Muslims but was defeated at Cotrone in 982. The emperor's efforts were subsequently continued by the popes with more success. In Palestine, an initial request for a military campaign was made by Pope Sergius IV (1009–1012) after the demolition of the Church of the Holy Sepulchre. But this call remained unanswered. In 1076, Pope Gregory VII repeated the call but was no more successful.[42]

Finally, in 1095, Pope Urban II (1088–1099) issued a call which met with a surprisingly large response mainly in Western Europe. An army of professional warriors got on its way in 1098 and was joined by civilian pilgrims.[43] During the following two centuries, seven large campaigns were fought over Palestine with some support from Byzantine armies; in the course of these campaigns some Christian rulers established themselves temporarily in Jerusalem and elsewhere in the area. In the end, however, various Muslim armies were able to repel the invaders and, in 1291, the last Christian stronghold in Palestine was given up.

The catastrophic end of the crusades demonstrated the powerlessness of the emperors, both in Byzantium and in the Occident. Thus, already in the middle of the twelfth century, William of Malmesbury (c. 1095–1143), an English historiographer, noted that the crusades had proved that the emperors were inept as the representatives of Christendom.[44] The crusades also put a heavy burden on Byzantium. The fourth crusade (1202–4), which did not reach Palestine, led to severe unrest in the city, the expulsion of the Roman Emperors from the city and the establishment of a non-traditional Latin Empire which continued until the Roman Emperors were restored in 1261.

Indeed, during the period under review, conflict loomed large. Under the conditions of an experience of time as an indefinite process and of perceptions of groups as inhabitants of territorialized polities, it became difficult to conceive universalism solely in religious terms. Territorialization fuelled the demand that the Roman Empire ought to be defined as a veritable institution of universal rule extending across the entire tricontinental *ecumene*. The consequences of territorialization for the Roman Empire were grave. Those who insisted that the Roman Empire was an administrative entity extending across the *ecumene* had to present schemes for the extension of its boundaries to the fringes of the *ecumene*, mainly through extensive warfare.

Those who took the contrary view that the Roman Empire had always existed and should therefore continue to exist within certain boundaries were faced with three difficulties. First, they were forced to limit universalism to religious matters only and to secularize imperial politics in confinement to rule over a certain territory. Secondly, they had to present designs for the conduct of relations between the emperors and rulers beyond the confines of the Roman Empire who would not accept imperial suzerainty. According to this second view, the Roman Emperors were merely one category of actors who competed with a large number of other actors within the European international system. Thirdly, they had to specify the principles according to which the relations between the emperor and other rulers inside the Roman Empire were to be established and maintained.[45]

The conflicts of the twelfth and thirteenth centuries therefore promoted a sense of crisis which led to fundamental questions about the nature and the conditions of international relations. As religious universalism could no longer be taken for granted and as secular designs for rule over the *ecumene* were in vain, the question came up of what would happen if the Roman Empire were to come to its end. The question itself raised anxieties which became manifest in radical ascetic movements. But the fact that no practical answers were offered to the question further deepened the sense of crisis.

After the crusades, both universal rulers and autonomously acting groups disappeared as international actors and were replaced by kings and other territorial rulers as well as by the councils of towns and cities. Emperors could have an impact on international relations only to the extent that they could act as territorial rulers. In the Occident this remained possible in a number of cases but in Byzantium the rule of the emperors became ever more narrowly confined to the city and a few areas in its vicinity. In consequence, Muslim Turks could penetrate into Asia Minor and the Balkans and establish there an empire of their own. This raised far-reaching questions about the boundaries between the two empires, and answers to these questions were most commonly sought through war. Thus, different from St Augustine's and Dante's international theory, the decisions about peace and war no longer fell into the province of the universal ruler but became the business of antagonist territorial rulers.

The later Middle Ages witnessed the growth of three theoretical responses to the crisis of universalism which followed the failure of the crusades. The first theory was conventional. Its proponents, among them Dante, demanded that the Roman Emperors should assume the powers of veritable ruler of the *ecumene*.

The second theory appeared as an innovative design early in the fourteenth century and seems to have been composed in order to cope with the widening gap between institutions of universal rule on the one side, and territorial polities and urban communities on the other. Its proponents, among them Engelbert of Admont, assigned the entire *ecumene* to the institutions of universal rule as its spatial substrate and derived its legitimacy from divine will. But they categorized territorial polities and urban communities as clearly demarcated spaces of regular communication which were derived from human will and whose governments were established by contracts in their favour.

The third theory was also innovative and was formulated in the context of considerations about divinely willed natural law. Its proponents, among them St Thomas Aquinas, tried to rescue universalism by de-institutionalizing it. They sought to identify as universalism all those rules and norms which they considered to be valid for and inalienable to humankind and derived them from natural law. In retrospect, it is clear that only the third theory has continued to have influence and has become the foundation of present human rights thinking. But that this theory would win out remained concealed up to the end of the fifteenth century.

The crisis of religious universalism was thus productive. It generated, among many other things, a corpus of international theories which came along in texts pertaining to the novel genre of political theory. This genre was novel because the question of who had the legitimate right to execute power was new. The question had never been asked in the early Middle Ages because power had been considered as a personal gift. Therefore, the power of a religiously legitimized universal ruler could then have been taken for granted, opposed or simply ignored.

In the later Middle Ages, the potential for conflict between religious universalism and group-bound particularism vanished because religious universalism was no longer tenable as the source from which institutions of universal rule could be legitimized and because the group-bound tradition to which particularistic norms and rules had been attached disappeared. Thus universalism was redefined in secular terms and territorial polities were delineated as spaces of regular communication. Under these conditions, those who articulated proposals for universal rule had to compose them as schemes for the subjection of the tricontinental *ecumene* to the manifest control of one and the same ruler. Because this was impossible in practice, such designs were rendered untenable. That meant that institutions of universal rule could be conceived, if at all, only as secular agencies overarching the multifarious territorial polities and urban communities.

The consequence of the secularization of universalism was that power could no longer be defined and measured in terms of influence which persons could yield over groups. Instead, the exercise of power was a corollary of legitimate control over land and peoples, with the proviso that only one institution could be in charge over one space of regular communication. Power in the sense of legitimate control over land and people was supreme when it could not be shared among institutions whose rulers or representatives held power legitimately and with justice. This meant that only those rulers of territorial polities and councils of urban communities who were recognized as the holders of a supreme power could be admitted as actors in international relations, whereas all other holders of offices, rights and privileges were mediated and became subordinates who, whatever their wealth and influence, were private persons.

Not all spaces of regular communication were large-sized entities. Indeed many urban communities, some of which were densely populated, were confined to narrow sites. Thus there were many international actors who competed among each other by military means, political strategies and economic measures. Although the *ecumene* continued to be depicted as integrated, it was in reality deeply divided and no one could truthfully deny that international relations as the conflictual interactions across the boundaries of spaces of regular communication were in operation. Therefore, one consequence of the crisis of universalism was the extension of military activity.

From the beginning of the thirteenth century, the international theories which ordained monks and secular scholars proposed helped to establish the criteria which territorial rulers and councils of urban communities could use to decide what kind of wars were just, and, in order to accomplish this task, further criteria had to be provided to determine when and under what conditions power was to be exercised legitimately and with justice and, last but not least, who was an international actor. International theory was thus, first and foremost, designed for the conduct of practical politics.

Theorists as well as practitioners identified the sources of power for the conduct of international relations more frequently with offices than in the early Middle Ages, and rulers were more often than before found to devote their power to the demarcation of territories through the use of martial arms. The goal of enforcing, maintaining or restoring universal rule continued as an unquestioned derivative of religious dogma, while theorizing about the hypothetical contract emerged as the centrepiece of political philosophy.

THREE

The Globalization of Secular Universalism

The secularization of universalism promoted critical inquiries. While St Augustine had taken the view that faith in God was the source of all knowledge, late-medieval scientists began to distinguish between believing and knowing and insisted that knowledge should be testable on empirical grounds. These tests also affected the world picture. Even though the fourteenth-century fictitious traveller Sir John Mandeville still used the Bible as a guidebook, the biblical world picture became subject to alterations where it appeared to contradict empirical evidence.[1] Such evidence was increasingly brought to Europe by the merchant traders who visited distant places ever more frequently and interacted with their colleagues in the world system of trade that spanned the *ecumene*. Under these conditions, it made sense to demand that the precise locations of places should be established and mapped and that distances should be measured as meticulously as possible.

Critical enquiries resulted in controversies. In the fifteenth century, there were several of them. One concerned the circumnavigability of Africa, another the traversability of the ocean from Europe to Asia. With regard to Africa, the question was whether a sea route existed around the southern tip of the continent. Medieval *mappaemundi* suggested that this was the case and that the circumnavigation of Africa allowed the passage to Asia. But the geographical knowledge of antiquity, namely that enshrined in the work of the Alexandrine geographer Ptolemy (*c.* 100–*c.* 160), told a different story. Ptolemy had assumed a hypothetical fourth continent, which fifteenth-century cartographers believed connected Africa with Asia and thereby turned into an inland lake the water basin now known as the Indian

2 Fra Mauro, Map of the world, 1459.

Ocean. If the map-makers were right, Africa was not circum-navigable and there was no sea route from Europe to Asia. Ptolemy had to his credit that his work was of great antiquity and that it was supported by a seemingly sound argument. Ptolemy had postulated the fourth continent in the south as a counterbalance to the land masses of the northern hemisphere and had argued that the southern continent was necessary in order to preserve the stability of the earth (illus. 2).

As the problem was not solvable on theoretical grounds, empirical tests were necessary. It is not surprising that, in the course of the fifteenth century, mariners and traders from southern Europe, mainly Portugal, became involved in the tests after Genoese and Iberian sailors had begun to penetrate into the waters west of the Strait of Gibraltar in the second half of the fourteenth century. Portuguese kings and other members of the royal court supported these tests and launched a series of expeditions directed southwards along the African coasts throughout the fifteenth century.

The mid-fifteenth-century state of knowledge is reflected in a map painted by the Venetian monk Fra Mauro (d. 1460) for King Alfonso V of Portugal (1438–1481) in 1459.[2] Like other map makers, Fra Mauro provided a fairly precise and detailed outline of the West African coasts down to what is now the Bight of Biafra but reconfigured the coasts with the ocean so that a hypothetical fjord came into existence. He then let the coast proceed southward before it bent to the east and gave way to a stretch of water between Africa and Asia. However, Fra Mauro chose a layout for his map which was highly unusual in the Occident. Rather than the east, the south was featured at the top where Africa was conspicuously displayed.

The reason why he chose this layout becomes clear from an explicit verbal statement which he inserted into the map. In this statement he claimed that Africa was circumnavigable. Fra Mauro's explicitness on this point suggests that he wanted to solidify the position which the Portuguese kings had taken in the circumnavigability controversy. He thus gave his map a distinctly secular purpose and layout. For instance, Fra Mauro included paradise but banned it from the *ecumene* to the lower left of his map beyond the ocean. Moreover, he showed

Jerusalem as a magnificent city but placed it far away from the centre of the *ecumene*. Likewise, he respected tradition by displaying many islands off the Asian coasts but added a large rectangular form which is identifiable as the island of Zipangu of which Marco Polo (1254–1324) had provided a description.[3]

Finally, the layout of the map seems to indicate that Fra Mauro had an idea of the Indian Ocean which had been conspicuously absent from the medieval *mappaemundi*. As *mappaemundi* with the south at the top were characteristic of Arab map-making, as Arab sailors were knowledgeable about the Indian Ocean already in the eleventh century[4] and as Venice was the locale through which much of Arab culture passed into Europe during the later Middle Ages, it is likely that Fra Mauro drew on Arab knowledge and not on the Byzantine tradition of ancient Greek geography which was represented in Ptolemy's work. Because the earliest printed version of Ptolemy's geography appeared in the Occident only in the 1470s and because these maps described the waterway in question as an inland sea under the name 'Indian Sea', Fra Mauro cannot have used this work.

Unburdened by the traditions of antiquity, Fra Mauro provided the stimulus which may then have been necessary to keep the Portuguese expeditions going up to the time when, two generations later, Vasco da Gama (*c.* 1460–1524) was ready to go (illus. 3).[5]

The traversability of the ocean from Europe to Asia was a controversial issue because the size of the ocean strip was difficult to determine. The Bible provided relative assessments which allowed for a variety of specifications. Ancient Greek geographers had assumed various lengths of the circumference of the earth, ranging from reportedly 250,000 stades (Eratosthenes, *c.* 284–*c.* 202 BC, approximating 40,000 km) to 180,000 stades (Ptolemy).[6] In any case, it was necessary to measure the continental extension of the *ecumene* first in order to be able to relate it to the circumference of the earth. These measurements could be determined only on the basis of data which were derived from land travel of the kind that the Polo family had undertaken to the eastern coasts of Asia around 1300.

Only in the late fifteenth century did scholars, among them the Florentine mathematician and astronomer Paolo dal Pozzo Toscanelli (1397–1482), begin to work themselves through Marco Polo's travel report.[7] However, as Marco Polo had seriously overstated the distances which the group had covered in the course of their journey, Toscanelli had to arrive at an assessment which greatly exaggerated the extension of the *ecumene* at the expense of that of the ocean when he sat down to calculate the extension of the *ecumene* on the basis of the distances which Marco Polo had recorded. Nevertheless, evidence seemed to exist that supported Toscanelli's calculations.[8] Naturalists had reported that elephants lived in the east of Asia and in the west of Africa, and this was understood to indicate that the eastern and western fringes of the *ecumene* could not be far apart.

3 Ptolemy's map of the world. From Hartmann Schedel, *Das Buch der Croniken* (Nuremberg, 1493), fols 12v–13r.

Moreover, bamboo had been found drifting in waters around the Azores and Canary Islands; as bamboo had been known to grow in Asia the conclusion was accepted that it had floated across the ocean and that this had been possible because the gap between Asia in the west and Africa in the east was not wide.[9]

THE TRANSFORMATION OF THE EUROPEAN WORLD PICTURE

The members of the Portuguese royal court and the scholars and sailors around them became the pioneers in the organization of maritime expeditions and the collection of empirical data during the fifteenth century. They were convinced that it was easier to reach the coasts of Asia by a sea route that circumnavigated Africa rather than by traversing the ocean.

Around the middle of the fifteenth century, the world picture enshrined in the medieval *mappaemundi* was temporarily confirmed in that the western coasts of Africa switch from a southward to an eastward extension south of Cape Verde, a relocation which was in line with the rounded shape that the *ecumene* took in the medieval *mappaemundi*. However, the eastward turn as observed by the mid-fifteenth-century voyagers was sharp and occurred at a point which appeared to be located too far north to be identical with the supposedly smooth eastward turn of the entire African coastlines towards Asia. It was therefore decided that the expeditions should be continued further to the south. The Cape of Good Hope was reached in 1488 but no further penetration into the Indian Ocean took place until 1497–9, when Vasco da Gama availed himself of Arab nautical knowledge and carried out an expedition across the Indian Ocean to the southwest Indian coast. When Vasco arrived at the court of the Zamorin of Calicut in southern India in 1498, he was reportedly asked about the purposes of his voyage. If the recording of the report is correct Vasco replied that he was in search of spices and Christians.[10]

The fusion of commercial and religious motives in the latter fifteenth century appears to be trustworthy because it can be related to what is on record in contemporary sources. The

Portuguese kings may have set higher goals for themselves than the mere gathering of empirical data.[11] As the expeditions proceeded further southward, they began to claim for themselves the title Senhor do Guinea (Lord of Africa) in order to articulate some form of suzerainty over the newly 'discovered' areas. However, they did little to substantiate their claim, although, in 1481, they ordered the building of the fortress El Mina in what is Ghana today.[12]

When the Emperor of Mali sought to establish an alliance with the Kings of Portugal, the latter declined the offer because, apparently, they did not want to get involved in internal African affairs.[13] Nevertheless, Africa did become an important market for manufactured goods to be shipped out from Europe and an equally important source for attractive commodities to be imported to Europe. Among the latter were gold, spices, ivory and slaves. The motive of finding safe routes to profitable markets where precious goods could be obtained had been present in the minds of long-distance traders since the crusades and, consequently, it was not surprising that the Portuguese kings supported the establishment of foreign trade relations when they commissioned Vasco da Gama's expedition.

The religious motive of finding Christians added a political dimension to the enterprise. The search for Christians could make sense only if it was understood as a search for potential allies as partners in the struggle against Muslims. The crusading idea had not faded in Portugal since the thirteenth century[14] and was recast into a design for military campaigns against the Ottoman Turkish Empire after the conquest of Byzantium in 1453. Consequently, it made sense from the point of view of the Portuguese kings to use the spirit of enterprise of their sailors and merchants to establish an alliance among rulers on either side of the Ottoman Turkish Empire. In fact, the Portuguese kings had, throughout the fifteenth century, made repeated efforts to involve the Emperor of Abyssinia in plans for a crusade. This policy seemed to succeed when Vasco da Gama reported that he had met an embassy of the ruler of Abyssinia on Mozambique Island[15] and that he had seen many Christians at Calicut, as he mistook the Buddhists of southern India for members of a Christian sect.[16]

In summary, the combination of commercial and crusading motives directed the Portuguese kings and the explorers whom they commissioned to areas which could, on the one hand, be exploited as sources for human as well as natural resources and as outlets for manufactured goods while, on the other, they could be used as a *glacis* for future military campaigns against the Ottoman Turkish Empire.

These concerns were, however, not shared everywhere. In the core Italian commercial cities, mainly Genoa, and in Catalonia, Castile and other Spanish parts of the Iberian peninsula, rival attitudes prevailed which were oriented towards the increase of profits from trade and the expansion of territorial rule. Yet there was a clear division of labour. On the one hand, the commercial goals were pursued mainly in the cities while, on the other, the administrative goals were harboured in some of the Spanish royal courts. In both cases, they were part of a time-honoured legacy. Since the crusades, merchant traders had displayed their growing interest in expanding the ever more closely knit networks of trade across the *ecumene* as they had launched daring expeditions into the oceanic waters.

In the 1450s, the results of these expeditions were laid down in *mappaemundi*[17] which were strikingly similar to the one created by Fra Mauro for the King of Portugual. Hence there was a sense of rivalry between the Portuguese seafarers and the merchant traders in the western Mediterranean. Likewise, since the crusades, the rulers of the several then existing Christian kingdoms in the Iberian peninsula conducted a rigorous policy of reconquest of Muslim territories in the area. As the reconquest advanced and the Christian kingdoms were allowed to consolidate, internal rivalries emerged which were strongest between the King of Portugal and, on the Spanish side, the King of Castile.

By 1455, these rivalries focused on the sea routes of the ocean to the west and south of the Iberian peninsula and were strong enough to cause the intervention of Pope Nicholas V (1447–1455). His intermediation accomplished an agreement that established a demarcation line which was formally agreed at Alcaçovas in 1479. It ran east to west across the ocean north of Lisbon and divided a Portuguese zone of influence to the south from a Castilian one to the north.[18] The agreement banned further Castilian expeditions along the African coastline. Early in 1492, the last Muslim rulers in the Iberian peninsula withdrew peacefully from their stronghold in Granada, thereby allowing the reconquest to be completed.

While the Portuguese expeditions and the Spanish reconquest were going on, there was little room for the idea of expanding trade and conquest beyond the ocean to the island world which was believed to hedge the Asian coasts against the ocean waters. That meant that the proponents of a westward voyage across the ocean had a difficult time in the Spanish Kingdoms. In Portugal, this scheme was considered after it had been proposed by a Genoese named Columbus (*c.* 1450–1506) in the 1480s. But Columbus was then unsuccessful, mainly because the Portuguese expeditions were pushed towards the south rather than the west and, secondly, because of the clumsiness of the evidence that he had in support of his plan.[19]

In 1492, however, after they had occupied Granada, the Kings of Aragón and Castile issued a joint mandate to Columbus authorizing him to conduct expeditions across the ocean to Asia with their financial support on condition that he placed all newly found 'islands and firm lands' under their control.[20] This formula, which reappeared in all major documents relative to Columbus's expeditions, reflects the belief, also recorded in medieval *mappaemundi*, in the existence of many islands in the ocean off the Asian coast, together with the belief in the hypothetical fourth continent in the south. The formula also proves that the islands in the ocean as well as the southern continent were considered *terrae nullius* (no man's land) which, even if inhabited, could be occupied and subdued to the rule of their presumed first visitor. It excluded mainland Asia as part of the *ecumene* and, consequently, turned mainland Asia into an area that could not be the target of conquests.

Columbus's first voyage, which lasted from September 1492 to March 1493, upset the treaty of 1479 in two respects. First, on his return, adverse winds drove him further south than he had intended and forced him to land at Lisbon. This was a breach of the treaty of 1479 because Columbus was sailing in Castilian service. The violation gave the Portuguese king the chance of issuing a protest and, more importantly, offered him an opportunity to interrogate Columbus and obtain first-hand knowledge about the expedition before Columbus could proceed to the court of the Spanish kings. Secondly, Columbus had proved that there were many islands in the ocean west of Europe and Africa although at a greater distance than had been anticipated by scholars like Toscanelli. Thus Columbus's return sparked hectic diplomatic activities to reconsider the demarcation line of 1479.

However, there were two problems with this demarcation line. First, given the existence of many islands in the ocean, seemingly off the Asian coast, the line of 1479 required that the Portuguese king follow the lead of the Spanish kings and commission westward expeditions across the ocean to take possession of whatever islands might be located in the ocean south of the line. But this request militated against the main strategy of pushing southwards along the African coast and then further eastwards to the coast of Asia.

Secondly, the line of 1479 placed the presumed southern continent into the Portuguese zone thereby preventing access to the Spanish. After lengthy negotiations mediated by Pope Alexander VI (1492–1503), both parties agreed to draw a new demarcation line from the northern to the southern pole, to locate it 370 nautical miles west of the westernmost islands of the Azores and Canaries and to allocate to the Portuguese that part of the ocean which was next to Africa and Europe. This solution allowed the Portuguese to continue their south- and eastward expeditions without disturbance and without forcing upon them more than casual westward voyages across the ocean; it confined the Spanish to remote areas in the far west, of which little was known, and it divided the hypothetical southern continent equally between both parties. The agreement was included in a treaty which was signed at Tordesillas in 1494.[21]

The division of the ocean between the King of Portugal and Spanish kings was not confined to quantitative matters.[22] Instead, it turned into a qualitative one and allowed the formulation and execution of rival and partly incompatible strategies on either side. In what was the old tricontinental *ecumene*, the Portuguese king was entitled to pursue his strategy of combining commerce with campaigns against Muslims, whereas, in the world of new islands and firm lands, the Spanish kings could continue their strategy of fusing commerce with conquest. But this qualitative division was defective in one conspicuous respect. For, while the Tordesillas line demarcated the Portuguese and Spanish zones in the ocean west of Europe and Africa, no attempt was made to delineate both zones of influence on or outside the Asian continent.

This defect became painfully obvious when Magellan (*c.* 1480–1521), who travelled in Spanish service, appeared in Asian waters in 1520 into which, according to the stipulations of the Tordesillas treaty, he ought not to have penetrated. The defect was remedied through the treaty of Saragossa in 1529 which established a dividing line east of the islands later called the Philippines. But unlike the Tordesillas line, the Saragossa line did not achieve lasting validity in international law, as King Philip II of Spain (1556–1598) conquered the Philippines even though these islands had clearly been assigned to the Portuguese zone.

Around 1500, the rival Portuguese and Spanish strategies created the platform from which a new world picture emerged. In this world picture, an ever-increasing portion of the globe's surface was recognized as being covered by water, and from the island worlds emerged the American continent as an entity in its own right. In the new world picture, there was no permeable *ecumene*, and no claims towards universal rule could be drawn on concepts of territorial rule alone. Instead, universal rule had to be conceptualized in terms of seaborne empires which were to emerge either from direct conquest or from some kind of overlordship over local rulers.

In any case, universalism could no longer be confined to a world picture which described the world as a spherical tricontinental land mass. Instead, it had to be tied to a picture of the world as the globe where land and water were interspersed in the complicated way that happens to be the case. In such a world picture, the empirical pluralism of islands and continents, of religions, of government institutions, of laws, of customs and ways of life was placed in contrast to the theoretical universal principle that all humankind is one.

Reconciling the emerging geographical, religious, political, legal and moral pluralism with the postulates of medieval universalism became not only a difficult task of theorists but also a controversial one. The change in the European world picture led to confusion, which made it difficult for theorists to lay down their thoughts in systematic writings at the time of the controversy. The more the continental extension of America came into the sight of European geographers, the more urgent became the recognition of the fact that the globe consisted of a pluralism of unconnected continents. The more frequent and intense the interactions between European traders, military men as well as clergymen and the non-European world grew, the more urgent was the appreciation of the global diversity of religions, government institutions, legal systems, customs and ways of life. All of these stood against the universalistic postulate that the Christian religion, the Roman Empire, Roman law and its believed or manifest derivatives as well as occidental customs and ways of life represented the global standard. The responses of theorists to this difficulty were varied.

THE THEORY OF NATURAL SLAVERY

John Major (1469–1550), a Scottish theologian writing at the University of Paris, was among the first to take up the challenge. In a commentary on the *Books of Sentences* of the twelfth-century philosopher Peter Lombard, published in 1519, he attempted to defend medieval universalism and, to that end, availed himself of a political theory the origin of which he found in Aristotle's theory of slavery.[23]

According to Aristotle, there were slaves by nature, namely people who had no chance whatsoever of being or becoming human beings in a moral sense and could only lead their lives as commanded by their masters.[24] Major used Aristotle's theory of natural slavery in a controversy over whether native Americans could legitimately be subjected to the control of European conquerors and whether they ought to be converted to Christianity through missionary efforts. Major gave an affirmative answer to the first question and a negative answer to the second. He argued that native Americans could and, of right, ought to be subjected to harsh treatment because the islands and firm lands on which they happened to live were not part of the tricontinental *ecumene* and, therefore, *terrae nullius*. Because *terrae nullius* became the property of their conquerors, the conquerors had the right to impose their will on the inhabitants.

In accordance with Aristotle, Major concluded that native Americans were slaves by nature because no one other than slaves could be forced to accept someone else's commands. This conclusion led Major to postulate that the fate of native Americans, as slaves by nature, was certain as the divinity had willed them to go to hell. Therefore, Major took the view that missionary efforts were in vain and that, instead of converting native Americans to Christianity, it made more sense to put them to death immediately.[25]

CREATING THE CONSCIOUSNESS THAT ALL HUMANKIND IS ONE

John Major's argument heated up the controversy. Already in 1502, Pope Alexander VI had decreed that native Americans ought to be converted to Christianity[26] and, in fulfilment of this papal decree, missionaries followed the conquerors. Among them was the Dominican friar Bartolomé de Las Casas (1474–1566), who devoted much of his long life to the missionary task. He arrived in the Caribbean in 1502, became active as a preacher in 1510, joined the Dominican Order in 1522 and headed the missionary bishopric of Chiapas in Mexico until 1551.

As a missionary, Las Casas was self-evidently convinced that native Americans ought to be converted to Christianity. He abhorred the genocide which the conquerors inflicted upon native Americans and persuaded Emperor Charles V (1519–56), who was also King of Spain (1516–56), to enforce laws against the abuse of native Americans. His main counter-argument against Major was drawn on St Thomas Aquinas's theory of natural law that humankind as a whole was one single moral unit by nature and divine will so that no human being could lose or be denied his or her moral or legal status as a human being.

Las Casas's recourse on natural law theories promoted his view that humankind was itself a moral category which could only be universal if it were applied to the globe at large.[27] Consequently, he took the view that Major's attempt to dehumanize native Americans was in itself immoral. He advanced his own counter-position that there were standard moral norms and rules which ought to be applied to all humankind regardless of the diversity of their places of settlement, their religious and political institutions, their legal and moral norms and rules as well as their customs and ways of life.[28]

Las Casas did not, however, disapprove of Aristotle's theory of slavery where slavery could be traced back to human decisions. Where persons were turned into slaves through their own fault or what appeared to be so, Las Casas advocated the use of forced labour by these slaves and, in 1517, recommended the purchase and deportation of African slaves across the Atlantic as a means to relieve native Americans of the workload which was imposed on them by the conquerors. Like most of his contemporaries, Las Casas saw no problem at this time with the deportation of Africans to America as forced labourers, though he later regretted having made the recommendation and withdrew his support for the African slave trade.

In order to advance his views in Europe, he reported on the acts of barbarism which were committed by Europeans in pursuit of their conquest. These reports became best-selling literature throughout Europe where they helped to activate support for the Catholic mission in America and led Pope Paul III (1534–49), to issue a bull in 1537 which banned acts of discrimination against native Americans and once again demanded missionary efforts.[29] Las Casas's views were taken up by Jesuit missionaries who began to spread their activities to South, Southeast and East Asia in the 1540s.

Cardinal Tomaso de Vio of Gaeta, who called himself Cajetan, (1469–1534) took Las Casas's natural law theory a step further and used it for arguments against universal rule. The cardinal was deeply worried about the self-righteousness with which European rulers claimed titles to rule over areas beyond the tricontinental *ecumene*. Like Las Casas he was shocked by the barbarism with which European control was imposed upon the native Americans who survived. But he went beyond Las Casas in questioning the authority of the pope to intervene in the political and administrative affairs of America.

Not unlike Bartolus of Sassoferato, Cajetan took the view that the globe was under the control of a variety of rulers who, if they claimed autonomy from the Roman Empire, could do so on just and legitimate grounds. However, Cajetan was faced with a problem that had not existed for Bartolus, namely what the legal status of the newly recognized islands and firm lands was. In the fifteenth century, Popes Nicholas V and Alexander VI had become involved as arbiters in the rivalry between the Portuguese and the Spanish kings on the grounds that the ocean strip and the islands located in it were areas outside the tricontinental *ecumene* and fell under the lawful control of the popes.[30]

Cajetan rejected this position as unfounded because the papal claim stood against the fact that islands, such as the British Isles, were not under papal control although they were situated in the ocean. Hence, setting apart in legal terms the tricontinental *ecumene* from the encircling ocean strip made no sense. Cajetan then concluded that, while the islands and firm lands did not indeed belong to anyone among the inhabitants of the tricontinental *ecumene*, they did not thereby acquire the status of *terrae nullius*. Hence he opposed the argument that these islands and firm lands could be the targets of lawful occupation by European conquerors.

Instead, he took the view that, as these areas were inhabited, they were under the lawful control of their inhabitants and that neither the popes nor the Roman Emperors nor anyone else from the tricontinental *ecumene* had any right whatsoever to them. Consequently, Cajetan argued in favour of the principle that native Americans were by nature free and had the inalienable right to govern themselves. By these standards, the European occupation of America could not be founded on any lawful grounds but resulted from nothing other than the application of physical force.[31]

THE EMERGENCE OF INTERNATIONAL LAW

Cajetan's theory turned the conquest into an undeclared war fought by Europeans against native Americans for morally undefendable grounds. From this point of view, it became possible and even cogent to apply the theory of just warfare as it had been conceived in the thirteenth century.

Before the end of the sixteenth century, two theorists issued works in which they supplied an ethics of warfare from which the criteria for judgements of what was just and permissible in this war could be derived. One of them was Francisco de Vitoria (c. 1483–1546), a Spanish Dominican who taught at the University of Salamanca. In 1543, Vitoria delivered lectures on the legal status of 'the newly found Indian islands'. In these lectures, he advocated the position that warfare in America could be just only if it followed natural law. That meant, first and foremost, that native Americans had to be accepted as human beings. Vitoria also insisted that the rule of just warfare which Aquinas had specified had to be accepted.[32]

The Protestant Italian émigré Alberico Gentili, who lectured on moral philosophy at the University of Oxford late in the sixteenth century, followed suit and added the demand that the rules of just warfare, as general principles of justice, ought to be applied to believers of all religions.[33] Hence, in the course of the sixteenth century, the law of war was recognized as a moral code which was to be universal in the sense that it was regarded as applicable to all humankind.[34] At the time, the law of war was not to be sanctioned and executed by any institutions, universal or otherwise, but a purely moral code to which, its supporters argued, rulers were bound to subject themselves in their own legitimate self-interest. For only such actions of rulers could be expected to receive political support that followed from morally defendable principles and intentions.

CONQUEST, TRADE AND PEACE

Among many other things, the catastrophic end of the crusades had entailed the consequence that the Roman Emperors were given the major task to salvage the Roman Empire as a would-be territorial polity. The crisis of the Roman Empire was much aggravated by the Turkish conquest of Byzantium in 1453 and by the end of the rule of the Roman Emperors in the eastern hemisphere in 1461. In due course, the conquest promoted designs for further crusades but these designs were not issued by the then reigning Roman Emperor of the Occident, Frederick III (1440–1493).

Instead of him, the Portuguese kings, as has been mentioned above, made preparations, and they were joined by George of Podiebrad, the Hussite King of Bohemia (1455–1471). In these preparations, Pope Pius II (1458–1464) played an equivocal role as he tried both to placate Mehmed II (1451–1481), the Turkish Sultan who had conquered Byzantium, and to raise resistance against Turkish rule. On the one hand, he promised to cede all of the Balkans to the control of the Sultan if he became a Christian.[35] The proposal did not get anywhere because the letter does not seem to have been dispatched. On the other hand, Pius gave full support to the idea of a crusade which, however, was not any more successful.

Subsequent efforts to forge a working alliance with the Zamorin of Calicut and other rulers in South and Southeast Asia failed miserably after the Portuguese decided to deploy and use martial arms to advance their position in the Indian Ocean.[36] And the Portuguese push to Abyssinia in a pincer movement against the Ottoman Turkish Empire materialized only after 1520 when the Portuguese position in the Indian Ocean had been solidified.[37] But then the Portuguese became involved in domestic warfare in Abyssinia and had no chance to advance the crusading idea. As neither strategy led anywhere, the Portuguese kings buried their plans for a crusade in the middle of the century.

Whereas the Portuguese kings had tried to organize the crusades on their own, George of Podiebrad proposed a union of Christian rulers in 1462–4 in order to prepare for what he considered to be a decisive strike against the Turkish Sultan.[38] George's proposal consisted of an elaborate scheme which was to unite the Christian rulers of Europe into a confederation in which all disputes among the members were to be resolved by peaceful arbitration. The confederated rulers were to renounce the use of force among themselves and to appoint a judiciary institution whose judgements they were to pledge to accept. Rulers were then to unite their forces in a campaign against the Sultan.[39]

George took great pains to publicize his proposal but, perhaps because he was a Hussite who had questioned the authority of the Roman Emperor, his plan did not lead anywhere. In summary, the international theory behind these schemes was entirely informed by medieval religious universalism and was bound to implode with the transformation of the world picture around 1500.

WORLD EMPIRE AS LORDSHIP OVER THE GLOBE

Until his father Frederick III died in 1493, Maximilian (1486–1519) displayed himself to be open to the crusading idea. Born in 1459, he had been raised when the Turkish advance on the Balkans was underway.[40] While his father was alive, he spent much time reorganizing the administration of the Roman Empire for the purpose of preparing a crusade. Even after his father died, he continued to work towards that goal. Thus we find him actively campaigning for a crusade at the Worms Diet of 1495 at which the principles of reform of the empire were scheduled for approval.

But in the years that followed, the goal of reforming the empire evolved into an end in itself, and Maximilian developed new priorities beyond the crusading idea. He began to promote his dynastic relations with the Kings of Portugal and Spain in the southwest[41] and with the Kings of Bohemia and Hungary in the east of Europe. He then set out to authorize the making of elaborate pieces of imperial propaganda to the end of portraying himself in the centre of all rulers in Christendom and the true heir to Charlemagne, Clovis and the Roman Emperors of antiquity.[42] He cooperated closely with the leading geographers, cartographers and mathematicians of his time,[43] tried to keep himself informed about the ongoing expeditions[44] and filled his imperial propaganda with symbols which expressed his claim that, as a Roman Emperor, he was the overlord over large parts of the globe. These symbols showed Maximilian to be the lord of the people of Calicut with whom the Portuguese king had established relations, and the ruler of the many islands in the ocean which had come under the sway of the Spanish kings.[45]

At a time when theorists were plagued with difficulties resulting from the collapse of the medieval world picture, Maximilian began to devise his own international theory and had his imperial propaganda composed to articulate it. To that end, he not only hastily integrated every new revision of the medieval world picture but early on grasped the core of the consequences of the disintegration of the medieval land-based world picture. The logic of the newly emerging world picture in which land and water were interspersed was that claims for universal rule could no longer be confined to rule over land, let alone only the tricontinental *ecumene*. Instead, Maximilian was the first to map out universal rule as an overlordship over large parts of the globe covering land and water and to present imperial rule as control over global international relations.

However, Maximilian's heroic attempt to employ the ongoing changes of the world picture as an ideological basis for the globalization of universal rule failed dramatically. Maximilian and the scholars assisting him had to capitulate in the face of the dimensions and the rapidity of change that they tried to control. Already during Maximilian's lifetime, it became clear that the Portuguese kings would not make efforts actually to rule over the areas which had been assigned to them as zones of influence in the Tordesillas treaty; and where there was no actual rule there could be no overlordship. It also became clear that the Spanish conquest of the Caribbean and Central and

South America was an enterprise far more extensive, time-consuming, expensive, hazardous and, last but not least, morally questionable than the subduing of islands and firm lands as purported *terrae nullius* in the ocean. Moreover, where there was no right to rule, claims to overlordship were vain.

Maximilian's imperial propaganda thus collapsed with his death in 1519. His grandson Charles V, King of Spain from 1516 and successor to the imperial throne, carried on the imperial propaganda, but, in the end, he gave up. When he abdicated in 1556, he allocated rule over the overseas islands and firm lands to his son Philip II, who was to succeed as King of Spain. By contrast, Charles's brother Ferdinand I, who had become King of Hungary and Bohemia in 1526 and succeeded as emperor, remained confined to Europe. This decision revealed that what had remained of the claims to universal rule was turned into an appanage of the King of Spain and became dissociated from imperial rule.

The collapse of Maximilian's imperial propaganda indicated the breakdown of the political dimension of universalism. Instead of continuing efforts to globalize universal rule as manifest administrative control of large parts of the globe, recognizing the pluralism of contending rulers became inevitable. Consequently, designs for the establishment, maintenance or restoration of universal rule gave way to strategies for the 'balancing of power'. Establishing, maintaining and restoring the balance of power emerged as the prime political concern for international theorists in the course of the sixteenth century. However, universal rule continued to occupy people's minds, although it did so not as a verifiable claim but as a bone of contention in controversies among diplomats and disputes among intellectuals.

Up to the beginning of the nineteenth century, any ruler whom someone wished to attack for attempts to misappropriate power could be libelled a universal ruler. Charging a ruler with attempts to create a universal empire became a powerful means to rally opposing rulers, to forge alliances and to justify wars. This happened to the Habsburgs, who were attacked on these grounds by French diplomats and pamphleteers in the sixteenth century, to the French kings who were accused of similar charges by the British and the Dutch in the later seventeenth and the early eighteenth centuries and, self-evidently, to Napoleon in the early nineteenth century.

But such quibbles only showed that the charges were arbitrary. None of the rulers who were attacked for allegedly striving for universal rule made any attempt whatsoever to establish themselves as rulers or overlords over large parts of the globe as Maximilian had. In fact, the process of the globalization of secular universalism led to its depoliticization. Secular universalism ceased to be a platform from which ideologies as well as political decision-making could be informed. Yet secular universalism, unfettered by the politics of making or defending universal rule, was sustained as a global framework for the pursuit of ethics which was based on the recognition of the unity of humankind.

Under these circumstances, international theory began to establish itself as a body of theory of its own in the later part of the sixteenth century. It branched off from the foundation which fourteenth-century political theorists had laid. In the fourteenth century, theorists had made efforts to explicate the dualism of one divinely ordained universal empire and the plethora of urban communities and territorial polities and, in this context, international theory was part and parcel of an integrated secular political theory whose main goal was to justify the variety of existing polities. In the sixteenth century, practical politics did much to solidify the existing territorial polities and urban communities and advanced the reforms which transformed the Roman Empire into a would-be territorial polity.

Even the popes followed suit. Through their own strategy of converting their secular titles to rule into a veritable territorial polity, the popes ceased to be contenders for universal rule in the sixteenth century and confined themselves to the management of religious universalism. Political theorists, such as Niccolò Machiavelli (1469–1527), reflected on the intensifying administrative concerns for territorial polities and urban communities and narrowed the focus of political theory to the affairs of the territorial polities and urban communities, while they were less concerned about international relations.

These concerns were taken up by theorists who were attracted by affairs relevant to humankind. Such theorists set out to provide a new understanding of universalism. If they were clergymen and missionaries, they wrote theological tracts and missionary reports through which they recast universalism in religious terms and placed Christianity as a universal religion into global competition with other religions. In their view, the mission was mandatory as an effort to globalize Christianity as a universal religion.

After the clergymen came the moral philosophers who, as trained theologians, delivered university lectures for the advocacy of the globalization of natural law as universal ethics. They insisted that this ethics should be global in the sense that it should overarch existing territorial polities and urban communities, and should in this sense be non-political, guide rulers and be applied in warfare among contending parties everywhere on the globe. While the protagonists of European religious universalism continued to pursue the advancement of Christianity, the supporters of the newly emerging ethical universalism as an international theory demanded the abidance by moral norms for the purpose of the reconstitution of humankind as a moral community.

PART II

Organizing the World

The globalization and depoliticization of secular universalism opened the debate over whether the world, now understood to be a globe, ought to be organized as a single global entity. Three answers are principally possible, first that there is a need for volitional acts in support of world organization, secondly that there is no possibility of effective world organization and, thirdly, that there is no need for volitional acts in support of world organization because the world has been organized by some non-human agent or has the capability of self-organization. Since the sixteenth century, both affirmative and sceptical views – as well as answers which suggest the irrelevance of the question – have all been argued at various times and on various grounds by various schools of international theorists. Therefore, the history of international theory between the sixteenth and the twentieth centuries has been the history of debates over the merits and demerits of world organization.

Theorists who took the view that world organization was not necessary prevailed throughout the sixteenth, seventeenth and eighteenth centuries. The nineteenth century witnessed the dominance of affirmative answers whereas at times during the twentieth century theorists who opted for positions of scepticism held sway. As in the Middle Ages, international theories were closely paralleled with broader patterns of culture. But the categories through which the parallelisms were determined differed. Whereas throughout the Middle Ages most theorists had taken the view that power was the personal or institutional capability to preserve the divinely willed order of the tricontinental *ecumene* and had devised various schemes to legitimate universal rule as rule over the *ecumene* and its inhabitants, theorists since the sixteenth century have sought to conceptualize world order in secular terms and have successively used various technical and biological models of the order of the world or its parts.

The term system came in use in contexts in which the order of the world or its parts were debated. The geographical range of the application of this term has varied. Whereas in the sixteenth, seventeenth and eighteenth centuries the term could variously be applied in confinement to Europe or to the globe at large, since the nineteenth century it has exclusively been related to the globe. Up to the beginning of the nineteenth century, European concepts of international systems competed with rival concepts elsewhere, notably in East, Southeast and South Asia as well as in various parts of Africa, where international systems existed that were both independent from and beyond the control of Europeans. Hence the secularization and depoliticization of universalism have amplified the variability of international theory and have sparked controversy among theorists themselves, between theorists of and practitioners in international relations and among practitioners themselves. When practitioners began to quarrel among themselves about matters relevant to the conduct of international relations, resorting to war was a frequently chosen means of settling these controversies during the sixteenth and seventeenth centuries.

FOUR

The Ethics of Self-Constraint

In the sixteenth and early seventeenth centuries, the globalization and depoliticization of universalism created a further potential for controversy and warfare. In Africa and Asia, wars resulted from the determination of local rulers to resist the invading Europeans, who were repelled in many cases. Within Europe wars were fought against parties that continued to support quests for universal rule in the earlier half of the sixteenth century, and throughout the period against parties which were accused of striving for universal rule. In any case, warfare was endemic, and there was no shortage of warriors ready to be employed in war.

Outside Europe, some rulers, such as in the Aztec empire, China, Japan and Java, mobilized armed forces with professionals or warriors recruited for long-term service whereas others, such as the Sultan of Malacca, relied on militia forces; and the Europeans came along with mainly small-sized mixed bands of semi-professional men who were ready to be employed as technicians and warriors. Within Europe, a growing group of professional warriors emerged who were willing to take fatal risks and hoped for decent pay, lavish prey and the honours that military success might convey.

These professional warriors were usually self-reliant people who ranked the accomplishment of personal success in battle over everything else. They were organized in self-controlled bands under the command of self-employed leaders who, as military entrepreneurs, respected little other than the assumed necessities of war or the commands of those rulers who were willing to use their services in return for payment.[1] A booming market for warriors allowed rulers to employ these bands in ever-increasing sizes provided they had the funds necessary to pay these armed forces. At the end of the sixteenth century, contingents as large as 70,000 men were conceivable as army units led into battle.[2]

Such daring required an optimistic anthropology[3] which suggested that human actors could and should use their own bodily energy to resist opposition and overcome obstacles.[4] In support of this belief, at the turn of the sixteenth century, artists such as Pollaiuolo, Michelangelo and Holbein[5] created a new image which displayed warriors using the energies contained in their bodies to overcome their foes. These warriors could be successful if they had a good deal of good luck and if they were willing and able to train themselves in the various bodily techniques *(techniques du corps)* required for the military profession, namely fencing, wrestling and other sorts of physical exercise. They had to acquire the technical skills necessary for the handling of sophisticated arms such as firearms, to act forcefully and yet in coordination with others when they were asked to use simple arms such as pikes, to observe the commands of their leaders and to abide by the law. In other words, there was a fine line between success and failure for these warriors. If they were successful, they could establish themselves as well-to-do people and lead a comfortable life. If they failed and survived, they remained confined to a life in misery as invalids about and for whom no one cared. In any case, war offered chances for those who had little to lose.

Emperor Maximilian I was among the first rulers to recognize that there was a long-term tactical advantage in requesting the full use by the warriors of the energies contained in their bodies and in combining with this request the demand for their subjection to the discipline of the warrior band.[6] But neither he nor his sixteenth-century successors had at their disposal an ethics which provided the general rules according to which human actors were to act both autonomously and with self-reliance as well as, at the same time, subject themselves to central command structures and the rule of law.

The condition for the promotion and acceptance of such an ethics was difficult to perceive or even to establish for a person like Maximilian who tried unsuccessfully to salvage the essentials of secularized universal rule. But it was an easy task for the theorists who operated with the depoliticized version of universalism as a category of ethics. Towards the end of the sixteenth century, these theorists began to argue that the rule of law and the execution of given orders were guaranteed if all individuals agreed on doing so and accepted constraints upon their capability to act autonomously and with self-reliance. They pleaded that acceptance of such constraints had to be voluntary and that the willingness to submit to them followed from the general capability of reason.

ACCEPTING HUMANKIND AS A MORAL ENTITY THROUGH REASON

Like medieval theologians such as St Thomas Aquinas, sixteenth-century secular theorists accepted the premise that acting in accordance with reason was identical with committing oneself to morally defendable actions or what was in accordance with natural law. But beyond their medieval predecessors they demanded that determining what was morally defendable and in accordance with natural law was to be accomplished through thinking and not through believing. This attitude was informed by the legacy of the ethics of antiquity, namely by the writings of the moralists of the so-called Middle Stoa, namely Epictetus and Seneca.

Their legacy was taken up first and foremost by the Dutch philologist and philosopher Justus Lipsius (1547–1606). Having studied Tacitus extensively during his early years and while he held the chair of classical philology at the Dutch University of Leiden, Lipsius began to subject to critical scrutiny the writings of Seneca as the most renowned moralist of antiquity. But Lipsius would not confine himself to mere bookish learning, as he intended to exploit the ethical thought of his Roman authors for the practical purposes of giving advice to rulers of his own time.[7] Advising rulers on what he considered to be proper behaviour before and during a war, Lipsius wrote:

> Neither ought you ever to begin any war but such as use and reason does admit. For there are laws belonging unto war as

well as to peace. And you ought to make war with no less justice than fortitude. And therefore in every commonwealth, the laws concerning war ought especially to be observed. For to run headlong to fight and rashly to come to handy strokes with our enemy carries with it a spice of cruelty and resembles the brute beasts. Which custom if we admit, what other thing shall we behold than war amongst all nations? And after the manner of barbarous people, we shall recompense death with death and satisfy blood with blood. Let it be far from you, and let these speeches never make breach in your heart, that there is right in arms and all things do belong to the strongest. Moreover, that the event of war, not the cause, is to be considered. And this most wicked saying that the conflict makes the conquered culpable.[8]

Through his demand that rulers should constrain their rightful competence to resort to war, Lipsius placed himself in opposition against the then current reason-of-state theories which sought to exempt rulers of territorial polities and urban communities from the constraints of ethics.[9] Instead, Lipsius argued that rulers should subject themselves to moral constraints in accordance with reason and act in accordance with such constraints even in the extreme circumstances of warfare. Following Aquinas, he demanded that moral laws of war should be accepted by all contending parties for the purpose of reducing the likelihood of wars and the amount of violence committed in their course. Further to this, he maintained that humankind existed as a metaphysical entity overarching the multifarious antagonistic warring territorial polities and urban communities and was manifest in a universal set of ethics. In this respect, he agreed in principle with the sixteenth-century proponents of international law, but emphasized more strongly the necessity that the universal ethics should and could be accepted voluntarily:

If we respect the whole nature of man, all these earthly countries are vain and falsely so termed, except only in respect of the body and not of the mind or soul which, descending down from that highest habitation, deems all the whole earth as a gaol or prison. But heaven is our true and rightful country, whither let us advance all our cogitations that we may freely say with Anaxagoras to such as foolishly ask us whether we have no regard to our country? Yes, verily, but yonder is our country, lifting our finger and mind up towards heaven.[10]

In this passage, Lipsius employed a series of conventions. He drew on ancient Greek philosophy for the juxtaposition of the body and the soul and also for the imagery of heaven and earth. Yet, unlike the authors of his Greek sources, Lipsius was not interested in ontology. Instead, he used the conventional phrases in the context of his international theory in order to demonstrate that the manifestly existing pluralism and divisiveness of earthly territorial polities and urban communities as antagonistic spaces of regular communication stood in opposition to the theoretical postulate of the moral entity of humankind as a whole. Hence, when relieved of the fusion of the Platonic body-versus-soul dichotomy with the Anaxagorean earth-versus-heaven imagery, Lipsius's international theory made explicit the demand that the idea of humankind should overarch the multitude of antagonistic spaces of regular communication in the world.

Lipsius justified this demand on the grounds of reason. He defined reason metaphorically as 'a true sense and judgement of things human and divine'[11] and accepted it as the ultimate source from which the principles governing humankind as a whole were to be derived. Lipsius argued that reason leads to 'patience', the 'true mother of constancie' which, in turn, he prescribed for rulers as 'a right and immovable strength of the mind, neither lifted up nor pressed down with external or casual accidents'. If necessary, 'the mind must be changed, not the place'.[12] On this basis, he could conclude that only acting in accordance with reason could usher in 'constancie' or steadfastness and thus contribute to the well-being of territorial polities and urban communities.

In Lipsius's international theory, 'constancie' had the dual meaning of *stabilitas loci*, the willingness to remain where one is, and *tranquilitas animi*, the stability of the mind; he expressed the latter through the technical model of the scales. This meant in the context of international relations that the several rulers representing the diversity of antagonistic territorial polities and

urban communities could commit themselves to the maintenance of the status quo as the condition of stability and peace if
and as long as they remained controlled by reason. However,
Lipsius was aware of the difficulty that rulers had the option of
acting unreasonably and could not be prevented from doing so.
Hence, with his bid for the constitution of humankind as a
single moral entity, he had to provide an explanation as to why
rulers of the manifestly existing antagonistic territorial polities
and urban communities might opt against reason. To that end,
Lipsius drew on the contractualism argued by fourteenth-
century political theorists:

> I confess, I say, that every one of us has an inclination and
> good will to his lesser country. The causes whereof I perceive
> are to you unknown. You would have it from nature. But the
> truth is, it grows of custom or of some decree and ordinance.
> For after that men forsook their wild and savage manner of
> living and began to build houses and walled towns, to join in
> society and to use means offensive and defensive. Behold
> then a certain communion necessarily began among them
> and a social participation of divers things. They parted the
> earth between them with certain limits and bounds. They
> had temples in common, also market places, treasuries, seats
> of judgment. And principal ceremonies, rites, laws. All which
> things our greediness began in time so to esteem and make
> account of as if they were our own in particular? And so be
> they in some sort, for that every private citizen had some
> interest in them, neither did they differ from private posses-
> sions saving that they were not wholly in one man's power.
> This consociation and fellowship gave the form and fashion
> to a new erected state which now we call properly the com-
> monwealth or our country. Wherein when men saw the
> chiefest stay of each person's safety to consist, laws were
> enacted for the succour and defence thereof. Or at least such
> customs were received by tradition from the predecessors to
> their posterity that grew to be of like force as laws. Here
> hence it comes to pass that we rejoice at the good of the com-
> monwealth and be sorry for her harm. Because our own
> private goods are secure by her safety and are lost by her
> overthrow.[13]

Lipsius used contractualism[14] to defend the existence of territorial polities and urban communities as institutions for the legitimate safeguard of private property and emphasized the voluntarism with which human actors enter into a contract and renounce some of their natural freedom. Admittedly, Lipsius did not employ the fully fledged phraseology of contractualism which Juan de Mariana (1536–1624),[15] Francisco Suarez (1548–1619),[16] Richard Hooker (c. 1554–1600)[17] and Johannes Althusius (1557–1639)[18] were to use shortly after him. But the voluntarism inherent in his concept of 'consociation' (which Althusius would later borrow from Lipsius) and the secular rationalism by which Lipsius derived the 'commonwealth' from custom or decree and ordinance,[19] and not – as his fellow Aristotelians would do[20] – from the divinely ordained world order or some natural sociability of human beings, display his efforts to disentangle customary and statutory law as the appurtenances of the voluntaristically established spaces of regular communication from the moral norms and obligations pertaining to humankind as a whole.

As Lipsius composed his international theory in the United Provinces, it was appropriate for him to avail himself of such contractualism. This was so because the United Provinces had been established as a polity through an actual contract which had been signed at Utrecht in 1579 in the form of a union treaty among the councils of towns and cities as well rural aristocrats who tried to free themselves from Spanish rule.[21] The Dutch towns and cities, like towns and cities elsewhere in Europe, had been established as contractual communities in the course of the high and late Middle Ages and therefore provided the best possible empirical support for contractualist political theories.[22] Such contractualism enabled Lipsius to juxtapose his ethical view of humankind as a lasting and stable moral entity against his legalistic perception of the diversity of 'commonwealths' as a local, law-governed, but antagonistic, competitive and constantly changing spaces of regular communication established for the defence of the specific belongings and interests of private individuals.

Because Lipsius was sceptical that rulers could be prevented from committing immoral actions, he needed to specify the conditions under which such actions could be punished in the interest of humankind at the level of international relations overarching the 'consociations' of territorial polities and urban communities. Lipsius demanded such punishments as mandatory coercive actions in defence of the moral integrity of humankind against those who wished to ignore the precepts of the ethics of self-constraint. The only available means to enforce such punishments was, according to Lipsius, warfare.

This conclusion was only apparently contradictory because Lipsius did take into account the absence of institutions of universal rule and had thus to permit resorting to war as a means to enforce acceptance of the ethics of self-constraint at the level of international relations. Hence, he demanded that wars should be limited to the use of force as a means to enforce sanctions against those who chose to act unreasonably and against the commands of the ethics of self-constraint. In order to explicate these views, Lipsius not only devoted to warfare the section on international relations in his book on politics but also produced two major and widely read works on the theory and practice of war.[23]

With regard to the theory of war, Lipsius drew on standard authorities available in the sixteenth century, mainly on the variations attached by Aquinas to St Augustine's scattered remarks on warfare.[24] Thus when Lipsius declared that wars could be just only on condition that they were declared by a legitimate ruler, conducted under defensive aims and concluded by a firm peace, he was almost entirely in agreement with the standards of just war theories of the then past 1,100 or so years. Likewise, when Lipsius, seemingly contradictorily, justified offensive acts against non-Christians, arguing that they endangered Christian 'manners of life',[25] this was merely a tribute to Augustine. But when he came to explicate his rules for practical military conduct, Lipsius offered a highly unconventional compound of moral principles, such as the following:

I have sufficiently (according to my power) debarred you from injustice, now I will likewise drive you from temerity. For I would not have you rashly, and upon every just occasion, enter into this field of Mars. It is a matter of great importance that requires deliberation and that with leisure. For know this that a war is easily begun but very hardly left off and the enterprising and end thereof are seldom in the power of one person.[26]

This implies that war was not only to be restricted to morally defendable acts but, more importantly, that not all just wars in Aquinas's terms could be regarded as morally defendable. Moreover, Lipsius assigned to rulers the obligation to constrain their military capabilities and, if wars were necessary and morally defendable, to conduct them solely under the government of 'discipline':

I shall call discipline a severe conforming of the soldier to value and virtue. The parts or offices thereof (being diversely dispersed) I shall reduce into a certain form of doctrine and do make them four in number, 1. Exercise, 2. Order, 3. Constraint, 4. Examples.[27]

'Exercise' was to denote the regular drill of the soldiers in the handling of the guns and other weapons as well as in the *techniques du corps* deemed necessary for the acquisition of physical strength. 'Order' was to be understood as the division of the fighting force into regularized 'legions, regiments and squadrons'. 'Constraint' was to represent a set of means 'which do repress and bridle the manners of the soldiers', namely 'continency in meat', 'modesty . . . in words, apparel, in deeds'. And 'examples' were to comprise 'reward and punishment'.[28] For all four items, Lipsius drew heavily on the military literature of antiquity but he modified them significantly by placing the rulers of urban communities and territorial polities in charge of organizing and controlling military drill.[29]

This literature had been available in print since the later fifteenth century without becoming the object of much serious and careful study for about a century when Lipsius wrote. In his own time, he was thus quite innovative, though not alone,[30] in subjecting this literature to a critical scrutiny and in making a conscious attempt to employ what could be used of its contents not only for the arcane requirements of general theory but also for the practical purposes of the organization of war. Lipsius was the first theorist to insist that the enforcement of control over the internal organization of armed forces fell into the legitimate competence of urban and territorial rulers, and, likewise, he was without predecessor in gleaning from the military literature of antiquity the conceptualization of war as an act of constraint in which volatility, forcefulness, rapid movements and the infliction of injuries were permissible only under the rule of discipline, for the restoration of the status quo, the accomplishment of a more stable peace and the absence of movement:

> Neither are arms to be directed to any other end (if you desire that they be just) but to peace and defence. Let war be undertaken that nothing but quietness may be sought thereby. Wise men make war that they may have peace and endure labour under hope of rest.[31]

Thus Lipsius set three levels of constraint against war: first, that war is permissible only if it is just; secondly, that only such just wars which are conducted with careful deliberation are morally defendable; and, thirdly, that only such just and morally defendable wars can be conducted as acts in accordance with reason in which temporary unrest leads in the end to a more solidified condition of peace and increased stability for which Lipsius used the words 'quietness' and 'rest'.[32] Thus, his ethics of self-constraint led Lipsius to the formulation of a theory of war according to which war could add to the achievement of a ruler if it was perfunctory to the enlargement and intensification of peace. In the more general terms of ethics, Lipsius expressed the same conviction again with the imagery of the scales in equilibrium: 'Virtue keeps the mean, not suffering any excess or defect in her actions because it weighs all things in the balance of reason making it the rule and squire of all her trials.'[33]

In summary, Lipsius rated the maintenance or restoration of peace as a condition of stability in an equilibrium the highest goal of political and military interactions among rulers of territorial polities and urban communities. Hence his sceptical assessment that wars were unlikely to be abolished once and for all was outweighed by his optimism that the ethics of self-constraint could limit wars to acts of reason conducted solely for the purposes of re-establishing the status quo and of enlarging and solidifying peace within and across the spaces of regular communication.

This conclusion now makes it easier to trace the sources of Lipsius's ethics of self-constraint. In fusing the ethics of the Middle Stoa with Aquinas's adaptation of St Augustine's theory of war, Lipsius was a Stoicist as much as he was a Thomist. And in demanding that international relations should be accepted as the interface between what should be accepted as humankind's being a moral entity and what constitutes the diversity of antagonistic spaces of regular communication, he betrayed a deep insight into the flaws of much of sixteenth-century European warfare. He tried to remedy these flaws through an appeal that individuals should voluntarily constrain their own physical energies, capabilities, wishes and passions and that they could keep them within their proper limits if and as long as they acted in accordance with reason.

CONTROVERSIES AMONG PRACTITIONERS ABOUT SOVEREIGNTY

Lipsius was overwhelmingly popular among academics. The two books in which he expostulated his international theory, namely *De constantia* and *Politicorum libri sex*, were translated into many vernacular languages. *De constantia* went through more than 80 editions, *Politicorum* through no less than 70, some of them with the then high print run of 1,500 copies.[34] Students from all over the continent flocked to Leiden to attend his lectures. Yet, his demand that humankind should be accepted as a moral entity met with little support from practitioners of his own time. This was so because there were few if any rulers who were willing to subject their actions to self-imposed constraints in service to nothing but reason. Rather than committing themselves to the principles of reasonable action they preferred to resort to reason-of-state arguments when they wished to go to war.

Conspicuously absent were multilateral peace treaties. Such treaties would have been indicators of the willingness of rulers to become involved in package deals and to take into account parties other than their direct opponents. But instead of recognizing international relations as a multi-dimensional set of interactions involving many actors simultaneously, rulers continued to adhere to the medieval practice of conceptualizing war as a bilateral contest with martial arms and the divinity as the judge and of concluding such contests with bilateral peace treaties. Hence no constraints on the sovereign war-making capability of a ruler were accepted until 1648, neither among European rulers nor in contests between European and other rulers, be they the Ottoman Turkish Sultans or rulers in Africa, Asia or America.

Controlling activities inside the territorial polities and urban communities was quite a different matter. Rulers had their own interest in mind when manifesting themselves as bearers of sovereignty not only vis-à-vis other rulers but also vis-à-vis population groups under their control. The latter interest was bitterly contested throughout the later sixteenth and much of the seventeenth centuries. Various institutions, such as the Church as well as a variety of different groups, among them the aristocracy, made efforts to defend whatever privileges they had or claimed vis-à-vis territorial rulers. Likewise, the councils of those urban communities which had established themselves as autonomous 'consociations' in Lipsius's sense asserted their rights against neighbouring territorial rulers.

Defenders of rulers' sovereignty maintained that rulers ought to have the legitimacy to enact laws and thereby impose their will upon everyone in the territory under their control in order to accomplish and maintain order.[35] In this respect, sovereignty was claimed in accordance with Lipsius's ethics for the ruler as an ordering competence and not as a licence for unlawful or illegitimate acts. Although rulers were not necessarily bound by the laws which were to be enforced through their officials and ministers, they were never free to act totally at their own discretion. Instead, the validity of 'fundamental laws' overarching the territorial polities and constraining the activities of their rulers or of natural law continued to be recognized.[36] Thus, sovereignty remained controversial. Among the many cases of violent protest against claims for sovereignty by territorial rulers during the sixteenth century, the one which occurred in the Netherlands was the most conspicuous.

When Emperor Charles V divided his realms in 1556, the Netherlands were allocated to the rule of the Spanish king. But Philip II's rule over the Netherlands was contested. The geographical distance between the Netherlands and Philip's court in central Spain promoted a sense of separateness which was strengthened by the fact that Calvinism had taken root in the northern part of the Netherlands. In that part of the country there were many wealthy towns and cities whose inhabitants wished to extend their autonomy and rights of self-government and even joined into a coalition with dissatisfied aristocrats in the area.

By 1568 both groups formed a protest and resistance movement against the King of Spain which was led by the aristocrat William of Orange and whose explicit goal it was to shake off Spanish rule and to constitute the Netherlands as a new polity independent from the Spanish king. The protesters formed the union which was finally agreed upon at Utrecht in 1579. The union constituted the Netherlands as a free and independent polity which stood under the control of a military governor (*stadthouder*) and in which sovereignty was claimed for the member provinces. The union was modelled upon the contractualism of medieval urban communities. But its goal was difficult to accomplish for two reasons: first because Philip II chose to ignore the protests and secondly because parts of the Netherlands were taken to belong to the Roman Empire. Hence the protesters had to seek independence through resorting to war, not only from the King of Spain but also from the emperor. The struggle was fought with some interruptions between 1568 and 1648 until the northern part of the Netherlands received its recognition as an independent polity in a bilateral treaty with the Spanish king. This act was, however, ignored by the emperor.

THE ETHICS OF SELF-CONSTRAINT IN PRACTICE: MILITARY DRILL

Not surprisingly, Lipsius's advice was taken seriously in the United Provinces during the Eighty Years War against the King of Spain. This was so not only because Lipsius's theory was drawn on the contractualism which was applied in practice in the process of the formation of the United Provinces but also because the struggle against Spain was fought mainly by militia forces. Prince Maurice of Orange (1585–1625), who had succeeded his father William as *stadthouder* when the latter was murdered in 1584, and his relative William Louis (1560–1620), *stadthouder* of Friesland, emerged as the leading army organizers and drew support from their relatives and Calvinist co-confessionals among the lesser territorial rulers in the empire.[37] In order to strengthen the armed forces of the United Provinces, they drew on three models: Lipsius's theories, the lansquenet mode of fighting and English trained bands.

Lipsius provided the reformers with knowledge about ancient Roman military organization which he had gleaned from historiography and military writings of the Roman Empire of antiquity. To these sources, the reformers added information which they took from ancient Greek and Byzantine military manuals[38] which were critically studied by classical philologists at the time. Lipsius and his fellow scholars described types of military organization which peaked in the position of a supreme military leader who was capable of enforcing strict disciplinary codes upon the warriors and left no room for private military organization. They urged rulers to develop their own military capabilities in order to promote the training and disciplining of militia-based armed forces under their direct command.

The lansquenet mode of fighting drew on the Maximilian enforcement of disciplinary codes which the warriors of each band imposed upon themselves. These codes included the obligation of each warrior to train himself in the use of weapons, to accumulate physical strength, to act in concert with other warriors in battle and to follow the commands of the band leader.[39] In the course of the sixteenth century, the lansquenets familiarized themselves with fighting in tactical formations made up from specialist bands of infantrymen, artillerymen and some cavalrymen, all of whom did battle according to designs and tactical schemes which they had prepared in advance.

However, by Maximilian's time, these battle designs and tactical schemes were already frequently at odds with the plans of the supreme commander, so that conflicts arose between what the lansquenet bands wanted and what their supreme commanded ordered them to do. In such cases, the commands of the supreme leader were frequently ignored even though autonomous action by the bands could lead to defeat in battle.[40] Likewise, the discipline of these warriors frequently ended when payment or reward for the services was deferred or refused. In such cases, bands could make their own decisions and deploy their arms against their previous commander or employer. Hence, the lansquenet mode of fighting presented a difficult legacy to the army reformers at the turn of the seventeenth century because, despite all their much cherished professionalism, lansquenet warrior bands were a source of unrest and disorder.[41]

Finally, the success in fifteenth- and sixteenth-century military practice of English trained bands seemed to prove that armies were successful when they were centrally organized under the command of the king as the supreme territorial ruler.[42] Already in the fourteenth century English aristocrats had agreed to renounce their privilege of leading battle on horseback. Instead, they accepted battle designs which forced them to dismount and act in support of lightly armed peasant infantrymen. Under this condition, the lightly armed infantrymen could be employed in large numbers with the longbow, a weapon which was effective only if its user was not heavily armed and was therefore unprotected against swords and lances of opposing cavalry.

In the campaigns of the Hundred Years War, English armies had developed elaborate longbow tactics and the organizational schemes necessary to establish and maintain socially cohesive armed forces. The major condition of the successful deployment of longbows was the training of the warriors in their use. To that end, the English kings began to issue commands in the fourteenth century that every longbowman should train himself continuously in the use of the weapon and increase his physical strength so as to be able to handle the bow at all times.[43]

At the end of the sixteenth century, drill was formalized and regularized to the extent that specific words of command were used.[44] English longbowmen had been used outside the kingdom in European battle grounds in the fifteenth century, and their deployment had been successful. Moreover, the sweeping victories which English armed forces had gained during the early phase of the Hundred Years War added to their reputation. The Dutch forces were supported by contingents of English forces from 1583.[45]

Apparently beginning in 1594, Maurice and William Louis developed several measures which created momentum for reform. They combined ancient Greek and Roman military practice for the purpose of creating mobile and highly flexible units or tactical formations in which the individual warriors were regularly trained to handle their weapons and to execute planned movements in their units under the control of the rulers or their appointed officers and according to prescribed words of command and battle designs. The reformers used ancient Greek and Roman drill where it was applicable, added certain drill patterns from the lansquenet mode of fighting and employed these patterns for the specific purpose of speeding up and regularizing the use of portable firearms. Finally, the reformers drew on English trained bands as the model of a disciplined army wherein militiamen and other warriors were accustomed to subject themselves unequivocally to the commands of their officers, control their movements and constrain their actions. The warriors were to be recruited from the local countryside and were organized as militia forces whenever possible.

Maurice and William themselves composed drill manuals and saw to it that they were published. These publications were lavishly illustrated with pictures and graphs which allowed the commanding officers to instruct their men properly and in accordance with the rulers' prescriptions.

During the first two decades of the seventeenth century drill manuals appeared in Dutch, English, French, Latin and German.[46]

The fusion of the three models culled from sources of antiquity, the lansquenets and the English trained bands produced a highly mobile, well-ordered and disciplined fighting force under the command of Maurice of Orange. During a twelve-year truce which he arranged with the Spanish king in 1609, the reforms took root and, when warfare was resumed in 1621, Maurice's armed forces could play out the tactical advantage achieved through the new organization. However, the success of this military organization hinged upon the willingness of the militiamen and other warriors to subject themselves to centrally commanded and supervised drill and to constrain and control their actions and movements in battle.

Such readiness was not self-evident as the failed attempts to emulate the Oranian reforms early in the seventeenth century made painfully clear. Reception began late in the sixteenth century in imperial estates whose rulers were related by kin and confession to the House of Orange. Foremost among them were the Earls of Nassau and the Electors of the Palatinate. Others who followed suit were the Landgraves of Hesse-Kassel and the Electors of Brandenburg. These rulers began to organize their own militia forces at the turn of the seventeenth century, trained them according to principles modified from the Oranian and the English models and devised elaborate defence systems for their territories.

Eventually, fully fledged military academies came into existence in Metz (France) and in Siegen (Nassau) in 1613. But when it came to battle, these militia-based armies suffered heavy losses and serious defeats against the professional warrior bands which were organized along the lines of the lansquenet mode of fighting. The reason for the defeats was that the militiamen were unwilling to undergo regular drilling and to enact the tactical schemes which the Oranian reformers had composed. This meant that, at the turn of the seventeenth century, the Oranian reforms succeeded only in the Netherlands. This was because Lipsius's ethics of self-constraint could be converted into principles of military organization only under the condition that the warriors were willing to increase their own capability for military action and, at the same time, to constrain and control themselves. They would be willing to do so if they understood that they were executing commands by rulers whom they had established by way of a contract.

In the Netherlands, this condition was fulfilled because contractualism was at the very bottom of the order of the territorial polity. Therefore, Lipsius's ethics of self-constraint formed the platform for both the legitimacy of the United Provinces as a territorial polity and the organization of the disciplined, well-ordered and minutely trained militia-based armed forces to defend it.

The period under review displayed war-proneness and diversity. These were the very factors that widened the gap between theory and practice of international relations. Already in the middle of the sixteenth century, theorists began to suggest universal norms and rules which they took to be globally applicable. These rules and norms were moral in kind and were drawn on the postulate that a framework of natural and fundamental laws existed which was apt to constrain the actions of every reasonable human actor. Hence international theories passed into the province of natural law theorists and moral philosophers who subscribed to the task of thinking of the world as a well-ordered entity for all humankind.

During the sixteenth and the early part of the seventeenth centuries, however, these theorists and philosophers were few in number. They were to be found in the universities as academic teachers and authors of scholarly printed works. Their audience were, again, primarily academics, although Lipsius's political and military works also penetrated into some rulers' cabinets and could be found on the desks of some military commanders. Still, the political impact of these works was indirect and depended on the position which they obtained in the academic discourse.

In a way, then, Lipsius and the natural law thinkers widened the gap between international theories and political decision-making because the theorists insisted that the world of international relations and the world of territorial polities and urban communities were organized along opposite principles. Such insistence had the merit of rescuing universalism for a globally applicable international theory drawn on ethics but it had the demerit of allowing political decision-makers to rank their interest as rulers above theoretical concerns for the world at large. The consequence was that, for the time being, international theory flourished in the ivory tower of academia with no more than occasional impact on the empirical conduct of the relations between rulers. Nevertheless, international theorists offered their suggestions regarding how the world was to be organized. The answer was that the world did not have to be organized at all.

FIVE

Mechanicism

The story of international theory during much of the seventeenth and the eighteenth centuries is the story of the rapprochement between theory and practice. This was accomplished through the gradual acceptance of the ethics of self-constraint as the first guideline for action in international relations. Two groups of theorists subscribed to the task of broadening the acceptance the ethics of self-constraint among the practitioners of international relations. The first and more numerous group specified the conditions for the establishment, maintenance and restoration of the balance of power, whereas the second group investigated the conditions for perpetual peace. Both groups of theorists operated on the joint platform of the conviction that the maintenance of stability was a positive value in its own right.

This conviction was in turn rooted in a tendency to compare living beings and indeed the whole inanimate world with technical devices, mainly the sophisticated machines (*automata*) which became fashionable in the course of the sixteenth and seventeenth centuries as the then most recent technological innovation. The purposes of these comparisons were: first, the tracing of similarities between living beings and the machine; secondly, the defence of the postulate that living beings as well as machines were well-ordered entities; and thirdly, arguing the hope that a well-ordered world represents a stable 'system' as the hierarchically structured assembly of interconnected or even integrated parts.

In the first half of the seventeenth century, Jan Amos Comenius (1592–1670) and René Descartes (1596–1650) were most explicit in arguing this mechanistic world view according to which the operation of machines was perfectly compatible with the principles of organization which were followed in nature.[1] This philosophical world view supported the perception of the world as a static entity all of whose principal constitutive parts, including living species, were believed to remain unchanged or to follow only well-ordered and repetitive cycles of change. Where change occurred, as in cases of cosmic irregularities, the incalculable ups and downs in everyone's life, the factuality of human mortality and the transformation or even collapse of polities, it was acknowledged with awe, deplored and attributed to the imperfection of the cosmos and the human world.

The most explicit expression of this perception, as far as life on earth was concerned, were Carl von Linné's (Linnaeus) (1707–1778) botanical and zoological tables which condensed the universe of nature into a static and hierarchically structured system of species.[2] This world view also generated theoretical and practical quests for stability in the relations among territorial polities and urban communities, and informed attitudes towards the balance of power as well as proposals for perpetual peace up to the end of the eighteenth century.

THE QUEST FOR STABILITY

In the seventeenth and eighteenth centuries Hugo Grotius (1583–1645) was the single most influential advocate of Lipsius's ethics of self-constraint. He did so mainly in his *opus magnum*, *De jure belli ac pacis libri tres* (*Three Books on the Law of War and Peace*) which was first published in 1625. As the title announced, the work consisted of three parts, one on what one can do in war, another on what one should not do in war and a third on the preparation for and conclusion of peace. Part One is a systematic list of the evils and miseries of warfare; Part Two is a register of arguments why rational actors, in pursuit of their own legitimate self-interest, should refrain from doing what can be done in war; and Part Three presents an outline of conditions of and procedures towards peace. Part Two is the most important one in the context of the history of international theories, because here

Grotius explicated his views on the morality of the conduct of international relations.[3]

He did so entirely in agreement with the principles which Lipsius had set out little more than a generation earlier. Like Lipsius, Grotius was a Thomist who believed in the divine origin of natural law in which he saw the source of the law of war and peace. He regarded the law of war as the universal moral code by which rational actors would continue to abide even when they had abrogated all other legal commitments. Consequently, Grotius categorized the law of war as an inalienable and divinely willed moral code which alone was capable of restraining the rational actions of actors at war. He was therefore willing to distinguish between the law of war and international law, the latter of which he confined to statutory rules in the Roman legal tradition.[4]

This position allowed him to integrate the arguments which Cajetan had adduced in his struggle against universal rule. When Grotius was asked for a legal opinion by the Dutch East India Company about the lawfulness of its overseas struggle against its competitors, he argued in agreement with Cajetan that the oceans were open seas and belonged to no one. Hence no one could prevent the company from extending its activities on to and beyond the oceans. Grotius thus rejected the idea that the Portuguese had obtained exclusive rights to conduct trade and other forms of international relations in the hemisphere which had been allocated to them by the Tordesillas treaty. Instead, Grotius insisted that trade was free to everyone by natural law and that this freedom included unrestricted access to the open seas.[5]

Later theorists who were less concerned with the world beyond the confines of Europe went further than Grotius and rejected his distinction between natural and international law. Instead, they took the view that international law, like the law of war, was natural law and could be supplemented only by statutes, but not principally changed. First and foremost among these theorists were Thomas Hobbes (1588–1679) and Samuel von Pufendorf (1632–1694) in the seventeenth century.[6] However, while disagreeing with Grotius about the conceptual reach of international law, they agreed with him in their view that international relations could be conducted in good order without statutory rules and in an inalterable systemic framework of inalienable rules rooted in natural law.

They also agreed in demanding that wars should be fought only for morally defendable reasons and only under the conditions which St Thomas Aquinas and Lipsius had specified. In this view, wars were temporary interruptions of periods of peace and were justifiable only if they led to the restoration of a more stable peace. Theorizing about international relations as peace–war–peace (rather than war–peace–war) sequences remained dominant up to the second half of the eighteenth century. Theorists following this approach demanded that stability of institutions should be promoted and that the effects of change when it occurred should be reduced, and they believed that the implementation of these demands was a condition for the accomplishment of happiness and a lasting peace.[7]

THEORIES OF THE BALANCE OF POWER

The search for a balance of power was a consequence of the depoliticization of universalism. If universal rule was an issue of the past and a bone of contention, it became necessary to determine the conditions under which various sovereign polities could coexist among themselves. Therefore, praise for mastery of maintaining the balance of power bore the hallmark of the unusual, and this was the very reason why, early in the sixteenth century, Lorenzo de' Medici was applauded for this capability.

Already late in the fifteenth century, conceptions of the balance among rulers were expressed in binary dichotomies.[8] The technical model of the scales achieved some currency during the sixteenth century[9] although its use was then overshadowed by the controversies over universal rule, and the model continued to be applied as a conventional phrase up to the twentieth century. But it was superseded in the seventeenth and eighteenth centuries by the machine model, for which an early record has been preserved in the political works of Francis Bacon (1561–1626).

Bacon was an established authority in the empirical natural sciences when he sat down in the early 1620s to prepare a speech, concerning a possible war with Spain, which he was going to deliver to Parliament in his capacity as Lord Chancellor. In the notes for his speech he tried to convince his compatriots that they ought not 'doubt to be overmatched' in a war with Spain, and he derived this conviction from 'experience' as well as from 'reason'. Under the heading of 'experience', he treated historical facts which appeared to tell him that Spain had never prevailed over England. Under the heading of 'reason', he adduced four indicators showing that England could not but win a future leadership struggle with Spain.

Bacon's first indicator was that Spain 'is a nation thin sown of men, partly by reason of the sterility of their soil; and partly because their natives are exhaust by so many employments in such vast territories as they possess'. Spain was thus not to be feared because of a lack of manpower. The second indicator was that 'if we truly consider the greatness of Spain, it consists chiefly in their treasure, and their treasure in their Indies (both of them) is but an accession to such as are masters by sea'. Hence Spain was vulnerable because the seas and oceans were open. The third indicator was that a future war between England and Spain would be a 'matter of restorative and enriching, so that, if we go roundly on with supplies and provisions at the first, the war in continuance will find itself'. Hence, for the benefit of his argument, Bacon accepted the current theory that the war could support itself and that English resources would not be overspent for the war.

The final indicator was

> that it is not a little to be considered that the greatness of Spain is not only distracted extremely and therefore of less force; but built upon no very sound foundations; and therefore they can have the less strength by any assured and confident confederates. With France they are in competition for Navarre, Milan, Naples and the Franche County of Burgundy. With the see of Rome, for Naples also. For Portugal, with the right heirs of that line. For that they have in their Low Countries, with the United Provinces. For

Ormus (now) with Persia. For Valencia with the Moors expulsed and their confederates. For the East and West Indies with all the world. So that if every bird had his feather Spain would be left wonderful naked. But yet there is a greater confederation against them than by means of any of these quarrels or titles; and that is contracted by the fear that almost all nations have of their ambition, whereof men see no end. And thus much for the balancing of their forces.[10]

This result of the analysis presented Spain as engulfed in a cobweb of pressures from 'all the world' acting primarily to 'balance' the forces of Spain. In order to accomplish it, Bacon 'reasoned' and drew a network of partly overlapping interrelations the causes and effects of which were subjected to analytical scrutiny. Such an analysis was incompatible with the previous scales model of the balance of power. A simple juxtaposition of Spain against the rest of the world was incompatible with the scales model, for no one could then imagine that Spain was able to counterpoise the entire world. And even if one could, the result would show Spain in an extremely strong position while Bacon's argument was directed towards the exactly opposite end. Hence Bacon employed the multi-dimensional and more sophisticated machine model. It suggested that Spain was no more than one part of the international system, and not a significant one at that.

The difficulty with Bacon's analysis is that one is left with doubt as to why England should be worried about Spain at all because Spain was presented by Bacon as a *quantité négligeable*, with very little value in itself. However, Bacon's analysis can be understood when placed before the wider background of the ongoing Thirty Years War and, more precisely, the impact of the Battle of White Mountain (1620). The flight of Frederick, the Protestant King of Bohemia and Count Palatine (1610–23), to England after the battle had suddenly drawn England into a network of relations with various other territorial polities.

It was within this system of relations that Bacon placed his analysis of England's Spanish policies. Thus Bacon was not describing bilateral effects of the changes in the relations between two territorial polities only. Instead, he was analysing the multilateral effects of a possible English interference with continental international relations. Furthermore, Bacon was not concerned with the establishment of stability and peace in Europe at large but treated what he perceived as the existing system of relations among the European territorial polities for the purpose of analysing possibilities and prospects of English interference with it.

That Bacon did not regard England's relations with Spain as bilateral or one-dimensional in the sense of the scales model of the balance of power becomes evident from a remark in a later essay which he wrote in 1625, entitled 'Of Empire'. This essay contains a 'rule' for the conduct of relations between neighbouring territorial polities:

> First for their neighbours. There can no general rule be given (the occasions are so variable), save one; which ever holds. Which is that princes do keep due sentinel that none of their neighbours does overgrow so (by increase of territory, by embracing of trade, by approaches or the like) as they become more able to annoy them than they were. And this is, generally, the work of standing councils to foresee and to hinder it. During that triumvirate of kings, King Henry the Eighth of England, Francis the First, King of France, and Charles the Fifth, Emperor, there was such a watch kept that none of the three could win a palm of ground but the other two would straightways balance it either by confederation or, if need were, by a war. And would not, in any wise, take up peace at interest. And the like was done by that league (which, Guicciardini says, was the security of Italy) made between Ferdinand King of Naples, Lorenzo de' Medici and Ludovico Sforza, potentates the one of Florence, the other of Milan. Neither is the opinion, of some of the school men, to be received that a war cannot justly be made but upon a precedent injury or provocation. For there is no question but a just fear of an imminent danger though there be no blow given is a lawful cause of a war.[11]

The term 'neighbour' is to be taken with a pinch of salt because England and the Habsburg imperial domains could then hardly be considered as adjacent territories. Consequently, the use of the term may be understood as a reference to a system through which the member polities become virtual neighbours and in consequence of which the causes and effects of actions undertaken within this system become multilateral in structure. Therefore, a multi-dimensional model was required to analyse them.

Bacon made this clear by adducing the example of King Henry VIII (1509–47), King Francis I (1515–47) and Emperor Charles V, all of whom he mentioned as members of a 'triumvirate' of territorial rulers. That term must be understood as indicating the equality of status among them so that, in Bacon's view, none of them exercised a prerogative over the other. Hence Bacon's analysis of the politics of Henry VIII differed fundamentally from those of sixteenth-century analysts, such as Geoffray Fenton[12] who had argued that Henry VIII had tried to act as a 'balancer' and to conduct relations only on a bilateral level.

On the contrary, Bacon's point was that the interactions among the three rulers were predictable to the extent that any attempt by one of them to upset the balance would entail combined counteractions by the other two for the purpose of preserving it. Consequently, Bacon neither made reference to rising or falling scales nor operated with the concept of a hierarchical superior 'balancer'. Bacon's model of the balance of power was thus multi-dimensional. Moreover, he admitted legal constraints to the end of maintaining the balance by claiming that the preservation of the balance of power was a just war aim and thereby amplifying the medieval just war theory.

Finally, Bacon's insistence that the emperor was a member in a triumvirate of rulers equal among themselves put on record his conviction that universalism had been superseded by balance-of-power considerations as the principle of the conduct of international relations.

THE MACHINE MODEL OF THE INTERNATIONAL SYSTEM

Bacon's arguments overlapped neatly with the mechanistic convictions of Comenius and Descartes because his model of the balance of power was the machine,[13] and they reflected contemporary conceptualizations of the international system. In the seventeenth century, words such as *societas* and *systema* were in use as terms for clusters of polities which were tied together by alliances and other forms of agreements.[14] Subsequently, further phrases such as 'European political system'[15] and 'European state system'[16] specified the spatial dimension of this system as a European one and laid emphasis on the fact that the relations among the polities in the system were relations among 'states'.

According to this concept, the system was a system of 'states' and formed the fixed outward frame for its member units. The polities forming this 'European state system' were thus tied together like parts of a machine. They represented a well-ordered, static and hierarchically arrayed assembly of units which was credited with the ability to repair itself, as Rousseau observed.[17] According to this concept, the system was equal to the total number of its units. It did not require its own laws and rules but existed as part of the divinely willed world order. It was not considered possible to change the number of member units in the system without seriously jeopardizing the entire system.

THE BALANCE-OF-POWER MACHINE MODEL DURING THE WAR OF THE SPANISH SUCCESSION

Whereas, in the seventeenth century, international theorists using this model remained in a minority position,[18] its use rose to dominance in eighteenth-century international theory. This was the case first and foremost for Jonathan Swift (1667–1745) who emerged as a foremost critic of politics and ways of life at the time of the War of the Spanish Succession (1701–13). Early in the eighteenth century, this war provided the background against which theorists advanced the use of the machine model.

The war was fought primarily over the question of whether the dynastic rights of ruling royal kin groups or the continuity of territorial polities should have priority in cases where one territorial polity might be united with another through the hereditary succession of one and the same ruler. This possibility seemed to exist when, after the death of King Charles II of

Spain (1665–1700), Louis XIV, King of France (1643–1715), tried to secure succession to the Spanish throne for his grandson Philip of Anjou. In the course of the war, the United Kingdom and the United Provinces (sometimes also referred to as the States General) concluded a treaty of alliance against France in 1709. Late in the seventeenth century, the United Provinces had repeatedly been attacked by French armies under Louis XIV.

To safeguard his polity against further French attacks, the Dutch *stadthouder* William of Orange (1672–1702) who was elected King of England in 1689 tried to obtain English support for the erection of a 'barrier' of fortresses against France in what is Belgium today. Swift opposed the treaty and took the view that it violated English self-interest by supporting Dutch policy without gaining anything in return. Instead, Swift proposed a theory of limited warfare and considered the following five war aims to be just:

> The motives that may engage a wise prince or state in a war, I take to be one or more of these: Either to check the over-grown power of some ambitious neighbour; to recover what has been unjustly taken from them; to revenge some injury they have received (which all political casuists allow); to assist some ally in a just quarrel; or lastly, to defend themselves when they are invaded. In all these cases, the writers upon politics admit a war to be justly undertaken. The last is what has been usually called *pro aris et focis*; where no expence or endeavour can be too great because all we have is at stake. And consequently, our utmost force to be exerted; and the dispute is soon determined, either in safety or utter destruction. But in the other four, I believe, it still be found that no monarch or commonwealth did ever engage beyond a certain degree.[19]

Swift followed Bacon in including the preservation of the balance of power as a just war aim but was more specific in spelling out the various dimensions of warfare. He admitted only one motive for going to a war which was to be fought to the bitter end and suggested that the four remaining motives should lead to no more than limited warfare in consequence of which no actor within the existing system would disappear. His introduction of the concept of limited warfare allowed Swift the combination of the pursuit of self-interest by actors in the system and the preservation of the entire systemic structure (except in cases of foreign interventions).

Swift provided the conceptual tools through which the machine model of the balance of power could be dissociated from the grand but impracticable goal of the pursuit of perpetual peace. He emphasized that peace should be generated through systemic stability which he posited as the ultimate goal to which all actors in the system should subscribe in the pursuit of their self-interest. It was Swift's achievement that he incorporated the struggle for primacy into the quest for the preservation of the systemic status quo by admitting preventive wars while banning offensive wars. This position led him to support the Tory government which decided in 1711 to reduce its terms for peace vis-à-vis France. Swift agreed that it is 'infinitely better to accept such terms as will secure our trade, find a sufficient barrier for the States, give reasonable satisfaction to the Emperor and restore the tranquility of Europe though without adding Spain to the Empire'.[20]

Swift avoided the use of the scales model because he focused on the distribution of power among many actors simultaneously engaged in a contest for primacy within the system of European territorial polities. Swift argued the position that the maintenance of the balance among all actors in the system was the first condition of stability in the system and should therefore have priority over the partial interests of the involved rulers and their dynasties. There is some indication that this position was debated during the Utrecht peace conference of 1712 and 1713 which ended the War of the Spanish Succession with the agreement that the ruling dynasties of the Kingdoms of France and Spain should be separated. In the text of his so-called renunciation, signed on 24 November 1712, the Duke of Berry gave up all rights to succeed in Spain for himself and his heirs and joined Swift in regarding the balance among the several territorial polities in Europe as superior to the interest of a single ruling dynasty.[21]

The Duke, like Swift, used the balance to describe the complexity of partly contradictory, partly overlapping factors in the network of multilateral relations within the system of European territorial polities. The peacemakers at the Congress concurred. In one treaty, the balance of power was referred to as an element of the status quo which the contracting parties wished to restore as a condition for a lasting peace.[22] Whoever considered inadequate or inappropriate such descriptive use of the machine model of the balance of power at the time did so either because such an analysis was regarded as incompatible with the conventional scales model[23] or because the price to be paid for the establishment of a balance by means of a preventive war was taken to be too high.[24]

By contrast, the Utrecht settlements gave priority to maintaining the status quo inside Europe by preserving a mechanistically conceived balance. The machine model of the balance of power could be used to show that the destruction of even small interacting units would entail the destruction of the system as a whole. Therefore, the machine model could be used to justify the coexistence of units with unequal capabilities but equal rights within a principally stable frame.

THE BALANCE-OF-POWER MACHINE MODEL AFTER THE CONGRESS OF UTRECHT

After the Congress of Utrecht, several international theorists attempted to demonstrate the long existence in history of the machine model of the balance of power. Not unlike political theorists in general, several international theorists went to great efforts to collect evidence for what they believed to have been the Greek origin of the balance of power, although they agreed that the words and the term had not then been in use.[25]

Such repeated insistence can be understood only by assuming that at least some of these theorists accepted the heritage of Greek and Roman antiquity not just as quarries for random evidence but as manifestations of the continuity of territorial polities of antiquity into those of their own time. In other words, they must have assumed that the use of evidence from sources of antiquity in the eighteenth century was possible without interruptions and fundamental changes. Following this assumption, one theorist could argue that the balance of power could emerge as an instrument regarded as so widely spread across time and space that it could be characterized as a ubiquitous, inalterable and 'natural' feature pertaining to any ordered community of men:

> All nations are compelled by a natural obligation to maintain the equilibrium; that is what has brought most among them and particularly several rulers of Europe to introduce it into treaties and conventions and to turn it into a rule, a principle of government. Consequently, rulers appearing to threaten that equilibrium and aspiring to a power with which they can be able to exercise just fear must cede those parts of their empire which could make the balance incline towards their side. Hence, the harshest remedies, the most intensive wars have been inflicted upon nations which have placed themselves on to this dangerous track; and, on the opposing side, those who have fallen into decay have been relieved by the defender of the common equilibrium.[26]

In this statement, the emphasis has shifted towards preventive war which, unlike Swift, the author ranked as the most intensive of all wars, although they were not considered to be wars of annihilation. The argument implied that the constraints upon rulers increased because they could be forced to refrain from aggression by the joint efforts of other actors in the system. It was no longer regarded as sufficient to tie actors in the system together only by bonds of morality. Instead, it was now considered that these bonds need to be tighter:

> Nations are obliged to cooperate more for the common utility than for their own particular advantages, and they must even neglect their own law . . . In the Balance of Europe, we find a sort of ostracism which, however, is less a pain than a means of banning envy because it diminishes the risks attached to too great a power.[27]

Territorial polities were regarded as personifications of individuals.[28] In the same way as an individual was held to be able to find security against unjustified attacks from another individual through subordinating himself under the authority of a ruler,[29] any single government was believed to be able to protect its subjects against attacks by other governments through a legally binding framework for rules, and the balance of power was the core structure of that framework. Theorists not only assumed that this framework was capable of reducing the sovereignty of the actors in the system but also took for granted that it was just and legitimate to limit the sovereign rights of these actors. Such rigidity of the application of the balance-of-power rules meant that infringements of these rules were to be identified as a just cause for war.[30]

The author from whose work the above quotations were taken was Ludwig Martin Kahle, a professor of philosophy at the University of Göttingen who submitted his work as a dissertation to the law faculty of his university. The original Latin text was immediately translated into French and appeared in print at Berlin and Göttingen. Written and printed during the War of the Austrian Succession (1740–48), in which King Frederick of Prussia (1740–86) intervened in 1740 with the military occupation of the Austrian provinces of Silesia and Glatz, the work provoked an intensive debate over method and matter as it was arguable that Frederick's action was a breach of balance-of-power rules.

In methodological respects, critics called into question the validity of Kahle's argument that the balance of power was a time-honoured principle of the conduct of international relations appearing already in ancient Greek times. Doubt was raised that Kahle's position was supported by historical evidence and that his interpretations were tenable. But the majority of theorists followed Kahle.[31] However, more important than methodology were two ontological problems in Kahle's theory. First, was the balance of power in truth a legal framework and could its maintenance be a just cause of war? Was its underlying assumption, that any increase in the power of a territorial ruler could result only from territorial expansion as Kahle maintained, acceptable? If not, was it just to punish the inhabitants of a territorial polity for being industrious and well-governed and thereby prosperous? These questions remained issues of public debate well into the 1780s and demonstrated the continuing relevance of this problem.[32]

The second problem was to determine the ontological status of the balance of power. Where was it? Was it perceptible and measurable by everyone objectively, as a thing in the world? Or was it a subjective construct in the minds of gifted propagandists? Whether or not the balance of power was a chimera – this problem, although then not altogether new, prompted perhaps the hottest debates among international theorists throughout the eighteenth century. While the majority of theorists appear to have considered the balance to be objective and tangible, the problem of measurability remained a source of constant worry. One could placate the critics by pointing to the vast, elaborate and sophisticated 'statistical' literature.[33] This literature seemed to meet the requirement of the public accessibility of data relating to economic as well as military capabilities and political goals. But even if one was willing to accept as trustworthy the data contained in this body of literature, what was it that one was going to measure?

A seemingly ingenious solution to this problem was offered by Antoine Pecquet (1704–1762), a French diplomat, political theorist and follower of Kahle. In 1757 he published a treatise on political theory issued as a sequel to Montesquieu's *Esprit des Lois*. Pecquet distinguished between 'primary' and 'secondary' balancing factors, the first including physical force, that is the size of the territory and of the armies available in it, and the second such less tangible matters as the spirit of rulers. Pecquet then assumed that primary as well as secondary factors could be subjected to a sufficiently rigid measurement which allowed uncontested perceptions of the operation of the balance of power.[34]

In other words, theorists who, like Pecquet, claimed objective existence for the balance of power were obliged to take for granted a highly conventional and normative communicative code apt to promote agreement over matters admittedly wide apart and would make comparable the variegated economic, military and political features of each territorial polity and urban community in the international system. In short, the logic of the eighteenth-century mechanistic balance-of-power theory was that it induced governments to follow the same standards, conventions as well as norms and act uniformly. If all rulers did the same at the same time, abiding by the same rules, making their intentions known and controlling themselves as well as each other, the balance would work and everyone would benefit.[35]

But even this solution could not provide an absolute guarantee for the stability of the system even if all actors abided by the balance-of-power rules. It was still possible that several territorial rulers concluded an agreement for the purpose of dismembering or annihilating another territorial polity or urban community and of sharing the spoils equally among themselves. This was exactly what happened on the occasions of the partitions of Poland of 1772, 1793 and 1795 which ended with the destruction of Poland as a polity. The partitions added to the size and power of the polities under the control of the partitioning rulers, namely Catherine II, Tsarina of Russia (1762–96), Frederick II, King of Prussia, and Maria Theresa, heiress of the Habsburg hereditary lands (1740–80), and Frederick's as well as Maria Theresa's successors.

Even though these rulers argued that the partitions were contributing to the maintenance of the balance of power in East Central Europe, the argument met with no support among non-involved parties elsewhere in Europe and was staunchly refuted by Polish émigrés who criticized the partitions as incompatible with balance-of-power rules.[36] Nevertheless, few European territorial polities and urban communities disappeared in the course of the eighteenth century.

THE BALANCE OF POWER IN THEORIES OF INTERNATIONAL LAW

If it was possible to conduct a just war against those who chose to break or act otherwise against the balance-of-power rules, determining the conditions for their enforcement fell into the province of jurisprudence. The juristic question was whether the binding force of the balance of power was strong enough to serve as a legal norm and in that quality as an instrument of diplomatic and military coercion. This expansion of the argumentative reach of the mechanistic balance-of-power model is not to be belittled, for the model added greatly to the ideological tools at the disposal of rulers and their capacity to influence and shape 'public' opinion among their own subjects as well as those in other territorial polities in Europe. In this sense, the juridification of the balance of power was in itself a contributor to the growing political interdependence among the several actors making up the international system of Europe.

Nicolaus Hieronymus Gundling (1671–1729) appears to have been the first jurist to ask whether it was lawful for a ruler to intervene in neighbouring polities when their rulers appeared to increase their power. Drawing on natural law, Gundling construed the argument that a ruler, when powerful, cannot be prevented from committing unlawful acts against the community of territorial polities in Europe and that, consequently, each government had the right to act in defence not only of its own security, but also of that of the entire system.[37] In this way, Gundling justified preventive warfare for the preservation of the balance of power. But the double-edged character of this argument became clear little more than forty years later at the time of the Seven Years War. Gundling's theory was then used to confirm the Austrian position that the Prussian king Frederick II had unlawfully acquired an excessive amount of power through his occupation of Silesia and Glatz and that Prussia ought to be reduced by force to its size before 1740.[38]

The most elaborate juristic explication of the eighteenth-century 'political system' of Europe was provided by Emer de Vattel (1714–1767), the Swiss-born legal adviser to the Elector of Saxony, in his widely read work *Le droit des gens*, which was first published in 1758. In his description of the European international system, Vattel pointed out that the balance of power was a means to foster close ties among the polities of Europe and to advance the mutual interdependence and vulnerability of territorial rulers:

Europe forms a political system in which the nations inhabiting this part of the world are bound together by their relations and various interests into a single body. It is no longer, as in former times, a confused heap of detached parts, each of which had but little concern for the lot of the others, and rarely troubled itself over what did not immediately affect it. The constant attention of sovereigns to all that goes on, the custom of resident ministers, the continual negotiations that take place, make modern Europe a sort of Republic, whose members – each independent, but all bound together by a common interest – unite for the maintenance of order and the preservation of liberty. This is what has given rise to the well-known principle of the balance of power, by which is meant an arrangement of affairs so that no state shall be in a position to have absolute mastery and dominate over the others.[39]

The common interest was focused on the uniting of the territorial polities of Europe and the maintenance of the status quo in Europe – a recasting into legal diction of Kahle's main argument. Vattel proceeded to tackle the problem of how to deal with those tending to break away from the common interest in order to pursue their own particularistic interest. His solution was an elaborate casuistry through which he tried to outline the conditions under which preventive warfare was justified when, 'in the midst of a profound peace, a neighbouring sovereign constructs fortresses upon our frontier, fits out a fleet, increases his troops, assembles a powerful army, fills his magazines, in a word when he makes preparations for war'.[40]

If such a thing occurred, Vattel first obliged rulers to distinguish between an increase of power which a ruler undertook with the determination to do harm to someone else and an increase of power which a ruler promoted in service to the population under his or her control. Vattel then argued that only increases of power which had been undertaken as a threat of injury could be considered as a reason for a just preventive war. He added that two further conditions must be fulfilled before a just preventive war for the maintenance of the balance of power could be launched. These conditions were, first, that several such suspicious acts should be on record and secondly that rulers could be suspected of planning acts of aggression against others only if they were well known and easily recognizable from past experience as untrustworthy people.

Finally, Vattel insisted that alliances for balance-of-power wars should be concluded only if the parties threatened by aggressive neighbours were incapable of defending themselves alone. In fact, these rules raised the threshold for the launching of a just balance-of-power war to a level where hardly any justification for such a war existed.

Like Gundling and Kahle, Vattel assigned to rulers the task of eternal vigilance and the readiness to intervene against attempts to upset the balance of power. He assumed that preparations for war could be known to all interacting partners in the system so that neither surprise attacks nor clandestine actions would occur. He was certain that there were general standards for the evaluation of rulers' characters and moral qualities and he expected that disputes about the correct interpretation of 'statistical' facts could not arise. Vattel's casuistry reflected the genuine difficulties into which the Prussian king had manoeuvred himself. Frederick's opponents had a legal title to intervene against Prussia on the grounds that Vattel specified at the time when the conflicts between Prussia and the Habsburgs about Silesia and Glatz were going on.

REVISIONS OF THE CONTRACT THEORY

In the middle of the eighteenth century, some theorists shifted the focus of their work from the study of the process of the establishment of legitimate rule to the conditions under which groups came into existence as manifestations of some form of domestic political order. For one, Francis Hutcheson (1694–1746) investigated the conditions for the formation of political order and took as the starting point of his investigation the assumption that there was no 'natural' force that compelled human actors to accept such an order. Instead, Hutcheson claimed, it was the rational consideration of human needs that accomplished this task.

He adduced as proof for this assumption that rational actors would sooner or later accept the premise that they could protect themselves and their belongings more easily if they joined in a group with others and subjected themselves to the order that was necessary to keep such groups in operation. Nevertheless, Hutcheson was sceptical enough to admit that not all human actors are rational, capable of recognizing the dangers of a lonely and unprotected life and ready to subject themselves to the discipline of a group as a protective organization. Hutcheson saw the problem that contractualist theory must provide an explanation as to why eventually all human actors residing in a given area could have been induced to enter into such groups. His solution to this problem was to bring in wisdom as a factor:

> Wise men by considering or experiencing these dangers, and representing them fully to others, have probably engaged great numbers to concur in the only remedy against them, viz. constituting some men of approved wisdom and justice the arbitrators of all their differences, and the directors in all measures necessary for the safety and prosperity of the whole; arming those rulers also with sufficient power to enforce their decisions and orders.[41]

Hutcheson thus argued that it was the task of rulers to use their power for the purpose of maintaining order and stability in polities and protect those entrusted to their control. His point was that rulers succeeding or even excelling in this task would provide a high degree of stability and security in their polities and thereby induce an ever-increasing portion of the resident population to accept rule in return for their own safety and protection.

This argument that the legitimate use of power at the hands of a ruler should contribute to stability and serve the well-understood needs of a resident population group in a given polity was shared by other eighteenth-century theorists who argued that the preservation and enhancement of stability through the ruler in a given polity and in international relations was the core condition for the growth of the population,[42] the acquisition of public and private wealth[43] and the accomplishment of happiness.[44]

Through these considerations, the emphasis shifted from the contract of a population with a ruler to the contract which, according to contractualist theorists, human actors must first conclude in order to establish a group which can then enter into another contract with a ruler. This stage of contractualist theory-making was reached when Jean-Jacques Rousseau (1712–1778) proposed his theory of the hypothetical social contract, which he envisaged as the constitution of some 'general will' as the property not of the individual group members, but of the group as a whole.[45]

The revision unleashed a substantive political momentum because it implied that rulers of territorial polities and the councils of urban communities had to become more elaborate and specific in justifying the privileges of government in these polities. Theorists who were called physiocrats sought to solicit support for rulers with utilitarian arguments. These arguments were drawn on the observation that the decisions of rulers were, and of right ought to be, beneficial and useful for the ruled.

Two such arguments mainly circulated in the second half of the eighteenth century. Proponents of the first argument contended that there was a community of interests between the ruled and the ruler. Among others, François Quesnay (1694–1774) insisted that this community of interests demanded obedience from the ruled so that the ruler could help control nature and organize the world in a stable way and allow the ruled to lead a prosperous and comfortable life.[46] Supporters of another argument, such as Johann Heinrich Gottlob von Justi (1717–1771) and Johann Peter Süßmilch (1707–1767), added that the rulers had the further duties of monitoring an active immigration policy and of providing security, health care and other measures through which untimely deaths could be avoided among the populations under their control.[47] These arguments generated a concept of rule according to which practical success in controlling nature and organizing a stable world served as the measurement for the fulfilment of the contracts between the rulers and the ruled.

The most influential legal document resulting from the revision of contractualism was the Declaration of Independence of the thirteen British colonies in America of 1776. The authors of the declaration used the medieval natural law tradition as a source of what they termed inalienable human rights and positioned against the contractualist obligation to fulfil the existing contract with the ruler. They took the view that the reigning British king had grossly violated the human rights of the British colonists in America, and they went on to say that through these violations the king had acted in breach of the contract. Thus the larger part of the text of the declaration is filled with accusations of the alleged abuse of power on the side of the British king.

But, unlike sixteenth-century monarchist theory, their conclusion was not that the king of right ought to be replaced or even killed, but that the colonists obtained the right to renounce the contract as invalid and declare the colonies independent. This conclusion was surprising as it was not prepared through the format and in the main part of the text of the declaration. The declaration did not specify an addressee and it was not sent anywhere. Instead, it served the purpose of mobilizing resistance against British rule among the colonists themselves. The declaration was not addressed to the British king whom the colonists would have had notify officially of their abrogation of the contract; there was no international institution of arbitration or higher ruler who could possibly have recognized the colonies as sovereign independent polities. Hence the implication is that the authors called for divine support for their cause.

Anticipating that the declaration would enlarge the already ongoing skirmishes into a fully fledged war, the authors, indeed, invoked the divinity and claimed that it was on their side. Therefore, the authors of the declaration continued to adhere to the medieval view that warfare was a quasi-legal trial with the divinity as the judge. However, they employed this tradition in a bid for changing the status quo, thereby creating a precedent for successful revisionism and confirmed the changeability of polities. Nevertheless, in its own time, this aspect of the declaration had few repercussions in Europe for the sole reason that the war took place on the other side of the Atlantic Ocean.

Still in the early 1780s, there was little sense of the interdependence between European and other parts of the world. The revolutionaries could expect to be able to accomplish independence only if they could take for granted that the British colonists in North America had already constituted themselves as a group that was distinct from the other population groups under the control of the British king in the United Kingdom and elsewhere in the British Empire. The belief that this was the case confirmed Rousseau's theory of the social contract and helped bring about the change of the mechanistic order of the world.

Mechanicism also informed proposals for perpetual peace. Peace was defined in the wider sense as a contractual agreement about indefinite reconciliation through amnesty, amity and the existence of good neighbourly relations between the contracting parties, and was sharply distinguished from the truce which stipulated the cession of military activities but not the conclusion of war. Thus, on the one hand, theorists classed peace as a partial contractual agreement between two parties concerning their bilateral relations whereas, on the other, they insisted that the more often peace treaties were concluded and were observed by rulers with a willingness to abide by the rules set forth in these treaties, the more the growing network of practical peace treaties would eventually evolve into a general and perpetual peace in which the maintenance of stability was possible.[48]

The concerns for the maintenance of stability were promoted early in the eighteenth century by the French philosopher Charles Irenée de Castel, Abbé de Saint-Pierre (1658–1743). He published a substantive treatise on perpetual peace at the time of the Congress of Utrecht to which he had been admitted as an observer. The Abbé took a highly sceptical stand against the peace treaties which were concluded at the Congress. He argued that the peace treaties alone could hardly terminate quarrels among rulers and that there was no certainty that the signed pledges in favour of the maintenance of peace would be fulfilled. His conclusion was that 'it is absolutely impossible that treaties will ever produce sufficient security for the period of peace'.[49]

He regarded the mere conclusion of peace treaties among rulers as imperfect because there was, in Europe, no superior agency equipped with the ability to enforce such treaties as binding. Instead, the Abbé criticized the Utrecht negotiators for having accomplished no more than an equilibrium. This equilibrium 'might well allow a short cessation of movement, some truces; but it is far from producing a solid rest, an inalterable peace'.[50] Instead, he asserted that the opportunity of the negotiations should have been used to accomplish a multilateral agreement on the 'system of the permanent society of Europe'[51] which could serve as an adjudicative institution and could enforce sanctions against rulers who decided to infringe upon the peace.

Saint-Pierre was not the first to use the word 'system' as a descriptor for agglomerations of territorial polities and urban communities whose rulers had concluded alliances and other formal agreements among themselves. But he was a pioneer in demanding that such a system should have a stable institutional framework. Drawing on the Westphalia peace treaties of 1648, he modelled this framework upon the Roman Empire wherein, he thought, 'the boldest and most restless are constrained by the fear of the Imperial Ban' and saw this as the most important condition for the maintenance of a lasting peace.[52] Hence, through Saint-Pierre's international theory, the Roman Empire was elevated into the pivotal point for peace in Europe of which the Abbé was certain that it could be accomplished in the foreseeable future.

That these views were grounded in the mechanistic international theory of the age was well understood by Jean-Jacques Rousseau, who apparently prepared a new edition of the Abbé's work in 1756. In what may have been conceived as the introduction to this edition, Rousseau wrote a short and sceptical summary of the Abbé's theory in which he referred to the Roman Empire as the centrepiece of the balanced 'system of Europe' and described the 'balance of power in Europe' as a static, self-adjusting, perpetual machine and a safeguard against the potentially disruptive passions of rulers.[53]

The differences between the Abbé de Saint-Pierre as well as Rousseau on the one hand and, on the other, the international theory informing peacemaking at Utrecht were thus more about the method of accomplishing a lasting peace than about the goal. Both agreed that the balance of power was a stable condition in which European territorial polities and urban communities had, in their view, existed for a long time. They also agreed that a lasting peace could be accomplished through successive treaties and other contractual agreements.

These convictions were called into question only at the very end of the eighteenth century in a short treatise in which Immanuel Kant (1724–1804) critically reviewed previous peace proposals, including those by Saint-Pierre and Rousseau. The piece was first published in 1795. Kant arranged his treatise as a hypothetical peace treaty. In the preamble to the First Definitive Article, he said that peace must be willed explicitly. Kant thus denied that there was an automatism by which perpetual peace could be accomplished incrementally. He explicitly rejected Saint-Pierre's and Rousseau's proposals and criticized them for having been overly optimistic that a lasting peace could be accomplished within the foreseeable future. Kant would only admit that the eventual accomplishment of a lasting peace was possible in the more distant future through some metaphysical plan of nature in accordance with which, he trusted following Lipsius, human actors, specifically rulers, were obliged to act as rational beings.

Against his predecessors in the eighteenth century, Kant took the view that perpetual peace as a universal condition of international relations was categorically different from partial peace treaties. According to him, the points of difference were that, while peace treaties emerged from temporary conditions, peace could be perpetual only if it was universal, if it was concluded without any reservation whatsoever to go to war, if there was a general guarantee for the continuing existence of polities, if standing armies were abolished, if no subsidies were accepted from foreign governments, if international relations were conducted solely on the principle of non-intervention in the domestic affairs of other polities and if international relations were conducted by morally defendable means.

He further requested a specific domestic condition within each polity, namely that the rule of law should be accepted as the very basis of what he referred to as a 'republican' constitution. This was a constitution in which rule was accepted as rule by law and by the consent of the ruled and in which the ruler's competence was confined to the exercise of force against those who chose not to abide by the law. Kant saw in what he termed a 'republican' constitution an essential condition for a lasting peace because he believed that polities with a 'republican' constitution would not develop attitudes of aggression towards their neighbours. But he insisted that 'republican' constitutions were possible only within sovereign territorial polities and urban communities because only in such polities could rule be rule by consent. He denied that a 'republican' constitution was conceivable for frameworks overarching sovereign polities because rule over sovereign polities would be an illegitimate reduction of the rights of the ruled to appoint and sanction their rulers.[54] This conclusion was viable only because Kant rigorously adhered to contractualism.

BALANCE-OF-POWER DIPLOMACY AND THE TAMING OF BELLONA

Unlike the sixteenth century, the second half of the seventeenth and much of the eighteenth century witnessed a substantive receptivity of practitioners in international relations to the demands of theory. Although they could and frequently did break balance-of-power norms and rules, supported revisionist strategies and launched offensive wars, many practitioners were in fact guided by the expectation that international relations within Europe should be calculable, stable and informed by morally defendable principles. Evidently, not all battles were indecisive, not all wars ended in equitable settlements and not all diplomatic interactions were well designed, friendly and guided by mutual respect among all involved parties.[55] But practitioners seem to have had in mind that this was what they should accomplish.[56]

The platform which gave rise to these expectations was the Westphalia peace treaties. Concluding the Thirty Years War (1618–48), the two treaties technically represented bilateral agreements between the emperor and the King of France signed at Münster as well as the emperor and the King of Sweden signed at Osnabrück, but they contained regulations which had a fundamental impact on many other territorial polities and urban communities all over Europe. It became a convention to refer to these agreements in many subsequent peace treaties to the end of the eighteenth century.

Theorists regarded the Westphalia agreements as the foundation of the balance of power in Europe,[57] and peacemakers used them as legal references to the status quo treaties which they claimed to restore or confirm through their own treaties.[58] The Westphalia treaties accomplished the integration of the Roman Empire into the European international system, wherein the empire turned into a kind of switchboard for relations all across Europe, as the Abbé de Saint-Pierre had described it. The empire fulfilled this role despite serious problems which were conditioned by the controversy over where sovereignty resided in the empire.

All three possible solutions to the problem were discussed. Proponents of the first possibility assumed that each of the several rulers in the empire was sovereign. This position implied the assertion that the empire was a kind of federation among the territorial rulers and councils of urban communities with no sovereignty being allocatable to the emperor.[59] It did, however, militate against the treaties of Westphalia, which had been concluded by the emperor on behalf of the empire, and this could manifestly have been done only by a sovereign ruler. Hence, the second position was that rulers and councils in the empire should not be sovereign and that, instead, sovereignty should be reserved for the emperor alone.[60] But this position militated against the stipulation of the Westphalia treaties that the rulers and councils in the empire were entitled to enter into alliances with rulers outside the empire which, obviously, only sovereigns could do. Hence, the third position was argued that sovereignty should be divided between the emperor and the rulers in the empire.[61] But this position was at odds with the logic of the concept of sovereignty which implied that, in a given polity, sovereignty could not be divided.

In any case, the territorial polities and urban communities inside the empire received the privilege of concluding alliances with any ruler, provided these alliances were not targeted against the emperor, the empire and the Westphalia treaties. This privilege promoted networking among the European rulers and amplified the range and numbers of treaties concluded among them. Since the end of the seventeenth century, the publicly concluded treaties were assembled in multi-volume collections which served as permanent and easily accessible records of international law.[62]

International relations evolved around the balance of power as a core concept. Like theorists, practitioners conceived the balance in mechanistic terms, even though their contests about it were not infrequent and manipulations of it were attempted. A case for the latter occurred in 1717 when King Philip V of Spain (1713–24, 1724–46) had launched a war against the emperor and had attacked Sardinia in breach of the Utrecht settlement. In his defence, Philip sent out a special envoy, Beretti Landi, to persuade other rulers that the power of the emperor had become formidable and a menace to others and that, therefore, the Spanish action had been justified. Landi is recorded to have argued:

> The equilibrium has been the reason for the latest war. His Majesty [i.e. Philip V] is requesting to consider whether it is really the case that the equilibrium has been preserved in this way. Or whether it might not have been true, on the other hand, that a contribution was made towards the aggrandizement of the power of one prince by whose manipulations no other interest is pursued than that of the enlargement of his own influence, and who, it seems, will not hesitate to direct [his evil intentions] precisely at those whose closest ally he is.[63]

However, Philip's manoeuvre failed because his arguments were too threadbare.[64] Therefore, the case illustrates the possibility of manipulations together with their limitations. Common sense and, perhaps, the amount of information available on the news market were sufficient to disclose Philip's manoeuvre as a shabby intrigue. The consequences for Philip were severe. On 2 August 1718 the emperor and the Kings of France and the United Kingdom concluded an alliance against Spain for the purpose of 'establishing a more durable equilibrium in Europe' and 'of observing the rule, necessary for public tranquillity, that those rulers who by right of birth have the right to succeed in either kingdom [of Spain and of France] have solemnly renounced their claims for themselves and their posterity'.[65] The Spanish manoeuvre of 1717 ended not only with a military defeat of the Spanish side but also with a confirmation of the Utrecht settlements. As a ruler who had claimed to act legitimately in pursuit of the interest of his territorial polity, Philip was subjected to the common interest of the 'society of Europe'.

Later in the century, the most serious threat to the equilibrium came from the Prussian King Frederick II. His invasion of the Austrian territories Silesia and Glatz ushered in three wars which were fought with balance-of-power arguments. The struggle ended in a draw. In the peace settlement of 1763, Frederick was finally allowed to keep the territories he had annexed but only at the price of his pledge to observe the balance-of-power rules in future. Prince Wenzel Anton Kaunitz-Rietberg (1711–1794), Frederick's main contender on the Austrian side, summed up the Austrian position in retrospect in a memorandum written in 1764:

> [The Prussian King] had provided the most convincing proof of how disadvantageous and dangerous it can be for a sovereign if he acts as a conqueror, proceeds despotically and does not preserve loyalty and faith, thereby compelling other courts to take joint measures and to form alliances... Unfortunate is the power which is forced to rely mainly on allies and their discretion. In the end, such a power will fall victim to its selfishness.[66]

Neither the staunchest defenders of the balance of power among the international theorists nor the proponents of perpetual peace could have added substantively to this argument. Hence practitioners made efforts to follow balance-of-power rules even if they knew well that they might fail.[67]

The Westphalia peace treaties did not end all warfare nor did they prevent rulers from keeping troops under arms in large numbers and at considerable cost after the conclusion of the peace.[68] These 'standing armies' even became the hallmark of the age until, late in the eighteenth century, the debate on them emerged[69] which was reflected in Kant's treatise of 1795. Again, these armies were organized in accordance with the principles of mechanicism. Following the precepts of the Oranian reforms, manual drill was introduced in virtually all European armies during the second half of the seventeenth century.

It was conducted as a well-ordered pattern of constrained behaviour in which the infantrymen were to be drilled to handle their arms, to enact commanded movements with precision by themselves and in battalion and to do so under the supervision of rulers and their commissioned officers. Eventually, in the first half of the eighteenth century, these patterns of constrained behaviour developed into the system of linear tactics in which troops were expected to execute minutely the designs which were made up of preconceived movements and manoeuvres as if they were battle choreographies.[70] In these choreographies, the common warriors were to act as if they were parts of a smoothly operating machine.[71]

A typical eighteenth-century drill command read as follows:

It must be the first goal of the exercise to drill the man and to give him the air of a soldier, so that the peasant is removed. To that end, the man has to be taught, first, how to keep his head, namely not to have it hang over to any side and not to close his eyes; instead, when under arms, the man has to look to the right with the head straight upwards and, when parading, he has to look straight into one's eyes. Secondly, the man shall march stiffly with his feet and not with bent knees, with his toes pointed to the outside when placing the tips of his feet on the ground. Thirdly, a man shall keep his body upright, shall neither lean backwards nor have his stomach stuck out to the front; instead, he shall bring out his breast well to the fore and contract his back.[72]

In the same stiff way, rules were prescribed for marching in rank and file and for walking elsewhere. The Saxon drill manual of 1776 ruled for the latter: 'In all circumstances the man must be required to walk with decency in the streets outside rank and file, without swinging his arms, but with a firm body and with stiff knees, and with his feet stretched to the outside.'[73] Thus most eighteenth-century drill manuals agreed that it should be the goal of military drill to 'transform' ordinary subjects into 'blindly obedient soldiers'[74] who were capable of displaying a distinctly military behaviour as the ruler's men. It was also understood that this goal was to be accomplished by way of training peasants to accept and perform specific military postures and movements which were new to them and that, through the specificity of these postures and movements, the infantrymen were to obtain a distinguished 'bon air', namely the 'air of the soldier'.

The term 'air' then had a technical meaning which was distinguished from the meanings of the related terms 'mine' and 'port'. 'Air' was defined as a 'facial expression which one chooses on particular occasions in order to display a particular passion and of which, consequently, there are as many as there are passions'. In its changeability the air differed from the mine as a permanent bodily expression and the port as the bodily comportment.[75] Hence the term 'air' denoted the change of bodily expressions for a variety of passions and was thus suitable to a practice according to which men were requested to change behavioural patterns upon their entry into the armed forces. Manual drill was the first and foremost means to organize this change under the control of rulers, and reviews were held for the purpose of demonstrating the result. This practice was Europe-wide in the eighteenth century and was followed not only in the armies of the larger territorial states but also in the many lesser courts.

Composing armies in this way was like putting together well-ordered machines. Armies thus had the primary task of displaying order and constrained behaviour. The warriors were to make clear that they would use their physical force and their weapons only by command and with utmost self-constraint. Such armies were pleasing to look at when they were garrisoned in towns and cities. They were useful in war as long as all engaged parties followed the rules of the game prescribed in linear tactics. But they were a nuisance for all those who preferred to use them in service to their own rigorous self-interest at the expense of all others.

No doubt, warfare in eighteenth-century Europe was as bloody as warfare always has been. But the ethics of self-constraint did contribute to the reduction of the battle dead from about 50 per cent of a fighting force in the sixteenth century and at the time of the Thirty Years War to about 10 per cent at the time of the Seven Years War. The containment of the destructive capabilities of the armed forces was perhaps the single most important factor of keeping the 'society' of European territorial polities and urban communities stable and in balance.

The international theory of the period was almost entirely secular in kind. Compared to the sixteenth century, the most significant change of the careers of international theorists was that, in the seventeenth and eighteenth centuries, almost none of them was a theologian. Apart from the Abbé de Saint-Pierre and Hobbes, no international theorist had a theological background or an affiliation with the Church. Instead, most of them were university professors or practising jurists. Their fields of study were mainly law and philosophy, although few of them were actually members of law schools. Pufendorf, for one, held a chair of international law at the University of Heidelberg, but was assigned to the School of Arts and Sciences.

The reason was that international law was then considered a branch of moral philosophy. In the eighteenth century, the number of moral philosophers theorizing on international relations declined. Rousseau, if he counts as a moral philosopher at all, was drawn into discussions on international relations through his study and appreciation of the work of the Abbé de Saint-Pierre. So was Kant in his critical approach to the Abbé's work. Hence, the jurists came to dominate the field. Their impact shaped the textual genres in which international theory was laid down.

There were three relevant genres, theories of international law which were explicated in bulky handbooks and general surveys, doctoral dissertations on details of the balance-of-power norms and rules, and proposals for perpetual peace. They supplemented each other. Handbooks of international law were composed in order to document the necessity and possibility of moral constraints upon the actions of sovereign rulers, doctoral dissertations in law documented these actions and evaluated them in the light of theory, and proposals for perpetual peace outlined the prospects for the maintenance of stability and the accomplishment of a lasting peace. Despite a plethora of writing on nearly all aspects of war and the military, not a single general theory of war was published during the seventeenth and eighteenth centuries.

Theorists' preoccupation with stability created a highly conservative attitude towards international relations and the changes which accompanied them. Practitioners shared this attitude. Theorists were busy applying the ethics of self-constraint to international relations and depicting the European international system as a pre-existent and static assembly of territorial polities and urban communities which had no need for specific human action in its favour. Practitioners frequently complained that they could not control rulers' actions, that the system was unstable, that norms and rules were violated and that the balance of power was being upset. But in doing so, they only articulated their belief that their expectations about the conduct of international relations were in line with the positions argued by the theorists. Theorists and practitioners availed themselves of a mechanistic imagery, characteristic of the period, in order to give expression to their basic conviction that international relations were in principle measurable and calculable as part and parcel of a well-ordered world. They all agreed with Lipsius that human actors were neither able, nor did they have any obligation, to organize the world. What they could and ought to do was implement and improve the stability of the existing world order.

There was some parochialism in the seventeenth- and eighteenth-century international theories of Europe. Despite the universalism which was at the bottom of these theories, their geographical reach was confined to Europe. Although the concept of Europe changed during the period through the incorporation of the Ottoman Turkish Empire, European overseas relations operated on principles which were of no concern for the theorists who, with the exception of Grotius, displayed little if any concern for the European conquest of America and for the dealings of European trading companies in Africa and Asia.

SIX

Biologism

Reason is timeless. Using reason to make sense of the complexity of time is one thing; developing reasonable attitudes to the change which is inherent in time is quite another. Throughout the seventeenth and much of the eighteenth centuries, theorists as well as practitioners had tried their best to employ reason to fend off or at least minimize the effects of change. They had done so on the basis of the experience of time which had emerged in the later Middle Ages and which had juxtaposed astronomical time as the indefinite linear 'mover of all things' against historical time as the finite interval between the creation and the end of the world.

However, already while von Linné was working, winds of change encroached into this minutely composed system. In the middle of the eighteenth century, scientists launched inquiries which cast doubt on the stability of the order of the world, and philosophers began to conduct speculative investigations which questioned the finiteness of historical time. These efforts soon led to new experiences of and attitudes towards time and the world, awarded a higher significance to dynamic forces and suggested that human beings should adapt themselves to these forces.

NEW EXPERIENCES OF TIME AND ATTITUDES TO HISTORY

After the American continent had come into sight of Europeans early in the sixteenth century, questions about the truth of what is recorded in the Bible about the world were opened, not only regarding the distribution of land and water on the surface of the earth, but also concerning the time-span between the creation and the end of the world. Whereas most issues regarding the spatial dimension had been settled during the sixteenth century, the temporal dimension had been left untouched by critical inquiries despite the felt need of an explanation for the problem of how life could have come to America after the Flood.

The difficulty was that migration could not be adduced as an explanation of this problem if the continental identity of America was taken for granted. But even the staunch traditionalists who still refuted the continental identity of America early in the eighteenth century and, instead, regarded America as a huge Asian peninsula[1] could not convincingly argue that all living species had migrated from Noah's Ark to the remotest parts of America across some Asian–American land bridge and that they had done so within the limited time-span of only the few thousand years that were allowed to have elapsed between the Flood and the present seventeenth and eighteenth centuries according to this view of biblical chronology.

For one, the theologian Thomas Burnet (c. 1635–1715) condensed the ante- and post-diluvial periods into the biblical time frame of the six world ages and gave the world 'no more than fifteen hundred years to go till the end'.[2] As Burnet continued to assign roughly a thousand years to each world age, the total age of the world could not be higher than six thousand years and, consequently, the Flood must have occurred in relatively recent times. In the eighteenth century, scholars such as Robert Hooke, (1635–1703) in a work published posthumously in 1705, and Giambattista Vico (1668–1744) as late as 1744 still agreed with Burnet.[3]

Moreover, sixteenth-century naturalists had already discovered many species which were peculiar to America and not known elsewhere. How would one account for the geographical variety of the post-diluvial distribution of species, the origins of which, according to the biblical traditions, would have to be traced back to one single spot on earth? In 1667 this problem was discussed by Sir Matthew Hale (1609–1676), a scientist of renown who investigated the 'primitive origination of mankind' on the basis of research on what could be ascertained about changes in other living species. Hale attributed the post-diluvial diversity of species to migration in the first place, to 'an anomalous mixture of species' in the second place and, in the third, to 'some accidental variations in the process of time'.[4]

These three factors, post-diluvial migration out of Noah's Ark, mutation in consequence of genetic irregularities and gradual adaptation, together served to support his conclusion that the unequal distribution of living species across the continents did not refute the truth of the Old Testament mythology of the Flood. However, the three factors disproved the postulate that, on principle, all species had been preserved in the forms which they had had as they walked out of Noah's Ark.

But the mythology of the Flood contained further pitfalls. During the second half of the seventeenth century, interest began to spread in the study of stones whose shapes were strikingly similar to those of living organisms. They were discovered all over the world and at odd places such as high on mountains. Immediately, the question arose whether these objects, called fossils then as now, were real stones or in fact petrified organisms of the antediluvial ages. The question was a difficult one because some fossils represented shapes which could not be linked with any living species. That brought on to the agenda the question of how such objects could appear in America and at the odd places where they happened to have been found. If some of the fossils were petrified organisms of extinct species, they provided the evidence that neither had all species made their way into Noah's Ark nor did all species still exist that had once descended from there. Hence the fossils placed the problem of the historicity of nature on the agenda. As yet, few were ready to accept the imminent conclusion that the Bible was wrong; instead, most scholars argued that fossils were a special kind of stone which had by accident been shaped like organisms and could be dismissed as jokes of nature.

However, only little more than thirty years after the publication of the third edition of Vico's work, Buffon's *Les époques de la nature* was published in 1778. In this work, Buffon (1707–1788) took a radically different view and argued that the current age of the world was about 75,000 years, that the world had undergone many changes during these many years and that it had about 45,000 years to go. In unpublished manuscripts written on the same matter since 1749, Buffon had gone even further, postulating an age of the world of roughly three million years. But he had hesitated to commit himself to this view in a published book.[5] In any case, in the second half of the eighteenth century, the biblical world chronology ceased to inform scholarly thoughts about the earth and what then came to be perceived as the many changes in its history.[6]

Eventually von Linné succumbed to the force of the new findings. In the twelfth edition of his botanical and zoological tables, published in 1766, he inserted a comment in which, for the first time, he admitted the possibility of biological evolution.[7] Summing up these thoughts in the four volumes of his *Ideas on the Philosophy of the History of Mankind*, Johann Gottfried Herder (1744–1803) attempted to show that 'our earth has undergone many revolutions before it became what it is now' and that the earth was a 'laboratory' from which successive sets of living species had emerged.[8] But the rejection of the biblical world chronology, coupled with the injection of dynamic views of the earth as an ever-changing entity, unleashed fears of instability and warnings that 'chaos and confusion are not to be introduced into the order of nature'.[9]

According to this view, human beings were given the task of providing for the stability of the earth. Along these lines, a sceptical Kant, already in 1784, tried to limit the range of human change-provoking action by insisting that there was a predetermined 'plan of nature' according to which the changes from the past to the future would proceed. Kant's was a conservative position which sought to counterpoise the fears of instability with the argument that nature would not allow its own destruction. But he could not prevent the dynamization of the experience of time and the widening use of the concept of biological evolution. Herder observed, using the evidence of fossils, that we 'can not deceive ourselves and deny that our earth has grown old in millennia and that this wanderer around the sun has changed fundamentally since its origin'.[10]

Herder applied his views also to politics. He insisted that, like individuals, 'peoples' have their continuously changing and improving gestalts. Postulating that polities have changed and would continue to change and adding a positive value to their changes, Herder saw the necessity of admitting the idea of progress into his theoretical reflections on history and politics.[11] If 'peoples' were credited with their own gestalts, it made sense to demand purposeful efforts to improve them in all cases where deficits or even defects were recognized. Such revisionism would then have to be targeted against all regimes whose supporters insisted upon the maintenance of stability and the status quo.

Herderian activism was a slap in the face for all those later eighteenth-century physiocrats who did their best to make the well-ordered world ever more perfect and who hoped to add to everyone's happiness. Such activism helped launch and gave support to the revolutionary movements in America and France, and it also impacted on international theory. Between 1786 and 1789, Jeremy Bentham (1748–1832), jurist, philosopher, free trader and political theorist, wrote a proposal for perpetual peace which took issue with then long-cherished convictions.

He identified four causes of war, the existence of overseas colonial empires, the conclusion of alliances, secret treaties to the disadvantage of non-involved third parties and the maintenance of naval forces.[12] Of these four causes of war, Bentham believed, the latter three were growing insignificant in his own time and could thus be neglected for the purposes of international theory. Instead, he identified the first cause as crucial. His argument for doing so was that maintaining and enlarging colonial empires prevented free trade and necessitated rivalries among the interested parties in Europe. Abandoning colonial empires was thus for him the first and foremost condition of perpetual peace.

But Bentham took his argument even further. First, like Kant, he obliged rulers to refrain from secret diplomacy and to declare all their intentions and goals to the public. Secondly, like Kant he was convinced that a growing network of peace arrangements and treaties could not automatically lead to a lasting peace but that the latter needed purposeful efforts in its favour. However, thirdly, Bentham was at variance with Kant over what was to be done in favour of a lasting peace. Whereas Kant sceptically rejected the idea of world rule and denied all hopes that a lasting peace could be accomplished in the foreseeable future, Bentham radiated optimism and insisted that a general council above the rulers of territorial polities and urban communities could contribute to the goal, because rulers as rational beings would, in their own interest, accept the decisions passed by that council. Therefore, the council would not require armed forces to have their own way. Instead, it would provide for world rule by peaceful means. The council's main task was to make sure that the self-equilibrating forces of the economy could operate freely without rulers' interventions on the world market and thus bar rulers from devising sinister schemes for aggrandizement and conquest.

Kant's and Bentham's proposals originated in similar observations but led to opposite conclusions. Kant classed perpetual peace as the condition of perfect stability and was thus deeply disturbed by the demands for change which Herder, his fellow theorists and the practitioners associated with the revolutionary movements in America and France articulated in the last quarter of the eighteenth century. Kant's response was to warn that too much human activism was not in agreement with the metaphysical plan of nature and was, consequently, dangerous.

Bentham employed the demand for change for his own purposes. He advocated the need for fundamental changes in order to increase human efforts towards the eventual accomplishment of peace, the benefit of which he saw as the advancement of free trade rules as a condition for unlimited competition among human actors. Unlike Kant, who was mainly concerned with European politics, Bentham made explicit his belief that peace in Europe was impossible without peace in the world at large and demanded the abolishment of colonial empires as the first condition of peace on the globe. He was thus completely in line with contemporary theorists who suggested that there was no such thing as a distinct European international system. Instead, conversely, he insisted that Europe was part and parcel of a single global international system and that this system had its own rules and ought to be manifest in specific institutions above the existing territorial polities and urban communities.[13] Much of Bentham's international theory had a lasting impact in the nineteenth and twentieth centuries.

New words coming in use at the beginning of the nineteenth century betray a concept of the international system that differed from that of the eighteenth century. Among the newly current phrases were 'community of states', 'world state system', 'general concert', 'cultural family', 'society of nations' and 'monarchy of nations'.[14]

These words denoted a system that either remained unconfined in terms of its geographical boundaries or explicitly engulfed the entire world. The system was larger than the sum of its constitutive parts which, as it were, it absorbed and covered like the skin covers the inner organs of a living body. The system was a mediating agent which constrained the activities of its member units and controlled the interactions among them and with the system's environment, and, vice versa, the environment was allowed to impact only indirectly on the member units through the system. The numbers of the member units in the system were variable. The system could endure pressure from without and a certain degree of resistance from within and could be destroyed only if members acted decisively against the system from within and if stress from the environment overpowered the system's 'boundary-maintaining capability'.[15] It had to be flexible and dynamic in order to be able to respond to the changes of its member units. The concept was drawn on the model of a living body and can thus be termed biologistic.[16] It no longer characterized the system as the derivative of its member units but, conversely, allowed the member units to appear as dependants of the system as an entity in its own right.

THE HUMAN BODY AS THE MODEL FOR THE BALANCE OF POWER

At the turn of the nineteenth century, biologism began to impact on balance-of-power theories and enhanced the employment of a new model of the balance of power. The

French Revolution paved the way for the recognition of dynamism as a factor of the balance of power. When the German philosopher Johann Gottlieb Fichte (1762–1814) published his appraisal of the French Revolution in 1793, he included the following sarcastic description of the operations of what he took to be the balance of power:

> The operation of the complicated wheelwork of that artificial political machine of Europe has always kept people moving. There was a perpetual struggle among conflicting internal and external powers. From within, the sovereign, by way of the wonderful masterpiece of the subordination of the estates, suppressed what was next to him in rank, these, in turn, pressuring what was inferior to them, and thence continuously down to the slave working in the fields. Each of these powers resisted the pressure and pressed upwards, and this confusing play together with the elasticity of the human mind preserved and inspired the machine, an artful masterpiece, offending nature with its composition and, although operating upon a single principle, yielded the most heterogeneous results: in Germany a confederate republic, in France an unlimited monarchy. From without, where there was no subordination, poise and counterpoise were determined and kept in a stable position by the steady tendency towards universal monarchy, the ultimate goal of all military campaigns even though it was not always made explicit. It destroyed Sweden, weakened Austria and Spain, in a single political row, and raised Russia and Prussia from nowhere and, among other moral phenomena, provided a new stimulus to humankind for heroic deeds, national pride without a nation. It may well be that the watching of that puzzling spectacle may offer a refreshing delight for the mind of the reflecting observer, but it can neither satisfy him nor instruct him on what he is in need of.[17]

In Fichte's description, the mechanistic balance of power turned into a chimera, something that idle or scrupulous propagandists strove for or argued with in order to defend sinister and, in any case, immoral goals. The balance of power was against nature and nonsensical, and its pursuit at the hands of a ruler was ludicrous at best. It produced instability, the opposite of what its protagonists claimed to accomplish. But Fichte's sarcastic tone also revealed some of his more far-reaching goals, namely his quest for the recognition of nationhood as it was being defined by the French revolutionaries.

From the point of view of nationalism, mechanistic balance-of-power politics indeed degenerated into petty suppressive strategies which, Fichte claimed, a ruler would pursue for no other reason than his 'own individual aggrandizement'.[18] Thus Fichte's conclusion was that the concerns for stability inherent in the mechanistic balance of power were vain pretences and had to be subjected to a critique of ideology. Concerns for stability could, in his view, not be genuine as they stood against the demand for change. Placing the machine in opposition to nature, Fichte argued in favour of a dynamism which was to bring about the collapse of the 'artful', repressive and unnatural balance of power.

Thus, by 1795 when Kant wrote, there was already a lack of confidence in the self-perpetuating capability of the European international system. Instead, there was an increasing readiness among theorists and practitioners to abandon the conventional machine model as obsolete, invalid and impracticable because doubt had arisen over whether lawful action within the system was truly calculable and predictable, whether the unconditional preservation of the status quo was beneficial and really a value in itself and whether it was genuinely impossible to call into question natural law and the feasibility of balance-of-power politics. Already in 1801, the Göttingen historian August Hermann Ludwig Heeren (1760–1842) warned:

> Even the most professionally calculated equilibrium system can never provide more than an insecure guarantee against the appearance of a favourable moment at which the nation, powerful through its resources or the talents of its leaders or through both, grabs the leadership which, after the usual course of events, will sooner or later degenerate into the repression of tyranny.[19]

Heeren was less radical in tone than Fichte but, in essence, shared his view. He admitted that the balance could be destroyed, acknowledged the lack of flexibility of the machine model vis-à-vis ongoing changes and thereby, somewhat clumsily, expressed the lack of confidence in the usefulness of this model at times of ongoing nation-building processes.

A few years later, the Scottish lawyer Lord Brougham and Vaux (1778–1868) was more explicit and precise in discerning the factors of insecurity. In 1803 he ascribed the lack of usefulness of the machine model to what he termed the 'capricious' movements of nations. Nations, he observed, acted incalculably, and an international system had to be capable of responding to such actions:

> The grand and distinguishing feature of the balancing theory, is the systematic form to which it reduces those plain and obvious principles of national conduct; the perpetual attention to foreign affairs which it inculcates; the constant watchfulness which it prescribes over every movement in all parts of the system; the subjection in which it tends to place all national passions and antipathies to the views of remote expediency; the unceasing care which it dictates of nations most remotely situated, and apparently unconnected with ourselves; the general union, which it has effected, of all the European powers in one connecting system – obeying certain laws, and actuated, for the most part, by a common principle; *in fine*, as a consequence of the whole, the right of mutual inspection, now universally recognized among civilized states, in the appointment of public envoys and residents. This is the balancing theory.[20]

Brougham's attitude towards the balance of power was more appreciative than Fichte's and more optimistic than Heeren's. But that was so because Brougham assigned new tasks to balance-of-power politics, first and foremost to absorb the 'passions' of nations. He took for granted that such 'passions' existed, that they could neither be measured nor calculated and, finally, could not be subjected to an ethics of self-constraint. Instead, the curtailing of these 'passions' was the task of the overarching international system for which Brougham sought to make specific laws. Thus the newly conceived international system was not to be the framework for measurable and calculable stability but the dynamic instrument for the taming of sudden movements and tensions arising from the 'passions' of nations.

A few years later, Friedrich von Gentz (1764–1832), subsequently Metternich's chief aide at the Congress of Vienna, cast these perceptions into solid terms. He reviewed eighteenth-century criticisms, denounced the mechanistic balance of power as a 'chimera' and made an effort to produce a new definition of that allegedly chimerical 'constitution':

> What is usually termed a balance of power is that constitution which exists among neighbouring states more or less connected with each other, by virtue of which none of them can violate the independence or the essential rights of another without effective resistance from another quarter and subsequent danger to itself.[21]

Gentz abandoned the multilateral concerns for stability as the overall common goal of all actors in the system and, instead, limited his concept to the balancing of rivalries among contenders. Like Brougham, Gentz assumed that these rivalries could be contained only through some systemic force and not through the self-constraining capability of the actors in the system. Looking back on the eighteenth century, Gentz noted occasions such as the partitions of Poland on which the systemic containment had been unsuccessful and concluded that the balance of power had been 'deranged':

> In the physical world, a system resting on the counterpoise between opposing weights can be disturbed only if one or more of them loses their original energy from which results the dominance of the other and the ruin of the machine. A similar system, applied to human conditions, is exposed to a further threat. Since in the latter system the forces are characterized by freedom, one part can form an alliance at the expense of the others and can thereby effect (what it could never have achieved on its own) the ruin of those selected for sacrifice, and in this way the destruction of the machine.[22]

The dynamism which Gentz ascribed to the actors in the system with the word 'freedom' placed the international system in opposition to its eighteenth-century mechanistic counterpart and led Gentz to admit that the old system had been destroyed. It was then to become the task of the Vienna Congress to piece together a new international system.[23]

The balance of power featured prominently among the core delegates to the congress. But they disagreed about the geographical and substantive range of its application. The deputies of Austria and Prussia demanded that essential aspects of the eighteenth-century 'constitution' or system of polities, namely the large number of sovereign rulers on the territory of the Roman Empire, should not be restored. Therefore, the 'future repose of Europe and the balance' were to differ from what had existed in the eighteenth century. In the new system, the 'power of Germany, its unity under the decisive influence of Austria and Prussia, which are closely allied with each other, will be the veritable basis' for the balance of Europe.[24]

Talleyrand (1754–1838), the French representative, was vehemently opposed. In consequence of the changes of polities and the renunciation of the imperial crown by Emperor Francis II in 1806, he argued, a 'loss of its particular balance' had occurred in Germany so that it could 'no longer support the general balance'.[25] Neither position was accepted by the delegate from the Grand Duchy of Baden, who was fearful that the Prussian and Austrian rulers were attempting to divide Germany in their own interest but under the feigned commands of some 'balance of Europe'.[26] It is evident from the second comment that some Fichtean rhetoric had crept into the minds of the Vienna negotiators by the time they began to meet. Some of them still adhered to the conventional practice of counting souls and collecting military as well as trade data as 'quantities enumerated by political arithmeticians'. But this term, which had been respectable up to the end of the eighteenth century, fell into disgrace and oblivion in the nineteenth century.[27]

Consequently, the new balance of power was regarded as justifiable only if and as long as it was capable of mediating among conflicting national 'passions', smoothing or absorbing their antagonistic and possibly disruptive dynamism. The static model of the machine was incapable of performing such a task. A new model had to be found, and it was derived from the human body. In his memorandum of December 1813 on the constitution he thought ought to be created for Germany, Wilhelm von Humboldt (1767–1835), a foremost Prussian reformer of the Napoleonic era, remarked:

> The way used by nature to unite individuals into nations and to separate humankind into nations contains an impenetrable and mysterious instrument by which the individual, being nothing in himself, as well as the family, valuable only through the individual, may be kept on the true path of proportionate and gradual development of their energies. And, although politics is never bound to respect such views, it cannot be so conceited as to act against the natural order of things.[28]

In treating nations as 'natural' phenomena and obliging statesmen to respect their existence as inalterable, Humboldt joined Brougham who had observed in 1803 that nations,

> like the individuals, who compose them, are moved by caprice, and actuated by passions; excited to contention by envy and hatred; soothed to reconciliation when exhausted by the efforts of their enmity; leagued in friendship by the dictates of an interested prudence; united together by the thirst of plunder; or combined for the gratification of some common revenge.[29]

Both made use of the biologistic imagery which was to become dominant in nineteenth-century international theory.[30]

Up to the Crimean War (1853–6), theorists mainly followed the principles which were set out at the time of the Vienna Congress. Leopold von Ranke (1795–1886), who advanced the methods of historical criticism and organized the academic study of history, joined Gentz in 1832 with his argument that the eighteenth-century balance of power had been upset by the rise of nationalism in the latter part of the century and demanded the balanced coexistence of independent nations in Europe.[31] Many others praised the balance of power as a dynamic instrument which could help stabilize national 'passions', arbitrate over conflicts and serve as an agent of national independence.[32] But there were also some criticisms that the biologistic model of the balance of power was vague and allowed too many different interpretations. The most scathing of these criticisms was articulated by Richard Cobden (1804–1864), the entrepreneur and politician who, although he endorsed Bentham's praise of free trade, was primarily concerned with refuting the limitations and obligations burdened upon one actor in the interest of the balance-of-power system as a whole.

Cobden did not hesitate to extend the time-frame of the biologistic balance-of-power model back to the eighteenth century and emphasized its continuity down to his own day. Yet he observed that, 'after upwards of a century of acknowledged existence', the model had come 'to be less understood now than ever' and exhibited a jungle of misunderstandings. He concluded:

> The balance of power, then, might, in the first place, be very well dismissed as a chimera, because no state of things, such as the 'disposition', 'constitution' or 'union' of European powers, referred to as the basis of their systems, by Vattel, Gentz, and Brougham, ever did exist; and, secondly, the theory could, on other grounds, be discarded as fallacious, since it gives no definition – whether by breadth of territory, number of inhabitants, or extent of wealth – according to which, in balancing the respective powers, each state shall be estimated; whilst, lastly, it would be altogether incomplete and inoperative, from neglecting, or refusing to provide against the silent and peaceful aggrandizement which springs from improvement and labour.[33]

Cobden recognized the incompatibility of the mechanistic balance-of-power model with a biologistic international system that engulfed the entire globe and of which Europe was an integral part. Consequently, to him, any statement about a balance of power which was invalid for the globe as a whole was *per se* nonsensical. The change of models thus sparked controversy about the measurability and implementability of the balance of power and added to the contradictoriness of goals pursued by those claiming to act in its support.

Not only did the concept of system undergo a transformation during the period under review, but also the terminology of politics and international relations began to change at the turn of the nineteenth century. Old words, some of which had been in use since antiquity, took on new meanings. The most important were the words 'state' and 'nation'.

'State', a Latin derivative, had originally denoted stable or even static (that is, standing, immovable) conditions. This meaning continued to inform the use of the word up to the middle of the eighteenth century when polities were believed to be static and well-ordered parts of the world.[34] Subsequently, within two generations around 1800, the word 'state' abandoned this meaning in political contexts and began to denote integrated 'organisms' made up from sets of institutions of government for the ruled.[35] The new states began to be conceived in separation from incumbent rulers who were replaced as ultimate decision-makers by government institutions as executive bureaucracies. These states differed markedly from the previous multi-faceted polities in that they were definable in the terms of a united territory, a united population group and a uniform recognizable government.[36]

Likewise, the word 'nation' took on a new meaning. Again, since Roman antiquity, the word had denoted a group of people who accepted for themselves a belief in their common origin whereby 'origin' could be understood in geographical or genealogical terms, whether or not such beliefs were verifiable from independent sources. Nations in this sense had usually been small-sized and motley groups. After their territorialization in the course of the Middle Ages, nations became commonly identified as the groups of ruled under the control of territorial rulers. Well into the eighteenth century, the terms of the relations between the ruled and the ruler were believed to be grounded in the hypothetical contract, whereas beliefs in such biological categories as genetic homogeneity, such psychological categories as common identity or such cultural categories as joint collective experience were then absent as nation-building factors.[37]

However, at the end of the century, in the course of the French Revolution, the word began to adopt a new meaning. It then came to be used to denote the group of dissenters who were willing to manifest themselves against their ruler. When, in June 1789, the deputies of the Third Estate declared themselves to be the 'National Assembly' and claimed to represent the entire nation, they vocalized the conviction that the nation had an identity of its own which was independent from the ruler and was based on a social contract of its own.

Theorists concluded from these terminological changes that states and nations were 'organisms' that needed to be compatible. The boundaries of 'states' were to be identical with the 'living spaces' of the nations and, if nations desired revisions of the boundaries of their states, governments were expected to fulfil these desires.[38] Some theorists demanded that governments should take appropriate measures to shape the gestalts of the nations entrusted to their rule. Among others, Fichte argued that support for a nation or neglecting it was a matter of life and death, not only for the nation as a whole but also for each individual member.[39]

THEORIES ABOUT NATION-STATES AS ACTORS IN INTERNATIONAL RELATIONS

Georg Wilhelm Friedrich Hegel (1770–1831) was the first to advocate an international theory which reversed Lipsius's hierarchy of a morally constituted international order of all humankind and an order of polities determined by statutory law. Hegel insisted that the 'state' was the embodiment of morality (*Sittlichkeit*) and that the 'nation' was the manifestation of the collective identity of the ruled (*Volksgeist*).[40] He radicalized Herder's gestalt metaphysics and credited the *Volksgeister* with perennial existence. Consequently, Hegel envisaged a chaotic international system into which only the nation-states as organic institutions and the caretakers of the *Volksgeister* were admitted as actors.

The implication of Hegelian etatism for international, more specifically military theory became immediately evident.

Educated under the supervision of the leading Prussian military reformer, Gerhard von Scharnhors (1755–1813), and drawing on his own experience in the Napoleonic Wars, Carl von Clausewitz (1780–1831) spent much of his later life as the director of the Prussian military academy in Berlin composing what was to become the most influential general theory of war throughout the nineteenth century. He left this theory incomplete when he died in the plague epidemic which also killed Hegel.[41]

Clausewitz rejected many of the assumptions that had guided eighteenth-century military theorists. First and foremost, he argued that wars could be won only if they took place in a condition of tension. This argument was informed by the belief that wars should be agents for the promotion of change, whereas wars were unjustifiable and a nuisance when, like some eighteenth-century campaigns, they were fought for the preservation or restoration of the status quo. Clausewitz drew the conclusion that the tensions must be generated in such a way that they affected the contending nations entirely so that they could stand against each other as if they were unified homogeneous, quasi-bodily actors.

He defined the military as one part of these bodies which could operate effectively and win the decisive main battles only if it was supported by the entire nation. He assigned to politicians the task of providing for and increasing the coherence of the nation, rallying it to support the military and the proclaimed war aims. He gave military commanders the task of determining in advance when the tension was going to be highest and of conducting the decisive main battle solely under the circumstances of high tension.[42]

In his own time, Clausewitz's *faible* for the employment of tension in military contexts was neither new nor unusual as, already by the 1770s, tension had been observed to permeate many different aspects of life. In 1772 Jacques Antoine Hippolyte de Guibert (1743–1790), a French military reformer and critic of linear tactics, had already begun to revise rules for military movements and had demanded that warriors 'shall not stand like a lifeless machine but shall rather resemble an animated statue which can begin to work and to move at any moment'.[43]

Through the use of such phrases, Guibert had explicitly associated the machine with motionlessness which he had condemned. Instead, he had believed that it was 'natural' to create a tension between standing postures and the movements which were to follow from them. In this way, Guibert had called into question the hitherto ubiquitous belief that stiff or constrained movements were 'natural' and, instead, demanded that tensions should be recognized as 'natural' when they could be resolved in movements. Thus, by the 1770s, the machine and 'nature' had been placed in opposition to each other.

Later in the century, further critics, some inspired by the American War of Independence, questioned the previous belief that the patterns of constrained behaviour which had hitherto informed manual drill would allow the pursuit of meticulously planned war games, and they further raised the fundamental question of whether it made sense at all to compose elaborate battle choreographies. Instead, these critics pleaded for a dynamic activity that had no similarity with a smoothly operating machine.[44]

Already during the 1770s, the earliest drill manuals in which some of the reformers' demands were taken into account appeared. In 1791, a drill manual was put into effect in the French army through which the new rules of and goals for manual drill were enforced.[45] The results were: first, that infantrymen became flexible and dynamic actors; secondly, that manual drill began to follow the general principles of bodily behaviour which were observed in humankind as a whole; and thirdly that manual drill paved the way towards the socialization of war and allowed field commanders like Napoleon to lead large numbers of warriors in swift marches all across Europe.

THE JURIDIFICATION OF INTERNATIONAL LAW

The biologism informing Clausewitz's theory of war not only reflected Hegelian etatism and the imagery of the human body used in early nineteenth-century balance-of-power theories, it was also shared by scholars who made efforts to renovate theories of international law. The renovation was deemed necessary after nation-states had been recognized as paramount systemic actors in international relations and made it difficult to create overarching international institutions and organizations. If polities were to be understood as uniform 'states' and if 'states' were to be regarded as nation-states and the embodiment of morality, the monopolization not only of state law but also of morality for the nation-states left no possibility for the reallocation of state-bound rights and moral norms to international law. Under this condition, the question of how international law could be defined and justified had to arise.

An answer to this was first suggested in the 1840s by Johann Battista Fallati (1809–1855) who equated international law with the law of the world society of 'nations'. He constructed a hierarchy of biologistically conceived groups, at the bottom of which were the kin groups as seemingly natural assemblies of men and women. Clusters of kin groups were then ranked as hordes, clusters of hordes as neighbourhoods, clusters of neighbourhoods as 'nations' and clusters of 'nations' as the world society. Fallati assigned to each hierarchical level a specific set of laws and institutions governing them.

International law was thus neither derived from any type of 'state' law nor was it taken as the outflow of divine will or natural law. Instead, in Fallati's system, international law was a secular framework for the government of world society and, consequently, needed to be enacted and executed through world institutions, the establishment and maintenance of which Fallati ascribed as a task to the governments of the nation-states.[46] Thus in Fallati's metaphorical language, world society was the widest possible extension of the biologistic model of the human body. Moreover, he conceived his hierarchy of types of groups as the end-result of an evolutionary process through which human actors came to be integrated into an ever-widening framework of institutions until world society as the most developed stage of this process had been reached. In this sense, Fallati posited world society under the rule of international law as the highest accomplishment of social organization and thus created a powerful evolutionist paradigm which subsequent theorists of international law and social organization took up eagerly.[47]

Practitioners were divided between optimists who used the instruments of biologism in order to translate into reality their vision of humankind as a global entity, and sceptics who gave priority to the preservation of 'state' sovereignty. The most influential document resulting from the first attitude was the Declaration of the Rights of Man and the Citizen, passed by the National Assembly in Paris on 26 August 1789.

The seventeen articles of the declaration were approved in response to a popular demand that the natural rights of the individual should be laid down in writing and should be published and thereby be made accessible for everyone. Such demands had increased in strength towards the end of the eighteenth century in many parts of Europe because it had been felt that these natural rights should be made known in order to serve as justifications for resistance against what had been taken as unjust or illegitimate government under any condition, wherever, whenever and by whomever.[48] Therefore the declaration made explicit human rights as rights *per se*. That is to say that, whereas the American Declaration of Independence of 1776 had claimed natural rights solely for the British North American colonists, the French declaration of 1789 was not limited to members of the French nation nor, for that matter, to Europe or Europeans, but was addressed to the globe at large.

The universal validity which was claimed for the declaration of 1789 not only greatly eased the spread of its text and its contents but also served as an engine for the dissemination of the ideas and the ideals of the French Revolution and, eventually, gave expression to the conviction that natural law could be used as a source not only for an international ethics of self-constraint but also for rights as universal legal titles. Thus the declaration of 1789 for the first time elevated human rights to the level of international law.

Against this declaration of universal norms, the core interest of the sceptics among the practitioners was focused on the more sober matters of mapping out the new European system of states after the devastation and changes brought about by the Napoleonic Wars. After the end of these wars, these practitioners gathered at the Vienna Congress to settle the more imminent problems of European state-craft. Although it passed a manifesto on the global ban of the slave trade and slavery as well as some other acts relevant to global international relations, the Congress was mainly concerned with the structuring of new states. Against its declared restorative intention, the Congress approved all changes of eighteenth-century polities which the French revolutionary governments and Napoleon had effected up to 1804 and thereby rearranged much of the political map of Europe.

The Congress thus generated lots of precedents for state succession and thereby increased the potential for revisionism even though its decisions ignored demands for the creation of nation-states in virtually all cases. Vis-à-vis the Italian peninsula, the German-speaking areas, the Netherlands and, most notably, Poland, regulations were approved which openly militated against the revisionist quests for nation-states.

But the legitimacy for its proceedings and decisions remained questionable. The Congress had been called for in a peace treaty concluded in Paris on 30 May 1814 between France and its major wartime enemies. This treaty was considered insufficient by many as the platform on which the Congress could proceed to accomplish its self-imposed goal of providing 'real and lasting equilibrium' in Europe at large. Some critics complained that the negotiators at the Congress were unwilling to respect democracy and the sovereignty of the 'nation' which had been demanded in the declaration of 1789. Keener observers did not overlook that, against the intentions of its creators, the new international system might, in fact, have to respond to the national 'passions' in such a way that quests for a nation-state might have to be taken seriously.[49] Others drew attention to further consequences of the Congress's diplomacy that the structuration of the system would lead not only to the establishment of new states but also to the destruction of existing nations and that, if such were the case, the decisions accepted by the Congress might provoke further revisionism rather than reducing it.

For one, the philosopher James Mackintosh (1765–1832), who addressed the British Parliament in 1815 in an effort to save the Republic of Genoa from its destruction, argued that the international system ought to be a 'guard to national independence' and should placate the 'national spirits' of its members.[50] But neither Mackintosh nor the Genoese could prevent the absorption of their urban community into the state of Sardinia-Piedmont. The fate of the city of Genoa underlined the fact that the overall goal of the Congress's diplomacy was the establishment of new states in lieu of the polities of the *ancien régime*. The Congress thus adopted an uneasy middle path between the promotion of state succession and the rejection of more far-reaching nation-building designs.

The change from seventeenth- and eighteenth-century to nineteenth-century international theories was an integral part of the broader transformation of mechanicism into biologism. Once again, international theories did not change autonomously but as part and parcel of a more fundamental change in perceptions of and attitudes to the world. Around 1800 these changes affected descriptive and analytical models rather than the world picture. As a standard model, the static, well-ordered, smoothly operating and self-equilibrating machine gave way to the dynamic, integrating, conflict-absorbing and tension-provoking living organism represented as the human body. The victory of the biologistic model was close to complete, as only residuals of the machine model have continued to be employed as conventions in nineteenth- and twentieth-century discourse. Theorists and practitioners took a joint share in initiating the change and mutually stimulated each other in promoting it.

The years around 1800 thus witnessed close cooperation and mutual exchange among theorists and practitioners. This implied that theorists were to be found not only in the study rooms of the universities but also among parliamentarians, advisers to decision-makers in government and negotiators at congresses. Likewise, texts, such in as the Declaration of the Rights of Man and the Citizen of 1789, in which key political demands were articulated, abounded with international theory. Moreover, practitioners' work at the Vienna Congress was immediately subjected to critical scrutiny by theorists, and practitioners, such as Brougham and Cobden, did not shy away from taking issue with theorists.

Thus theorists and practitioners cooperated in order to make up for the loss of guidance which the collapse of mechanicism had caused. After the perception of the world in terms of the minutely structured and well-ordered international system had gone, Lipsius's distinction between the ethics of self-constraint as a universal moral principle and contractualism as a polity-centred theory of legitimacy withered away and had to be replaced by a new systemic structure.

Creating a new international system took some time. Specific human efforts to construct, map out and maintain the system were deemed necessary. Attempts to that end are already on record from the 1790s when biologistic imagery began to be employed in critical discourses on the balance of power. Soon theorists as well as practitioners familiarized themselves with the new perception that displayed the global international system as a living organism and cast it into the shape of an extended human body. Even military theorists concurred and employed biologism. A comprehensive general theory was composed by Clausewitz who, on top of a multitude of detailed observations and reflections on military matters, extended the spectre of international theory to include the theory of war.

As a quasi-living organism, the international system seemed to require specific efforts for its establishment and mainte-nance, appeared to be an entity in its own right, more than just the sum of its parts and therefore autonomous from them. But theorists and practitioners could not agree on whether such efforts could be successful and, in any case, whether they were legitimate at all. Consequently, the biologistic model of the bal-ance of power and the equally biologistic perception of the international system were contested. Sceptics among theorists and practitioners supported a negative answer and preferred to focus on the security of the newly created states. They domi-nated the Vienna Congress.

According to their position, the organization of the world into a single global international system was neither possible nor useful. Optimists took the opposite view and claimed that the global international system was both necessary and possible.

By the 1840s, they identified the globe as the world society of states and the embodiment of international law, demanded that institutions should be created for the enforcement of international law above the sovereign states and defined these institutions as global. In short, these theorists were of the opinion that the world as the globe had to be organized.

SEVEN

Functionalism

Since its victory in the early nineteenth century, biologism has continued to inform international theories to the end of the twentieth century. No single European or North American international theory is on record which has called into question or sought to refute the concept of the international system as an overarching organic entity in its own right and as larger than the sum of its parts. And no definition of an international system has been proposed which does not categorize such a system as if it were a living being. But biologism has given support to various approaches to the international system.

One problem has continued to be on the agenda since the early nineteenth century, and that has concerned the assessment of the relationship between the system as a whole and its member units. Broadly speaking, one group of optimistic theorists and practitioners have taken the view that the system has been in good order and has operated well whenever it has been manifest in globally operating institutions and organizations under the rule of international law. Optimists have also argued that these institutions and organizations ought to devote themselves to the promotion of peace and that they should take some degree of control over the governments of sovereign nation-states. The contending group of sceptical theorists and practitioners has believed that the system has been anarchic in the sense that it has neither allowed nor necessitated international institutions and organizations with the capability to reduce the rights of sovereign nation-states.

For a variety of reasons, these two groups have come to be known as functionalists and realists. Functionalism has undergone more substantive transformations than realism. Both theories have persisted with some variants far into the second half of the twentieth century although, at times, proponents of alternative theories have challenged them. Because functionalism, realism and their variants and challengers have coexisted during the later decades of the nineteenth and much of the twentieth centuries, the next three chapters, unlike the preceding ones, do not follow a chronological order.

FUNCTIONALISM UP TO WORLD WAR I

Until World War I, the assumptions and views of most functionalists echoed positions of one or the other brand of liberalism. Functionalism shared its liberal foundation with federalism and internationalism. All three of these theories were directed against conceptions and ideologies of the unitary nation-state which were articulated by nationalists. Against nationalistic unitarianism, liberals advocated the benefits of limitations on the sovereignty of nation-states; demanded priority of the rights and freedoms of the individual over perceived government interest; strove to make compatible concerns for social justice and welfare with efforts towards the maintenance of institutions of government and requested the subjection of government action to the constraints of international law, international institutions and organizations. In so far as these designs, expressed in terms of federalism, functionalism and quests for international order, were fed by liberalism they represented liberal options against the unitary nation-state.[1]

The concept of federalism embraced various forms of 'composite' polities and 'confederated' states and determined the relationship between statehood and sovereignty in three different, partly overlapping, partly mutually exclusive ways.[2] First, federalism could be regarded as enforcing the division of sovereignty among hierarchically arrayed, partly integrated state institutions. Secondly, federalism could be perceived as denoting overarching institutions which lumped together sovereign and non-sovereign states. Thirdly, federalism could be understood as a facade for the unitary sovereign state whose centralist features were concealed behind ideologies of power sharing.

The first approach to federalism originated from seventeenth- and eighteenth-century mechanism in conjunction with the use of contractualism as a theory of the legitimacy of polities. At that time, contractualists had admitted the possibility that several equally legitimate 'consociated' polities could be joined into a larger unit which then came to be referred to as *unum Reipublicae corpus*, a corporate polity in which sovereignty was divided between the federation and the member polities. This theory had also proved to be a useful tool for the description and analysis of the constitutional intricacies of the Roman Empire after the Westphalia peace treaties.[3]

The viability of this approach to federalism was called into question by the liberal jurist John Austin (1790–1859). In 1832 he argued that the protection of the rights of the individual could be guaranteed only in a law-governed sovereign state. He realized that it was difficult to reconcile the theory of the 'composite state' with liberal convictions. Hence Austin insisted that the theoretical admission of divided sovereignty had to result in one of the following three irregularities: first, that a 'government deemed imperfectly supreme' is 'perfectly subject to that other government in relation to which it is deemed imperfectly supreme'; secondly, that 'it is perfectly independent of the other, and therefore is of itself a truly sovereign government'; thirdly, that, 'in its own community, it is jointly sovereign with the other, and is therefore a constituent member of a government supreme and independent'.

Austin's conclusion was 'that no government can be styled with propriety half or imperfectly supreme' and that sovereignty is theoretically inseparable. Yet he admitted that sovereignty can be 'so shared by various individuals or bodies that the one sovereign body whereof they are the constituent members is not conspicuous and easily perceived'. The latter qualification constituted Austin's theory of federalism which he interconnected with the allocation of sovereignty among cooperating governments. According to Austin, there were two options. In a 'federation' as a 'composite state' (such as the USA), the 'several united societies are one independent society, or are severally subject to one sovereign body' in which sovereignty is allocated to the federation. Or, in a 'confederation' as a 'system of confederated states', 'the several compacted societies are not one society, and are not subject to a common sovereign' (such as in the German Confederation of 1815–20).[4]

Contrary to seventeenth- and eighteenth-century theorists, Austin took the view that the concept of divided sovereignty was a contradiction in itself. If this proposition had to be accepted, Austin faced the difficult choice of having to deny either sovereignty to the institutions labelled as members of federations or statehood to the institutions labelled as confederations. In any case, the allocation of sovereignty and statehood became the touchstone for the unity of the state. Therefore, federalists faced the dilemma that they either had to give up federalism as a form of the sovereign state or had to widen the concept of the state in order to be able to include non-sovereign institutions.

Giving up federalism was not viable because states with federal constitutions were on record. Therefore, the latter option was the one chosen by theorists who considered the second approach to federalism in studies of federal constitutions. In one case, the governments of the existing sovereign member states of the German Confederation of 1815–20, which had been transformed into the North German Confederation in 1867, agreed a constitution which, in 1871, established the German Empire as a sovereign federal state.

The fact that this constitution existed raised the theoretical question of what had happened to the sovereignty of the member states. Answers were given mainly by German jurists at the turn of the twentieth century. All participants in the debate accepted the biologistic model of the state which was defined as the triad of the unities of territory, population and government and tried to accommodate with it the diversifying impacts of federal constitutions. Among the various contending parties, the position articulated most vocally by the jurist Paul Laband (1838–1918) started from Austin's assumption that there was an important conceptual difference between a federation and a confederation and that this difference mattered for the allocation of sovereignty.[5]

Laband's argument was based on what he set as an analogy between international and state law on the one side and, on the other, the law of contract and the law of the firm. He equated the distinction between the 'contractual' confederation among states by international law and the 'corporate' federation by state law with the distinction between 'contractual' associations among individuals in accordance with the law of contract and the 'corporate legal person' constituted by the law of the firm. In either case, the distinctive criterion was the emergence of a 'corporation' as an institution with a degree of uniformity that allowed the application of the biologistic model of the human body for its description.

Where this was not the case, what came into existence was merely an association with a 'legal relationship' among individuals as private persons or as single states, none of whom would take any liability for the doings of the partners in the association. By contrast, Laband insisted that the formation of 'corporate' institutions transforms their individual members, be they states or private persons, into 'subjects of the law'. In these cases, the institutions as 'corporate bodies' can be subject to litigation with the consequence that each member becomes liable for the doings of all other members of the 'corporations'.

The conclusions which Laband drew from the analogy were first that federations were 'corporations' and, in this capacity, states composed of states, and secondly that in federations sovereignty resided with the federations and not with the member states, because they had become subjects to the state law of the federation. Thus the states lost their sovereignty upon entering into a federation, but they continued as states. On the other side, Laband argued that confederations were not 'corporations' but associations constituting 'legal relationships' among their members subject to international law. Thus states constituting a confederation retained their status as sovereign states.[6] However, this conclusion was not fully satisfactory, as Laband himself realized. For it was solely based on an analogy which, on its own, could not provide a cogent reason why, in a federation, sovereignty had to reside with federations.

Laband tried to resolve this defect in a way which displayed his underlying liberal convictions. He proposed to consider federations as a sort of direct democracy of a higher order in which the member states, like every citizen, are subject to 'state power and, at the same time, participate in the sovereign power', so

that the member states in a federation have 'the right of participation in the formation and the execution of the will of the
federation'.[7] The condition for participation in such a state was
acceptance of its sovereignty. Because Laband suggested giving
equal rights and opportunities to the federation and its member
states, he can be regarded as the representative of a liberal
theory of federalism.

However, Laband's liberal position met with the same fate as
liberalism in general at the same time: Laband's theory was
respected as a strategy for accommodation but it was no longer
well received because of the complexity of the arguments supporting it. The predicament of liberal functionalism grew early
in the twentieth century, when critics appeared who opted for
the third approach to federalism. These critics insisted that federalism was an agent of divisiveness and, of right, should be
admitted only as a means to accomplish a unitary state. They
argued that the admission of statehood for what they regarded
as subordinate, non-sovereign administrative entities equalled
the rejection of the unitary structure of the federate state. They
admitted that Laband's liberalism had constitutional stipulations to its support but that it did bad service politically to all
those whose intention it was to develop the German Empire
and other federations formally into unitary states.

This position rose to dominance in the early decades of the
twentieth century not only in Germany, but also in Switzerland
and France, and it became the guideline for British colonial
administrative practice in Africa and South Asia.[8] It was
founded on the belief that there was no crucial conceptual difference between a unitary and a federal state because in a federal
state the subordinate administrative entities not only were
bereft of sovereignty but did not acquire statehood either, even
if the member units of a federation were referred to as states in
constitutions. Instead, these unitarians argued that the subordinate administrative entities were mere provinces or local
communities with some sort of autonomy in the administration
of their internal affairs.

Although this position had the merit of reuniting a rigid concept of the unitary state with the concept of inseparable
sovereignty, it had the demerit of disregarding constitutional

stipulations. In the view of these theorists, then, federalism was of service only to those who tried to use liberal convictions for the purpose of draping their own concerns for the establishment of a unitary state. Consequently, liberal federalism was seen as militating against the territorial unity of the state from the standpoint of theorists who demanded that the state was taken to be a centrally administered, biologistically conceived corporate entity.

The nineteenth century witnessed not only controversial functionalist attempts to systematize the theory of law and the state but also the expansion of functionalist sociological theory. Theorists of society devoted their work to the analysis of the conditions for the advancement of social justice and the provision of social welfare as solutions to the social question. Functionalists emphasized the necessity of conceiving and implementing solutions for the social question whereby they envisaged solutions which were to be accomplished through institutions within the state or above the state.

Solutions were conceivable either with regard to specific nations or parts of them or with relation to the working class as a distinct social group crisscrossing state and national boundaries. They were accepted as betterments in the sense of liberalism if they focused on issues related to the strengthening of national identity, to the safeguarding of social justice to be manifested in separation from, though not necessarily in opposition to, the state and to the providing of social welfare by the state, however imperfectly.

Hence, the several liberal functionalist strategies for the purposes of conveying national identities, of maintaining social justice and of providing social welfare shared one common feature, namely that they were designed to reduce the scope of the activities carried out and of the services offered by the governments of states to the benefit of the self-organization of the population and the independence of the individual. This commonality included the provision of social welfare because liberals took the view that the goal of social welfare was to help its recipients become independent of it. Liberal functionalists therefore opted for a middle road between socialism and etatistic nationalism.

Liberal functionalist social theorists perceived the population of a state as a 'collective being' and variously described it as a nation, a 'social body', a society or a 'moral organism' which was held to create and maintain the state.[9] This perception of the state implied a sharp turn away from the early nineteenth-century Fichtean and Hegelian convictions that the state was a nation-building instrument or the moral embodiment of the nation. Both these perceptions had given primacy to the state over its population whereas, since the middle of the nineteenth century, the state came to be considered as a service institution and as the functional derivative of the population.

Furthermore, liberals believed that, in its 'function' as a service institution, the state was not alone but the governments of states carried out their tasks in competition with other parts of the all-embracing 'social body'. Within this school of sociological theory, the relationship between the state's population and the state was explicitly defined in terms of 'function'.[10] Liberal functionalists availed themselves of an imagery which was entirely biologistic in kind although, on occasions, they would quarrel with political and other social theorists, such as liberal federalists, about the applicability of certain biologistic phrases.[11]

Liberal functionalist theories supported the pragmatic view that the state 'acted' through its government in competition with other parts of the 'social body' for the accomplishment of the tasks of conveying national identity, maintaining social justice and providing social welfare. Concerning the conveyance of identities, state governments were regarded as salient and justifiable only when they were recognizable as successful competitors with, for instance, Church institutions and private social welfare providers at the local and international levels. In the words of a contemporary analyst, the state could be accepted as salient if it served the twofold task of 'positively and immediately maintaining the whole of the collective being' and, negatively, of 'regulating the self-controlled movement of all self-active members' of the population.[12] In other words, liberal functionalists arrived at the illiberal conclusion that governments of states succeeded as competitors with other parts of the 'social bodies' as long as they were able to reduce individual freedoms.

Therefore, it is fair to say that, at the turn of the twentieth century, liberal social theorists contradicted their own preference for the rights and freedoms of the individual in the same way in which, at the same time, liberal federalists impeded their own concerns for the maintenance of the rule of law by their adherence to the concept of inseparable sovereignty. The alternative was to admit that the state failed as a competitor in the conveyance of identity, the maintenance of social justice and the provision of social welfare, to denounce the state as militaristic, economically dissatisfying and morally corrupt and to open up a gulf between the state and its population.[13]

In this case, functionalists questioned the social unity of the state with the argument that, despite theoretical assumptions, the state had not actually evolved as the functional derivative of its population. However, one consequence of liberal functionalism was more dramatic than its logical inadequacy. In extreme circumstances, the functionalist paradox led to the justification of warfare as a means of strengthening the coherence of the 'collective beings' under the control of state governments. At the time of World War I, philosophers such as Georg Simmel (1858–1918) and Max Scheler (1874–1928) were convinced that these circumstances existed and they tried to rally the public to active support for the war.[14]

Although liberal functionalist social theorists took into account the international dimension of their demands for the conveyance of identity, the maintenance of social justice and the provision of social welfare, they were mainly concerned with the internal relationship between the state and the population and therefore were induced to focus on the domestic affairs of the nation-states even when and where they were sceptical about the salience of these institutions. By contrast, the third liberal option against the unitary state at the turn of the twentieth century was articulated by a group of internationalists who requested the curtailing of the activities of governments of states through the strengthening of the international order.

Internationalist demands were targeted against a conception of and attitudes to the kind of 'world politics' which was then being defined as 'great power politics within the emerging global system of states',[15] which in turn was regarded as an expanded European state system. It was believed at the time that this specific European state system had originated in the fifteenth century and was 'composed of a pluralism of powers each of which mutually recognized and respected each other in their independence and equity and among which persists a balance of power which, although of labile nature and exposed to frequent shake-ups, has persisted through all smaller and larger disturbances'.[16]

It was argued that, through the expansion of the European state system to the global level, an interdependent 'global society of states with a corporate structure' was in the making which was dominated by a number of globally operating 'great power' governments. According to this perception of 'world politics', the global system of states was without overarching institutions and consisted merely of the global interdependence of the actions and reactions among the 'great power' governments.[17] In other words, 'world politics' was then understood as the aggregate sum of mutually balanced actions and reactions among the 'great power' governments. These governments operated under the assumption that all of their actions and reactions would be relevant no matter which issues were at stake and which areas were the targets.[18]

Hence 'world politics' at around 1900 was perceived as existing mainly at the level of pragmatic interdependent decision-making, neither with explicitly and purposefully set rules nor under institutional constraints. In consequence of this perception, 'world politics' was and remained under the control of the interacting 'great power' governments and did not constitute a higher level independent from and autonomously impacting upon the governments in the global system of states. It is hard to dissociate this perception of 'world politics' from imperialist colonialism even though such a link was then explicitly denied.[19]

In opposition to the imperialist view of 'world politics', liberal internationalists claimed that the international system should be constituted by some international order as a higher level which was imagined to be independent from the actions and reactions of some globally operating governments.[20] Internationalists drew on earlier nineteenth-century biologistic conceptions of international law and further demanded that this higher level should become manifest in institutions established above the sovereign nation-states and that it should operate under the legally binding rules which were enshrined in the European tradition of international law.[21] The demand was explicitly designed as an attack on the machinations of imperialism,[22] and strategies for the accomplishment of the goal oscillated between federalism and functionalist social theory.

Adopting functionalist arguments, Lassa Oppenheim (1858–1919) and other internationalists insisted on the necessity of international conferences and conventions 'which are essential to the economic and social welfare of the Family of Nations – a family the members of which, whether they like it or not, are becoming every day more interdependent and more internationalized'.[23] He generalized from the experience of the second half of the nineteenth century that the growth in number and scope of international organizations and institutions had taken place mainly through conferences and that, moreover, plans for the promotion of peace in the world had been discussed on similar occasions.[24]

Oppenheim expected that the proposed League of Nations was the proper instrument for the handling of globally relevant international affairs. Thus he imagined that, although the international order had to come into existence through decisions by governments of sovereign states, once in existence, it was to be equipped with a dynamism of its own and the capability 'to organize the international life of the Family of Nations' in its own right.[25] Hence Oppenheim's vision of the international order was that of a defective state, at once resembling the state justified by its capability of providing social welfare, and different from the state in its lack of legitimacy for the autonomous use of force.

Oppenheim fully shared the liberal functionalist confidence in the rationality of the handling of the 'real state interests' under the Kantian premise that 'the victory everywhere of constitutional government over autocratic government' would eventually occur. He also fully subscribed to the biologism of the liberal functionalist conviction that the nations as the population groups of such states were a 'community of many millions of individuals, who are bound together by the same blood, language, and interests' and who 'think it necessary to have a state of their own'. Therefore, Oppenheim's vision of the international order was as biologistic as the liberal federalist and sociological perception of the nation-state whose significance Oppenheim set out to reduce.[26]

Liberal pacifist internationalists employed elements of liberal federalism, took a step beyond Oppenheim and attempted to transform 'the totality of states making up the present community of international law' into a community of 'the law of world communication' based on the 'commonality of international interest'.[27] Pacifists identified the common international interest as the maintenance and increase of interdependence of the emerging 'world economy', the broadening scope of international law, ongoing technological changes such as those caused by the invention of the telegraph and the telephone, the globalization of the use of steamships, the creation of continental railroad networks and, facilitated by these two developments, a dramatic increase in international migration around the world.[28]

Such economic, legal and technological interdependence was accepted as a stimulus for the conclusion of international treaties relevant to communication as well as for the foundation of specialized international organizations such as the Universal Postal Union (established in 1878).[29] It was assumed that these treaties, institutions and organizations would enhance what Theodore Roosevelt (US President, 1901–9) referred to as the 'tidal wave of internationalism', would develop international law into the law of international administration and would transform 'world politics' into the domestic politics of the world.[30] Consequently, pacifists described international institutions and organizations as 'federations of states' established for specific issues and appreciated them as stepping stones to the ultimate formation of a general 'world confederation of states'.

They hoped that international institutions and organizations would help transform the 'commonality of international interest' into the 'collective interest' vested in an 'international confederation'.[31] The speculative expansion of federalism to the boundaries of the globe and the demand for the allocation to the 'world confederation of states' of as many sovereign rights as possible were regarded as the first and foremost condition for the preservation of world peace. It was understood by pacifist liberal internationalists that federalism allowed the conceptualization of a peaceful organization of the world as, in terms of biologistic functionalism, a 'collective of independent states'.[32]

Pacifist liberal internationalists further assumed that the international economic, legal and technological interdependence among the sovereign states of the world would automatically and inevitably reduce the sovereignty of these states and oblige their governments to subject themselves to judicial arbitration through international institutions and organizations. They also believed that the reallocation of sovereign rights from the states to international organizations and institutions would help reducing the war-making capabilities of the governments of sovereign states. Finally, they expected that the governments of sovereign states would ultimately subject themselves to international regimes and pursue their legitimate self-interest with peaceful means. This vision did not differ fundamentally from the restatement of the Kantian 'plan of nature' by Victor Hugo (1802–1885) who in 1849 had assigned historical inevitability to the 'future superior unity' among the sovereign states of the world.[33]

Evidently, the pragmatic link between the formal actions of imperialist world politicians and the informal actions of pacifist liberal internationalists was established in the Hague conferences of 1899 and 1907 and the resulting conventions such as the Hague convention on land war and institutions such as the International Court of Law. Not surprisingly, the Muraviev memorandum of 12 August 1898, which launched the negotiations for the first Hague conference, took up the functionalist social welfare concerns and the pacifist demands for judicial arbitration. The memorandum was highly appreciated by pacifists who also welcomed in principle the outcome of the ensuing conferences and the stipulations of the concluded conventions, despite their criticism of shortcomings in detail.

It was also rightly observed that, simply by way of participating in the conferences and signing the conventions, the involved governments already renounced part of their sovereignty and that they did so consciously under an explicit *si omnes* proviso.[34] However, bargaining about the conference agenda and bickering over mutually distrustful assumptions about possibly malicious intentions hidden by some involved governments betrayed a widening discrepancy between pragmatic government concerns for the assertion of state interest at the expense of peace and the theoretical internationalist quests for curtailing the range of government decision-making capabilities.[35] Therefore, as a complex of theoretical designs, liberal quests for international order could support pragmatic administrative quests for the institutional unity of state governments only on condition that the nationalists regarded the internationalists as unwillingly serving the interest of the state.

WORLD WAR I AND AFTER: FUNCTIONALISTS IN OFFICE

World War I brought about a cessation of international theory almost everywhere in Europe and its relocation to North America. As liberal federalists, liberal social theorists and liberal internationalists gave in to the nationalist pressures which were mounting at the time of the launching of the war, concerns for the strengthening of the unitary nation-state held sway. The war was fought along the lines which Clausewitz's theory had sketched and, consequently, the divisiveness of federalism, the critical attitudes of social theorists to the nation-state and the opposition to nation-state sovereignty which internationalists articulated could then be considered as dangerous impediments against the build-up of a nation's fighting force. Thus functionalism and its liberal options against the unitary nation-state were suppressed and vanished from the European scene as the war dragged on. But, already late in the war, it was allowed to resurface as an international theory in a sudden and unexpected comeback in North America.

The restoration of functionalism as an international theory was the result of the work of the international peace movements.[36] Their pre-war commitment to the accomplishment of world peace through world organization created a demand for empirical research into basic questions: why do governments resort to war? Why do people want to fight? Are institutional constraints possible against the war-making capacities of governments and in favour of the preservation of peace? What is peace? And how can justice be guaranteed at the international level by peaceful arbitration? Not all of these questions were new. But the activists of the peace movements insisted that they had never been more urgent than at the end of World War I and that, indeed, they had never been answered on the basis of empirical data.

Hence the demand of the day was research, because it was expected to provide reliable answers that could, in turn, provide the platform for solid and responsible decision-making. But who was to do the research? In the United Kingdom, France and Germany, jurists specializing in international law took up the issue. But their approach appeared too narrow to functionalists, because the issues at stake were not primarily legal in kind. Instead, they were primarily political and social issues and, above all, they appeared to warrant serious historical inquiry as international relations covered a long time-span.[37] In other words, research into the conditions of world peace had to be interdisciplinary and multi-perspective. As qualified research could be done only by academically trained students, the organization of the interdisciplinary and multi-perspective study of international relations in the universities obtained high priority.

Among the first to respond to this demand prior to World War I were industrialists Alfred Nobel (1833–1896), who devoted parts of his fortune to rewarding efforts for peace, Andrew Carnegie (1835–1919), the steel baron who established an endowment for International Peace in 1910, and Sir Richard Garton, who donated a fund for the promotion of international studies in 1912. The Carnegie Endowment produced, among other things, bulky editions of the *Classics of International Law* which made accessible in reprints and translations the frequently used works by Grotius, Pufendorf, Vattel and others. Inside the universities, historians and political scientists took up the issue (in the English-speaking world first), offered courses on the history of international relations and took a critical stand against colonialism and imperialism.[38]

In 1916 the time was ripe for the publication of an *Introduction to the Study of International Relations*, which was edited by the British historian Arthur James Grant (1862–1948) and contained papers on historical, legal, political, economic and social aspects of international relations.[39] After the war, new research and teaching institutions were founded and chairs for international relations were established in universities. In 1919 Herbert Hoover, the distinguished administrator and 31st President of the USA (1929–1933), donated a grant to Stanford University, his alma mater, for the establishment of a research institute which became known as the Hoover Institution of War, Revolution and Peace. The institute had the tasks of collecting documents and making them accessible for research. Professors of international relations were appointed at the University of Chicago and Yale, Princeton and Harvard Universities during the 1920s.

In Europe, the governments of the United Kingdom and France pledged at the Paris Peace Conference to found two research institutes on international relations, one in each country. The pledge went into effect when the British government launched the Royal Institute of International Affairs in 1920 whose task it was to observe and comment on ongoing world affairs and to place them into a wider context. Initially, the context was understood to be historical so that the historian Arnold Joseph Toynbee (1889–1975) could work on and publish his ambitious multi-volume *Study of History* under the 'auspices' of the institute. Similar institutes followed in France and Italy.

The Graduate Institute of International Studies was established through a grant by the Rockefeller Foundation at Geneva in 1927 to conduct research, to offer advanced teaching and to review the work of the League of Nations which had its headquarters there. An institute similar to the Hoover Institution was established in 1919 in Germany at Stuttgart under the name Weltkriegsbücherei. In European universities, teaching positions for international relations were opened only slowly, first at the University College of Wales at Aberystwyth which received a donation to establish its Woodrow Wilson Chair of

International Politics from the Liberal MP David Davies (1880–1944) in 1919, and later during the 1920s at the London School of Economics and Political Science, the Sorbonne and the Universities of Berlin and Hamburg. In 1941, Stalin founded the Moscow State Institute of International Relations (MGIMO) as a research institute, think tank and advisory board for foreign policy. There were also international organizations devoted to the study of international relations, among them the World Peace Foundation which published the journal *International Conciliation*.

The research institutes, with the exception of MGIMO, operated along the directives which functionalists had designed, and most scholars teaching at universities were themselves functionalists. One scholar of renown was Sir Alfred Zimmern (1879–1957) who held the chair at Aberystwyth to 1921, attended sessions at the League of Nations from 1921 to 1930 and taught at Oxford from 1930 to 1944.[40] He devoted his life to research into the conditions of successful international organization and wrote extensively on the League of Nations.[41] Another eminent functionalist scholar was David Mitrany (1888–1975) who taught at the London School of Economics and Political Science and had a distinguished career as a government adviser.

Zimmern's and Mitrany's thought was informed by pre-war functionalism which they tried to apply to world organization. They argued that technology facilitated high-speed communication and created networks which were manageable only by international institutions and organizations above the sovereign states. They also insisted that global interdependence reduced the potential for worldwide conflicts. Mitrany became the most vocal and influential protagonist of world organization at the time of World War II through the publication of his proposal for a *Working Peace System* in 1943. In this pamphlet, the first edition of which was published by the Royal Institute of International Affairs, Mitrany provided core arguments in support of the foundation of the United Nations.[42]

Outside the newly established discipline of international relations which dealt with problems of world organization, functionalism was restored in the 1930s and 1940s as a theory of social organization on the basis of the biologistic concept of the system. During the late nineteenth and early twentieth centuries, scientists, specifically biologists, suggested that instructive parallels existed between sets of relations among units in the inanimate and the animate worlds and developed methods to break down the divisions between natural and social sciences.[43] Functionalists as students of social groups and social relations took up the proposal and suggested that human groups constituted social systems which were characterized by some 'boundary-maintaining capability' which would fend off stress from the system's environment. And they concluded that social systems would continue to exist as long as their 'boundary-maintaining capabilities' were stronger than the environmental assaults on the system.[44]

These social scientists, who termed themselves functionalists, availed themselves fully of the imagery of nineteenth-century biologism and developed articulate concerns for the preservation of systems which continued to be seen as equipped with the capability of absorbing a limited amount of change. When these functionalists became involved in colonial administration, they sought to determine the conditions of systemic stability in the social systems of the population groups under colonial rule in order to reduce the potential for conflict.[45] Systems theoretical functionalists remained influential in the social sciences well into the 1960s.[46]

Nevertheless, the effect of the work of functionalists in office was limited because functionalist assumptions remained unconfirmed by actual events. This was eventually detrimental to their influence since they had pledged to provide applicable knowledge to decision-makers. However, as events happened, decision-makers acting on functionalist premises and adopting strategies suggested by them met with serious obstacles which scholars did not anticipate and against which they found no counter-measures.

This was true first and foremost in the case of the politics of Woodrow Wilson (28th US President, 1913–21), and of the League of Nations. Lack of recognizable relevance of the results of functionalist research was characteristic mainly of Wilson's efforts. Wilson himself had initially been a scholar. At

Princeton he held one of the first professorships of political science, to which he had been appointed in 1890. He shared major functionalist convictions. As a governor of New Jersey (1911–12) he had made efforts to advance social justice and provide social welfare. As President of the USA he made further efforts to generalize these concerns into principles of the conduct of international relations, combined them with demands for the globalization of free trade rules and added the further demands that travel should be possible without limitation and that the human right of personal freedom should be guaranteed everywhere.

As these demands encountered opposition and met with resistance, mainly among the core colonialist governments of Europe and particularly in Germany and its wartime allies, Wilson ended up mired in the same conundrums as nineteenth-century liberal free traders. If there was opposition voiced against the quest for free trade, how would the supporters of free trade respond? Would they tolerate exemptions from free trade principles on the grounds that free trade was to be introduced through voluntary agreement, or would they demand the use of force? Wilson's answer was the use of force. When the German Kaiser, in response to Wilson's statement of the free trade principles on 22 January 1917, commanded unrestricted submarine warfare without exempting US ships, Wilson pushed through Congress the declaration of war on Germany by the USA on 2 April 1917. His explicitly stated war aims were first to remove 'autocratic' governments backed by military force, and secondly to bring together a 'partnership for democratic nations' as a 'steadfast concert for peace'.

Like functionalists, Wilson rejected the balance of power, which he categorized as a technique of clandestine action, an apology for secret government agreements and an ideology of 'autocratic' decision-making.[47] In 1917 he juxtaposed what he denounced as a sinister 'balance of power' against what he praised as a respectable 'community of power'. In 1919, he demanded the substitution of the balance of power as a 'weight which does not hold together' by the 'thoroughly united League of Nations'. When he made these derogatory comments about the balance of power, Wilson had in mind the kind of 'world politics' that had been cherished among core European colonialist governments before the war. He took a stand against these positions and advanced the liberal internationalist conviction that the world should be organized as a single coherent community.[48] But he soon came under attack. Already in 1919, the British Tory politician William Barry called Wilson a 'monist' with an unjustifiable desire to reduce the pluralism of political attitudes, goals and perceptions and complained that it was illusory to believe in world organization through world organizations. Others observed that it was unjustified to denounce all concerns for the balance of power as sinister strategies of 'world politics'.[49]

A further serious threat came from another functionalist in office at Wilson's time. The October Revolution in Russia brought Lenin to power; he immediately issued a Decree of Peace on 9 November 1917. In this decree, Lenin denounced as evil the practice of making secret agreements among governments, pledged to publish all of them as far as Russia was concerned and announced Russia's pullout from the war. Lenin thus became Wilson's formidable rival and added to the President's troubles. For Lenin's pledges were not only more radical and far-reaching than Wilson's, but Lenin also had the privilege of being able to act accordingly, whereas Wilson could do not more than to fight the war against Germany, hope to impose his principles on it after its end and, for the time being, try to persuade his own allies to implement them.

Moreover, whereas Wilson's demands were understood to be targeted primarily against Germany and its allies, Lenin's pledges were universal in kind. This meant that Lenin could use his pledges as anti-government propaganda everywhere in the world, for example as a means to support anti-colonial movements in Africa and Asia. When, eventually, the new Soviet government began open peace negotiations with the government of the German Empire, Wilson had to respond. The response was contained in an address which he delivered to the US Congress on 8 January 1918. In this address he discussed Russian affairs and then specified Fourteen Points as his peace programme. Whereas ten of the Fourteen Points focused on European affairs, four were of global significance: the universal demand for open diplomatic negotiations (Point I), the general guarantee for the absolute freedom of navigation (Point II), the multilateral pledge for the admission of free trade rules (Point III) and the agreement, among the signatories of the peace treaty, to install 'a general association of nations . . . for the purpose of affording mutual guarantees of political independence and territorial integrity, to great and small states alike' (Point XIV). When, on 3 October 1918, Germany offered a truce on the basis of the Fourteen Points, Wilson had won for the time being. The ensuing peace conference at Paris accepted his proposal for a League of Nations as the world organization of states and included the covenant of that organization into the peace treaty signed at Versailles with the German Empire in 1919.

The League began its operations in 1920. It became an umbrella organization for negotiations on disarmament in Europe as well as on a world economic policy and it provided crisis management. But it had the following serious defects:

Firstly, the US Congress turned down Wilson's request that the USA should join the League.

Secondly, the League failed to address important issues relating to disarmament in the Pacific. This issue was settled outside the framework of the League at an international conference organized by the US government and held in Washington in 1921 and 1922.

Thirdly, although Wilson had included a pledge to end colonialism in his Fourteen Points, the League acted manifestly as an agent of colonialism by excluding population groups in the colonies from membership and by giving out mandates for colonial rule to governments of its member states. The latter process occurred with regard to areas in Africa, Asia and the South Pacific which had been under German colonial rule up until 1918 and were passed on to the control of the governments of Belgium, the United Kingdom, France, South Africa, New Zealand, Australia and Japan. Through these decisions, the League actively denied to peoples in Africa, Asia and the South Pacific the right of self-determination. League attitudes were informed by the belief, rooted in biologism, that there was some gap of development between the allegedly advanced European peoples and those allegedly backward peoples of Africa, Asia and the South Pacific. According to this belief, the latter peoples were 'children and must be treated as children'.[50]

Fourthly, Wilson used the League as a fortress in his struggle against communism and made efforts to defer the admission of revolutionary Russia into the League. Therefore, the League was not neutral in ideological terms.

Fifthly, Germany, which had been categorized as the main defeated state at the Paris peace conference, was barred from access to the League for the time being. Hence, the League was not designed as a universal organization.

Sixthly, the covenant of the League, although a document of universal significance, was included into the partial peace treaty between Germany and its wartime enemies. This meant that the League as a whole could be identified as part of the policy of the victors.

All in all, the League did not grow to become a true world organization. Instead, it remained incomplete with regard to the number of member states, partial with regard to the ideologies it admitted and biased in favour of colonialism. With these defects of the League, functionalists in political office and academia lost their most important asset. When the League failed to respond to the new challenges emerging early in the 1930s, the then remaining functionalists faced serious opposition which put them on the defensive against rival theorists.

Functionalism was a branch of biologism. It started out as a liberal option against the unitary sovereign nation-state towards the end of the nineteenth century, and enshrined and elaborated the biologistic conviction that active contributions were necessary to organize the world. It was reconstituted after World War I as an international theory and a theory of society which was applied by administrators in Europe as well as in the colonies. It continued the demands and proposals of the pre-war world peace movement. It was primarily a brainchild of intellectuals, mainly scholars teaching in universities, who believed that better understanding of world affairs would lead to the improvement and solidification of world organization.

Functionalism was both a theory of the state and social groups and a theory of international relations.

As theorists of the state and social groups, functionalists not only sought to improve the conditions for the shaping of national identities, to promote social justice and to provide social welfare within the state, but also helped to stabilize European colonial rule; as theorists of international relations, they pursued the preservation of peace and social justice in the world at large. In either case, they took issue with incumbent governments who ranked the fostering of the unity of sovereign states and the increase of their military capabilities as higher goals than the preservation of peace, the promotion of social justice and the provision of social welfare.

The consequence was that the biologism of functionalist theories could be applied to the level of the state as a unit in the international system and, at the same time, to the level of the international system itself. If a conflict of interest forced functionalists to opt for one of these levels, most of them abrogated their internationalism as well as their liberal convictions and opted for the state. This was the case in July and August 1914 when all liberal options against the unitary sovereign nation-state collapsed under the pressure to contribute to the unity of the state as the war was launched.

Only the confusion in which the war ended in 1918 offered functionalists a second chance. They left domestic politics to socialists or conservatives and focused on international relations under the goals of promoting peace and providing social justice to the world at large. But most functionalists sought to accomplish these goals as academics. The only noteworthy liberal functionalist in a high government office, Woodrow Wilson, was a scholar himself who turned into a politician. Hence, much of functionalist theory-making, before and after World War I, had little effect on politics, even if the League of Nations was a result of functionalist efforts to apply their theories in practice and did in fact have an impact on international relations as well as domestic politics in Europe.

As scholars, functionalists were aware of the traditions of European political and international theory. Many functionalists appreciated late-eighteenth-century contributions to international theory, specifically those by Bentham and Kant. But they employed these mechanistic contributions into their own biologistic concerns for dynamism and the promotion of change and thereby reduced their argumentative force. While Bentham's plea for free trade had made sense in combination with his demand that colonial rule should be given up, functionalists compromised with their foes and promoted free trade together with colonialism. While Kant had argued that unequivocal acceptance of the status quo and the rule of law as well as the willingness to preserve the status quo were the most important conditions for a lasting peace, functionalists fused Kant's stability-oriented demands with revisionist schemes for the reorganization of states and thus added to instability, rivalry and inter-state strife.

In the end, the inadequacies of functionalist theories contributed more to their failure than the strength of rival theories. However, the fact that functionalists in office after World War I failed to implement the pre-war functionalist theories does not support the conclusion that functionalism had no lasting effects. Instead, the functionalist insistence that theory-making and attempts to understand world affairs on the basis of empirical evidence are values in their own right contributed decisively to the establishment of international relations as a field of study in the 1920s even though functionalists themselves soon lost control of it. The establishment of international relations as an academic discipline added greatly to the capacities for the study of international relations, but it could not stem the increasing power and influence of people like Lenin, whom the peacemakers of 1919 tried to ignore, and Hitler, who was determined to ignore the peace treaties.

EIGHT

Realism

In the course of the 1920s and 1930s, functionalists came under increasing pressure from challenges which originated first and foremost from the rise to government of fascists, militarists and national socialists in Italy, Japan and Germany. These movements represented challenges to functionalist theory because they vocalized opposition to world organization through international institutions and organizations, the acceptance of international law as a constraining force above the sovereign states, the recognition of the post-World War I peace settlements and disarmament agreements as well as opposition to the respect for and guarantee of the human rights and the principal freedoms of the individual.

The revisionist potential was strongest in Germany and weakest in Italy, while Japan took a place in the middle. Elsewhere, fascist movements or groups advocating similar ideologies gained importance in the later 1920s and the 1930s in Hungary, Portugal and Spain or were implanted under German, Japanese and Italian pressure in the Balkans and in East Asia. In Germany, the revisionism peaked in the promulgation and execution of laws through which entire population groups, first and foremost Jews, were singled out first for discrimination, subsequently for social isolation in ghettos and eventually for mass murder.

The activities of these governments and the people who supported them thrust upon functionalists the question of where liberal toleration against illiberalism and purposeful lack of toleration should end. The question pushed functionalists back into the dilemma which had haunted them since the beginning of the twentieth century: if they chose to continue efforts to maintain and strengthen world organization through international institutions and organizations, they would have to mobilize force against evident and purposeful violations of human rights and international law. If they opted for efforts to advance the unification and strengthening of the existing nation-states, they would have to respect the sovereignty of the nation-state, refrain from intervention and confine their international activities to the management of international crises through the League of Nations. Functionalists took the second choice and risked that the revisionist governments would not only sneer at the League but eventually depart from it. The governments of Japan and Germany did so in 1933 and the government of Italy followed suit in 1937, leaving the League without any legal possibility for intervention.

Functionalists could neither provide an explanation for the failure of international crisis management nor offer suggestions for responses against the revisionist movements of fascism, militarism and national socialism, and thus gave way to rival theorists who, at a later stage, identified themselves as realists.

FROM PRACTICE TO THEORY: THE GENESIS OF REALISM

Realism is a distant relative of functionalism. Both had their intellectual roots in biologism and shared the convictions that the world is engulfed by one single global international system as an ordering framework of its own, that this system is more than the sum of its parts and that the maintenance of systemic stability should be a core concern of theorists and practitioners of international relations.[1] Functionalists as well as realists believed that states were the constitutive units of the system, that they should be nation-states as the embodiments of homogeneous and unified population groups and that it ought to be the task of theorists to provide the intellectual tools for determining the relationship between the global international system and the sovereign nation-states as its members.

But functionalists and realists were at odds over how the relationship between the system and its units ought to be perceived.

Against functionalists, realists rejected the importance of trusting in general acceptance of the rule of law at the level of international relations and opposed the expansion of world organization through international organizations as well as institutions above sovereign nation-states, because they took the view that international organizations and institutions were unable to constrain the decision-making capability of the governments of these states.

Instead, realists relied on vigilance and control as principles of the conduct of international relations through the governments of sovereign nation-states and were prepared to accept the use of force as well as, if necessary, of physical violence, against states whose governments were seen to infringe upon international law or to act otherwise against the perceived interest of the international community. Against functionalists, realists predicted that there was a higher probability of breaches of set rules than abidance by them. Realists were convinced that the international system was innately 'anarchic' in the sense that there was no possibility of world government, and they were convinced that attempts to build a world government were futile.

Some of them even went so far as to claim that the maintenance of the international system in the state of anarchy was a just war aim because the anarchy of the system was the best possible safeguard against attempts at universal rule. Realists assumed that the anarchical structure of the international system could be controlled not by the joint efforts of all or the majority of its units, but merely by the governments of core states, namely those nation-states in which economic and military capabilities had accumulated. Some realists even limited the international system to such core actors and declared governments of all other states systemically irrelevant.

Against functionalists, realists further insisted that the only way to achieve systemic stability was through the maintenance of a balance of power between the core actors in the system. They argued that balance of power ought to be measured in terms of military strength and that its maintenance required vigilance as well as, where necessary, the use of physical force. Finally, realists radicalized biologism in that they ignored any categorical difference between states, their governments and their populations and categorized states as actors in the international system. They did so on the basis of the assumption that, as far as foreign policy and the conduct of international relations were concerned, states were homogeneous to an extent which allowed them to 'speak' metaphorically with one voice. To make this assumption explicit, realists availed themselves of the eighteenth- and nineteenth-century diplomatic jargon in which states or their capitals featured as quasi-animated agents which were given the capability of acting as if they were human beings.

Realism in the sense of a radicalized version of biologism originated in the early nineteenth century from the efforts to construct a new systemic order in Europe after the Napoleonic Wars.[2] Its earliest traces are to be found in diplomatic memoranda from the time of the Vienna Congress and the following years. An early statement of realist theory is contained in a remark by Robert Stuart Viscount Castlereagh (1769–1822), the British plenipotentiary at the Vienna Congress. In 1818, Castlereagh noted that the international system could accomplish the tasks assigned to it by the balance-of-power theorists of the time only if it was enacted through such activities as international conferences, the conclusion of treaties and the provision of cross-national assistance at times of crisis.

Through such instruments, he insisted, governments of nation-states could demonstrate their willingness to cooperate among themselves, to develop a consensus about their goals and to streamline their policies. But he added, in accordance with Kant's arguments, that these instruments did not accumulate into measures for the conclusion of a 'general alliance' as a 'system of general government', and that nothing would be less justifiable than the enforcement of a general peace at the discretion and with the power of only one interested party. Consequently, Castlereagh concluded, the international system had to remain disorganized until, at some time in the more remote future, a consensus about such a general peace might become possible.[3]

Castlereagh was as much in favour of the balance of power as a dynamic instrument for the maintenance of stability as other participants in and commentators on the European international system at the time. In a curious document which was submitted to the attention of the peacemakers at the Vienna Congress, Friedrich Karl von dem Knesebeck (1768–1848), a general active in the Napoleonic Wars and subsequently Prussian war minister, proposed the construction of a mechanical balance of roughly equal-sized core 'powers' around a central 'weight' made up from the German states and the United Kingdom (illus. 4).

He argued that this arrangement was a guarantee for stability because it appeared to him to contain no incentive for revisions. Knesebeck paid no attention to systemic constraints (in fact, a systemic frame is absent in the graph) but recommended that governments of the states in the arrangement should continuously be on guard against initiatives for revision. Knesebeck's proposal remained without influence as a general design during his lifetime but was taken up in 1854, at the time of the Crimean War. On this occasion, it was employed in support of arguments for the war against Russia, whose government was accused of trying to upset the balance as Knesebeck had envisaged it. That means that, in the middle of the nineteenth century, his proposal

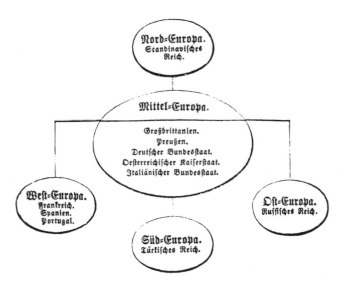

4 Scheme of the balance of power in Europe. From Friedrich Karl von dem Knesebeck, *Denkschrift betreffend die Gleichgewichts-Lage Europas* (Berlin, 1854).

was turned into an instrument to justify the ongoing war against Russia as an effort to maintain the balance of power in Europe and the Ottoman Turkish Empire.

In the nineteenth century, realism thus supported a set of preferences and assumptions of which diplomats and military men could avail themselves in the making of foreign policy concerning the European states and the Ottoman Turkish Empire. Although all nineteenth-century theorists and practitioners of international relations accepted the biologistic premise that there was only one global international system which engulfed the entire world, up to the 1870s practical foreign policy decision-makers exhibited little concern for the other continents and the open seas except in the United Kingdom.[4]

The European colonial empires in America collapsed in the late eighteenth and early nineteenth centuries, and only some spots in the Caribbean and on the eastern fringes of South America remained under European control. There was still little European penetration into the interior of Africa in the earlier nineteenth century and in Asia the only governments which made extensive use of military force were those of Russia (which subjected Siberia and the northern Pacific to its control) and the United Kingdom which, in succession to the English East India Company, expanded its control over the Indian subcontinent by means of conquest and provided military support for penetration into the South Pacific.

But the Opium War in China (1840–44), the forced opening of Japan to international trade (1853–68), the British, Dutch and French conquests in Southeast Asia around the middle and in the second half of the nineteenth century as well as, finally, the 'scramble for Africa' and the South Pacific in the 1880s and 1890s not only globalized the foreign policy decision-making processes, but also added to their antagonisms and made it impossible for competing, non-European international systems, such as the Chinese or the various international systems in the Pacific and the interior of Africa, to continue to exist.

With the partition of Africa and the South Pacific among European colonial governments and with the joint European intervention against the Boxer Rebellion in China in 1900, it became evident that indigenous Chinese, African and Pacific perceptions of the world, as far as they were incompatible with European perceptions, had to be given up. Indeed, around 1900, this evidence seemed to lend support to the functionalist conviction not only that the world was a single global entity but that only one perception of it was viable, namely the European one.

But the uniform Europeanized global world picture did not rule out realism. Instead, rivalries among European colonial governments increased, and these rivalries could be understood as indicating the justice of realist demands for eternal vigilance and concerns for the maintenance of the balance of power. These concerns informed, first and foremost, British foreign policy in the early years of the twentieth century. Sir Eyre Crowe (1864–1925), a senior policy-maker in the British Foreign Office, made little effort to conceal his worries about the growing likelihood of German aggression in 1907 and advanced his own proposal that the British government should make efforts to preserve the balance of power against states whose governments appeared to be unable or unwilling to control their incalculable 'ambitions'. In order to add weight to his argument, he awarded historical inevitability to the balance of power tantamount to a law of nature:

> History shows that the danger threatening the independence of this or that nation has generally arisen, at least in the past, out of the momentary predominance of a neighbouring State at once militarily powerful, economically efficient, and ambitious to extend its frontiers or spread its influence, power and efficiency, and to the spontaneity of 'inevitability' of its ambitions. The only check on the abuse of political predominance derived from such a position has always consisted in the opposition of an equally formidable rival, or of a combination of several countries forming leagues of defence. The equilibrium established by such a grouping of forces is technically known as the balance of power, and it has become almost a truism to identify England's secular policy with the maintenance of this balance by throwing her weight now in this scale and now in that, but ever on the side opposed to the political dictatorship of the strongest single state or group at a given time. If this view of British policy is correct, the opposition

into which England must inevitably be driven to any country aspiring to such a dictatorship assumes almost the forms of a law of nature.[5]

Crowe's preference for reactive interventionism to the end of maintaining the status quo, his insistence that the balance of power as a dynamic part of the natural world order needed to be actively and purposefully defended against revisionism, and his demand for strong political and military reactions against those whom he accused of attempts to upset the balance characterize him as a realist *avant la lettre*. He was willing to apply to foreign policy a set of general principles for which he drew on the sciences. The precedent of scientific method led him to consider as viable a determinism which subjected the making of foreign policy to seemingly unchanging regularities. He assigned the execution of these regularities to the practical tasks of diplomats. At the beginning of the twentieth century, realism had thus reached the level where it could be transformed into a fully-fledged theory in accordance with the scientism prevalent at the time.

Nevertheless, the realism advocated by Crowe was not then shared by many people elsewhere in Europe. Specifically, German commentators on British foreign policy assailed as propaganda the British quest for the maintenance of the balance of power. Not unlike eighteenth-century supporters of King Frederick II of Prussia, these commentators argued that behind professed activities for the maintenance of the balance of power were hidden strategies for the control of the world as a whole or the largest possible part of it.[6] The controversy displayed the lack of agreement among the European imperialist governments on long-term or strategic goals. Because there was this lack of agreement, it was unsurprising not only that the major European imperialist governments resorted to war eventually in 1914, but that the decision to go to war was fully supported by the realist convictions of the time.

No one made this clearer than US Captain Alfred Thayer Mahan (1840–1914) who, in 1912, took issue with the functionalist supporters of the world peace movement[7] and predicted that governments of sovereign states, such as that of the

German Empire, would continue to employ military force for the accomplishment of political goals, that the acknowledgement of legitimate self-interest was the primary condition for maintaining the balance in international relations and, consequently, for the preservation of peace.[8] Denouncing functionalists as materialists, he concluded:

> To regard mankind, in individuals or in states, as so dominated by material self-interest that the appeal of other motives – ambition, self-respect, resentment of injustice, sympathy with the oppressed, hatred of oppression – is by it overbalanced and inoperative, is not only to misread history, but to ignore it. Almost every war of the past half-century contradicts the assertion. Nations will fight for such reasons more readily than for self-interest.[9]

This statement was compatible with the contemporary conception of 'world politics' which was pursued by the government of the core imperialist states at the time.[10]

TURNING REALISM INTO AN INTERNATIONAL THEORY

Realism was transformed into a full international theory through historical inquiries. Realists assumed that empirical evidence from history was needed to support 'scientific' theories and, therefore, shared with functionalists the *fin de siècle faible* for historicism which also permeated economics, sociology and jurisprudence at the time.[11] But contrary to functionalists, who delved into the history of international organization in order to demonstrate its empirical possibility, realists plunged into the study of the changes and continuities of the balance of power gleaned from primary sources.

The group of scholars studying the balance of power was international. It included the Russian Alexander de Stieglitz, the French Léonce Donnadieu, Charles Dupuis and Gabriel Hanotaux, the Norwegian Olof Höijer, the Belgian Ernest Nys and the German Ernst Kaeber.[12] A few of them were professional historians, such as Kaeber; some were diplomats or people in government, such Hanotaux and Stieglitz; others were jurists, such as Höijer. They scrutinized the diplomatic correspondence as well as the theoretical tracts which they found in archives and libraries of many European countries. The results of all this research agreed with regard to the principal observation that the balance of power had been a flexible equilibrating device in European international relations since the fifteenth century and that its precise definitions, the range of territories to which it had been applied and the degree by which its rules had been regarded as binding had varied.

It was from the background of these results that realist diplomats, such as Crowe, could extrapolate their view that the balance of power was something equivalent to a law of nature. But the message which these historical enquiries left behind was more fundamental. It defined the realist conception of the balance of power biologistically as a moving equilibrium in the same way that some of the Vienna peacemakers had followed. Consequently, the late-nineteenth- and early-twentieth-century students of the balance of power not only assembled seemingly value-free historical material which later theorists could use as a quarry but also lent support to the view that the Vienna peacemakers had set the standards for balance-of-power politics pure and simple. This conviction continued to impact on realists up to the 1990s.[13]

Realists thus had solid grounds for theory-making after World War I. While functionalists strove to enact policies for the deepening of world organization and struggled over the establishment of academic institutions of teaching and research in international relations, realists combined their efforts to create a theoretical platform from which assaults against functionalists in office could be launched.

The first opportunity to do so was the debate in Congress over US membership in the League of Nations. Realists blamed Wilson for having condemned the balance of power without reason and justification. They contended that world organization had been in existence long before the war, that it had collapsed in the face of the aggressive policies of some governments, such as those of the German Empire, and that it had been discredited as ineffective thereby. They complained that further schemes for world organization could lead only to world government, which had no constituency to provide legitimacy for itself and was therefore undemocratic. They constructed the international system as an anarchical framework and concluded that the balance of power, although far from ideal, had been tried out, seemingly successfully, on many occasions as a reportedly useful instrument for the preservation of peace, whereas the success of world organization had so far failed.

Most of these arguments were far from obvious and conclusive. Hence their success, which killed Wilson's bid for US membership in the League of Nations, may not have been solely due to their innate strength but may also have depended on the impediments which the White House faced at the time due to Wilson's illness. However that may have been, the very fact that functionalists had been defeated in Congress counted as a defeat because it catapulted realist views into surveys of international relations produced for consumption in the universities on both sides of the Atlantic.[14]

In Europe, realist positions were voiced outside the academic world by Sir Winston Churchill (1874–1965) soon after World War I. In 1923, Churchill published an insider's account of the war in which he used the diplomatic jargon of states as animated actors and did much to popularize it. The work contains a lengthy discussion of the reasons for the war. It features Bismarck (1815–1898) as a thoughtful balance-of-power statesman whose moderation maintained Europe in a stable equilibrium, and condemns Kaiser Wilhelm II (1888–1918) and Bismarck's unwise successors for having changed the balance of power into two 'vast combinations, each disposing of enormous military resources, dwelling together at first side by side but gradually face to face'.[15]

Churchill deplored the impossibility of imposing international constraints upon the decisions of governments and, even more, the lack of human capability to control 'world fortunes'. Sceptically, he detected a willingness to suffer which smouldered beneath the surface of satisfaction in the Old World and concluded that, if people were willing to suffer, there was nothing that could be done about it.[16] Consequently, Churchill turned into a great, though temporary advocate of the balance of power which, in 1936, he praised as a means to preserve stability and as 'the wonderful unconscious tradition of British foreign policy'.[17] However, disillusioned by World War II, he rejected the theory as 'unsound' on the grounds that 'we cannot afford, if we can help it, to work on narrow margins, offering temptations to a trial of strength'.[18] Without returning to functionalism, Churchill became a critic of the balance of power, which he denounced as too shaky to be acceptable as the equivalent of a law of nature.

The same ambivalence of attitudes towards the balance of power also characterized realist theory-making in the USA during the 1920s and 1930s. The establishment of realism in academic circles was mainly the work of political scientists at the University of Chicago whose Department of Political Science was run at the time by Charles Merriam (1874–1953, at Chicago 1900–40, head of the department 1923–40). Merriam had produced a substantive study of the history of sovereignty[19] and thus combined his interest in history with his willingness to advise foreign policy-makers in government. He attracted to Chicago a number of similarly minded scholars, first and foremost Quincy Wright (1890–1970), who took office at Chicago in 1931.

Whereas Merriam had been a generalist who penetrated into various branches of political science, Wright concentrated his work on international relations. Trained in international law and offering courses in the law of war and the law of peace, Wright, upon arrival at Chicago, launched a long-term research project on war which went on throughout the 1930s and involved a large number of younger and émigré scholars. Among the latter were Arnold Wolfers (1892–1968) and Theodore Hermann von Laue (1916–) who had begun to establish international relations as a field of study in German universities during the 1920s before the rise of the Nazis forced them to emigrate.

At Chicago, Wright established an interdisciplinary study programme for international relations which put together international law, international politics and 'international sociology'. The programme was organized by a Committee on International Relations which Wright chaired and which served as the training ground for future international relations scholars. But, like Merriam, Wright was also active in public service, particularly at the time of World War II and during its immediate aftermath. For example, he joined the Nuremberg Tribunal as a consultant to Justice Robert Jackson. Wright confirmed Clausewitz's biologistic definition of war as 'an extreme intensification of military activity, psychological tension, legal power, and social integration'.[20] He added a tripartite classification of civil, colonial and international war all of which, he insisted, demanded specific approaches.

Wright and his team thus betrayed their dependence on Eurocentric attitudes by drawing a sharp line between international wars and colonial wars which they positioned in proximity to domestic wars.[21] The likening of colonial wars to domestic wars took the point of view of the European colonial governments and ignored the fact that this view was being challenged by anti-colonial resistance movements at the time. Moreover, despite his expertise as a specialist in international law, Wright took no notice of the fact that when they were allowed to continue under 'indirect rule' many traditional rulers, particularly in Africa, regarded themselves as heads of sovereign states and were justified in doing so on the grounds of the international treaties which they had concluded with the European powers.[22]

Wright and his colleagues drew heavily on the older histories of the balance of power[23] and generalized the realist position that the international system was anarchic and that war was an imminent factor of international relations which was unlikely to fade away. As war could not be removed from the world through human efforts because living beings seemed to share a 'natural' inclination to it, it made no sense to rely on international organization as a means to promote peace. Instead, eternal vigilance and ascertainable readiness to use military force were recommended as the best deterrents against war, even though Wright shared the critical position on the balance of power which Churchill adopted later in his life.[24]

At Harvard, the study of international relations was promoted by Carl Joachim Friedrich (1901–1984), another émigré scholar. Like Merriam and Wright, Friedrich understood international theory as a contribution to practical foreign policy decision-making. Friedrich was among the first to argue the necessity for a revision of the functionalist principles which had informed the international theory of the 1920s. In 1938, he gave a gloomy account of the anarchic and volatile state of international relations which concluded with a critique of the League of Nations and a plea for the disillusioned use of the balance of power as an instrument for maintaining stability:

> It is evident that international relations under either the balance of power or the league of powers are highly uncertain and dynamic. The league ideal, when coherent, transcends existing possibilities on account of the great diversity of political systems. The balance of power ideal likewise is impracticable on account of the complexity and constant change of the international alignments. There is no apparent balancer either within or without the League in its present or any conceivable reformed state. Yet, without an effective balancer, no order or balance can be expected among 'independent' states . . . [A] balance of power, though far from being a beautiful design, may yet be preferable to the international anarchy which is prevailing at present.[25]

Still in 1942, Nicolas Spykman (1893–1943) at Yale agreed with Friedrich expecting that, even after the end of World War II, an 'international society' would continue to exist 'composed of at least six great [powers] and a number of small [powers]'. He concluded with what he took to be a reminder of the fact 'that, whatever may ultimately be achieved in the form of integration and federation, we will start more or less where we left off when war broke out'.[26]

While Wright was absent from Chicago, his post was temporarily filled by Hans Joachim Morgenthau (1904–1980), an émigré scholar who specialized in international theory.[27] Morgenthau stayed on at Chicago for the rest of his life and took charge of international politics in the Chicago international relations programme. He became most widely known through his textbook *Politics among Nations* which has served as a cornerstone for realist theory. Morgenthau's approach in *Politics among Nations* differed little from Wright's. He drew heavily on history, dealt with the history of the balance of power at length, confessed his admiration for the Vienna peacemakers, declared the use of power to be at the core of international relations and urged eternal vigilance.[28]

Although not accepted in his own time, the Protestant theologian Reinhold Niebuhr (1892–1971) gained much influence after World War II. He shared basic convictions with realists without being influenced by the traditions of realist political thought, but had a great impact on wartime theorists like Morgenthau and Wolfers.[29]

In Europe, realism as an international theory advanced more slowly. In the early decades of the twentieth century, its most ardent supporters were German historians. Among them, the Berlin modern historian Friedrich Meinecke (1862–1954) published a book on the history of the reason of state in 1924 which is essentially an exercise in the history of grand political theory. Meinecke supported the view that the use of power in international relations was not subject to systemic constraints.[30] This view was shared by contemporary pragmatic historians whose work encapsulated the legacy of the political philosophy of Leopold von Ranke.[31] Theodore Hermann von Laue was one of their students.[32] In the 1930s, the historian Walther Kienast (1896–1985), a student of the Berlin medievalist Dietrich Schäfer (1845–1929), described the late-medieval process of the depoliticization and secularization of universalism in terms of decay and observed with much regret that the international system which, in his view, had replaced universal rule in the late Middle Ages was bereft of instruments to govern the world.[33]

The most momentous pronouncement of realist theory appeared in the summer of 1939, on the eve of World War II. Edward Hallett Carr (1892–1982),[34] who had just quit the British diplomatic service in order to take over the professorship of international relations at Aberystwyth, published his views on international relations under the title *The Twenty Years' Crisis*. In this work he recorded what he termed 'the abrupt descent from the visionary hopes of the first decade [after World War I, i.e. 1919–29] to the grim despair of the second [1929–39]'. He accused functionalists of taking 'little account of reality' and blamed Wilson for having vainly tried to call back eighteenth-century Benthamite doctrines which had long been 'hollow and without substance'.

Further denouncing functionalists as 'utopians' who fixed their 'eyes on the future' rather than on urgent problems of the present, he proclaimed himself as 'the realist' whose thoughts were 'rooted in the past' and insisted that the study of the history of international relations contained the keys to the solution of present problems.[35] Carr and Crowe had both worked in the British Foreign Office and they shared a sense of history. Like Crowe, Carr believed in the importance of applying the laws of nature (as scientists described them) in order 'to emphasize the irresistible strength of existing forces and the inevitable character of existing tendencies, and to insist that the highest wisdom lies in accepting, and adapting oneself to, these forces and these tendencies'.[36]

Carr relied on his experiences as a diplomat and on the empirical information which he had gathered in office in order to support his view that international relations were a perennial power struggle among nations or similar groups organized in states for political conflict.[37] His views were thus identical with the positions that had previously been developed in the USA. Carr's lasting contribution was, however, that he coined and popularized the word 'realism' for these positions and, at the same time, insisted that only realists were realistic in their assessments of international relations. He graciously admitted that functionalism had been a necessary stage in the evolution of international theory but confidently diagnosed that its time was over. In the preface to the second edition of his *Politics among Nations*, Morgenthau took over this label and thereby joined ranks with Carr.

THEORISTS AS PRACTITIONERS: THE COLD WAR

The leading position into which realists in the USA had catapulted themselves during the 1930s and early 1940s was further advanced after World War II. The coming of the Cold War had been foreseen by keen observers, such as William Thornton Rickert Fox (1912–) at Yale, during World War II.[38]

The principal contending issues debated during the Cold War were explicated in 1947 in a well-publicized article which appeared under the pseudonym X in the journal *Foreign Affairs*, but whose author was soon disclosed as the diplomat George Frost Kennan (1904–). In order to define the US position in the Cold War, Kennan employed much of the traditions of liberalism and elevated them to values of general validity. In doing so, Kennan observed that the values enshrined in the liberal tradition could not be observed in the Soviet Union and called for the containment of Soviet influence. He advised the US administration not to rely on military might alone but also to seek success in diplomatic skirmishes.[39]

The postwar realist who was most seriously involved with history was Henry Alfred Kissinger (1923–). In his Harvard doctoral dissertation he reviewed early nineteenth-century balance-of-power politics after the Vienna Congress. Kissinger was most explicit in associating his own realist convictions with what he took to be accomplishments of the Vienna peacemakers. He then implemented his theoretical plea for the maintenance of the balance of power while he was in office as a presidential adviser and secretary of state, and repeated his views when he returned to diplomatic history later.[40]

Other realists turned away from history to 'pure' theory. Foremost among them was John Hermann Herz (1908–). In his review of international theory published in 1951, Herz disagreed with Carr and attached to functionalism the new label of idealism. The new label lifted functionalism above utopian dreams but retained for realism the claim for methodological superiority.[41] Herz also retained the realist belief that the international system was anarchic and discovered what he called the 'security dilemma of men in groups and their leaders':

> Groups or individuals living in such a constellation must be, and usually are, concerned about their security from being attacked, subjected, dominated, or annihilated by other groups or individuals. Striving to attain security from such attacks, they are driven to acquire more and more power in order to escape the impact of the power of others. This, in turn, renders the others more insecure and compels them to

prepare for the worst. Since none can ever feel entirely secure in such a world of competing units, power competition ensues, and the vicious circle of security and power accumulation is on. Whether man is by nature peaceful and co-operative, or domineering and aggressive, is not the question. The condition that concerns us here is not a biological or anthropological but a social one.[42]

Herz's confidence in the methodological superiority of realism was challenged fundamentally in 1957 by Morton Kaplan (1921–), successor to Wright at Chicago. Kaplan denounced as unprofessional previous international theories because he thought they lacked a systematic approach. He criticized historical analyses as patchwork and theoretical explanations as inconclusive. He accused historians of having failed to provide in their work complete and reliable data and blamed theorists for having insufficiently clarified their tacit assumptions and implicit hypotheses

Kaplan came under the impact of Parsonsian systems theory and insisted that only the systems theoretical approach was acceptable. He believed that general and theoretically viable statements about international relations could emerge only from a study of recognizable actions and processes at the systems, i.e. the macro level of international relations. To him, the international system consisted only of core actors which he identified as homogeneous states. He used game theory in attempts to generalize on processes (as sequences of decisions of core international actors) and rejected as incomprehensible the empirical study of motives for actions. Instead, the study of processes at the systems level appeared to him to allow predictions about results.

On the premise of realist theory, Kaplan defined six hypothetical types of international system of which he credited only three with the possibility of empirical existence and selected only one for which he defined a number of theoretical rules. That system was the balance of power. The most important of these rules was that wars for the maintenance of the balance of power were just. This conclusion was explicitly made to justify military action against the Soviet Union if the Soviet government chose to upset the postwar balance of the superpowers.[43] Although Kaplan's radical rejection of the importance of the study of motives in international relations was soon refuted,[44] his work had profound influence on international relations studies throughout the 1960s and the 1970s.

In Europe, realism was elaborated in the United Kingdom in historical terms by Martin Wight (1913–1972). Wight had been a collaborator of Toynbee at the Royal Institute of International Affairs before taking up a teaching position at the London School of Economics and Political Science. Although a peace activist, Wight saw every reason to defend Carr's realist convictions in studies and lectures on the history of international relations. The importance of his few published works and many unpublished papers and lectures has increased since his premature death in 1972.[45] Together with the Cambridge historian Herbert Butterfield (1900–1979), Wight was the *spiritus rector* of the British Committee for International Relations, whose members met regularly during the 1950s and 1960s to discuss theoretical and historical issues of international relations.[46]

Wight's most important contribution to realist theory, which was popularized by Hedley Bull (1932–1985),[47] was his classification of three so-called traditions of international theory which he associated with Grotius, Hobbes and Kant. Grotius was categorized as the representative of the 'rationalist', Hobbes of the 'realist' and Kant of the 'revolutionist' 'tradition'. Wight associated Grotius with 'rationalism' because the latter appeared to have argued in support of world organization through international law as a set of rationally imposed rules. He labelled Hobbes a 'realist' because Hobbes had described the state of nature as anarchic, and Wight used this description as a model for his own realist perception of the international system. He placed Kant into the 'revolutionary' 'tradition' because he identified Kant as an early advocate of liberal internationalism.

None of Wight's ascriptions had, however, anything to do with Grotius, Hobbes and Kant. Grotius had not perceived international law as a set of rationally imposed rules but as an outflow of divine law. Hobbes had not described international relations as anarchic but as well ordered, and Kant had denounced as despotic the revolutionary movement in France, had praised Prussia as a model republican state and had envisaged world order in terms directly opposed to the views of functionalist internationalism.

Thus Wight betrayed his own realist bias through his insistence that Grotius and Hobbes were antipodes. But Grotius and Hobbes could only have been so under the biologistic assumption (which neither Grotius nor Hobbes nor, for that matter, Kant shared) that the international system was more than the sum of its parts. For it was only against the background of this assumption that Hobbes's perception of the natural condition of humankind before the emergence of society could have been applied by way of analogy to international relations. Only the realist belief that the international system was by nature anarchic could turn Hobbes into a realist *avant la lettre*. But, contrary to Wight's biologistic assumption, Hobbes would not admit that sovereign rulers behaved like human beings in the state of nature, but took it for granted that they were constrained in their decisions by overarching fundamental laws and a well-ordered mechanistically perceived international system. Hence Wight's classification of Hobbes as a realist *avant la lettre* was a realist misinterpretation of Hobbes which lingered on to the end of the twentieth century.[48]

Realism started out as a complex of preferences and values shared by a number of practitioners in European international relations in the early nineteenth century. It emerged against the background of biologism and was elaborated through the practical business of refurbishing the European states and shaping a new systems perception of the world. The pragmatics of realism established its own tradition in the course of the nineteenth century, at the end of which realist practitioners took issue with functionalist theorists about the problem of what conclusions were to be drawn from the expansion of the European international system to the boundaries of the globe.

Whereas functionalists demanded world organization, realists ascribed to the balance of power the status of a law of nature and thereby credited it with global validity. Realists developed a theoretical position of their own which they tried to glean from empirical research in the history of the balance of power.

Focusing on the preservation of the balance of power, realists defined conservative positions whose advocates were convinced that ascertained past experience could allow predictions of the future.

After World War I, realists quickly penetrated into the newly established academic institutions of teaching and research which they soon developed into bastions pitched against functionalism. A growing number of realist theorists took charge of institutions, many of which functionalists had helped to establish, and condemned functionalists first as utopians, then as idealists. During the late 1930s, the 1940s, the 1950s and the 1960s, realists held sway and remained in control of the core of these institutions in the USA and the UK, the only two states where institutions of research and training in international relations advanced significantly at the time. Some realists used their positions to impact on foreign policy making, particularly during Cold War, and a few of them took high offices in government.

Despite their *faible* for history, realists were hardly aware of the biologistic limitations of their theories. Carr, for one, was sure 'that group units in some form will certainly survive as repositories of political power, what ever form these units may take'. Emphasizing the unifying effect of the nineteenth-century nation-building processes, he concluded:

> Nationalism was one of the forces by which the seemingly irreconcilable clash of interest between classes within the national community was reconciled. There is no corresponding force which can be invoked to reconcile the now seemingly irreconcilable clash of interest between nations. It is profitless to imagine a hypothetical world in which men no longer organise themselves in groups for purposes of conflict; and the conflict cannot once more be transferred to a wider and more comprehensive field. As has often been observed, the international community cannot be organised against Mars. This is merely another aspect of the dilemma with which the collapse of the spacious conditions of nineteenth-century civilisation has confronted us.[49]

Carr's description of the international system was identical with that which functionalists provided, but he drew the opposite conclusion from it. While functionalists took the view that world organization had to be enhanced so as to allow the imposition of constraints upon the governments of sovereign nation-states, Carr, like other realists, withdrew to the sceptical position that the world could not be organized at all.

Realists were not always fair to functionalists. As theorists, they failed to appreciate that functionalists had brought the very institutions to a stage of development which realists were so eager to take over. Likewise, realists overlooked the fact that functionalists as supporters of the peace movement had been the first to demand and to undertake empirical research in international relations. And realists were not justified in denouncing functionalism as wishful thinking merely on the grounds that some functionalist assumptions were confirmed neither by empirical data gleaned from historical research nor by ongoing events. After all, post-World War II realists of the second generation applied the same criticism to pre-World War II realists of the first generation.[50]

As practitioners, realists often conceived *Realpolitik* in terms of the politics of the day. They thus found it difficult to formulate long-term goals and even more to accomplish them. The case in point was Churchill's attitude to the balance of power. He used it in his criticism of Wilsonian politics but, through his experience as the British wartime prime minister when he was confronted with the necessity of making tough decisions against Hitler, he cast the balance of power overboard with the argument that no time had been left for minute calculations. Churchill cared little that Wilson had used the same type of argument against Kaiser Wilhelm II.

Nevertheless, it would also be unfair to be harsh on realists for the inadequacy of some of their theoretical positions. The rise of fascism, militarism and national socialism was a formidable challenge for western democracies, and only realists offered the proper response.

NINE

Challengers, Rivals and Variants: Functionalism and Realism in Context

The clash between functionalism and realism dominated twentieth-century international theory but did not command it completely. Functionalism and realism had their challengers, rivals and variants. The very existence of such competitors indicates that the diversity of international theory has grown in the course of the twentieth century, especially since World War II. Moreover, both functionalism and realism developed at the time of European and US colonial rule over large parts of Africa, Asia and the South Pacific. They were consequently identified as theories of European and North American provenance and criticized as Eurocentric after the demise of colonialism.

Criticism became vocal first in Africa and Latin America during the 1950s and '60s. It added to the diversification of international theory. It seems obvious that this diversification was also the result of the widening scope of international relations as an academic field of study within which various schools of thought could easily be established and documented through the output of academic publications. At the same time, the growing diversity of available theories and the dwindling periods during which they flourished reduced the grip which any single theory could have on practitioners' minds and, conversely, strengthened its dependence on functionalism and realism as the core theories in the background.

After the demise of colonialism, essential convictions which functionalism and realism had shared were called into question. Among the more important of them was the demand that international theories should provide the tools for determining the relationship between the global international system and the sovereign nation-states as its members. The confidence that the governments of sovereign nation-states (or, as realists thought, a small number of states themselves) were paramount actors in the international system has become subject to serious doubt since the end of World War II. Such doubt has been informed by the coming into existence of a growing number of so-called non-state actors, the recognition of structural as well as contingent weaknesses of state institutions and by the admission that, in many parts of the world, state institutions represented a peculiar form of polity which could neither integrate or overarch nor annihilate or prevent from coming into existence concurring polities on one and the same territory.

The following description focuses first on the defeat by functionalism and realism of socialism and Nazism as their two major challengers; secondly on the attempt to revise functionalism and realism in the light of world systems theory; and thirdly on attempts to adapt functionalism and realism to the new conditions emerging with the demise of colonialism.

SOCIALISM AS A CHALLENGER OF LIBERAL FUNCTIONALISM

Socialism was functionalism without liberalism. The most important socialist challenge against liberalism was due to the fact that socialists reduced the role of the state as the paramount international actor and placed it in competition with classes. Already in its beginning, the socialist movement was decidedly internationalist, as the Communist Manifesto of 1848 made clear. The subsequently established socialist parties adhered to internationalism, forged party alliances across state boundaries and produced several elaborate theoretical schemes in support of the argument that the state was 'withering away'.

Against liberal functionalists, socialists described the state not as the embodiment of the nation but as a set of institutions controlled and manipulated by the ruling élites which they identified as the bourgeoisie. From this point of view, socialists could denounce liberal functionalism as an ideology supporting what appeared in their perspective as the dictatorship of the bourgeoisie, and they could point towards colonialism as supporting evidence. Using international finance data, socialists such as Rudolf Hilferding (1877–1941), Rosa Luxemburg (1871–1919) and Vladimir Il'ich Lenin (1870– 1924)[1] argued that European colonial expansion at the turn of the twentieth century had been triggered by bourgeois capitalists who had looked for the expansion of product markets and opportunities to cash in profits from investments of risk capital in the European colonies.[2]

Moreover, socialists identified World War I as a colonial war and urged their followers to use the war to precipitate the collapse of capitalism. In 1916 Lenin developed this vague demand into tactics of world revolution. He demanded that the suppressed peoples in the colonial peripheries of the world should stand up against their rulers, shake off their yokes by force and force into capitulation the colonial governments and the capitalists supporting them. When Lenin came to power in November 1917, he acted accordingly, pulling Russia out of the war and urging the workers of the world to demand the same from their governments.

But socialism shared a number of crucial features with liberal functionalism. Lenin's theory of world revolution was a case in point. He postulated global interdependencies between colonial centres and colonial peripheries. This postulate implied the perception of the international system as a global entity of its own which demanded positive action in favour of its continuing existence. Its implementation required the advancement and efficient use of communication technologies in order to promote the interaction between the centres and the peripheries. Functionalist supporters of the world peace movement could not have agreed more on these points. Moreover, Lenin identified capitalists as well as workers as global actors and, like functionalists, demanded the promotion of social justice through the advancement of technology. Subsequent socialist international theorists did no more than canonize Lenin's work.

After World War I, functionalists in office took measures against the challenge of socialism. They barred Russia from access to the League of Nations. The League of Nations agreed to admit Russia only after Lenin had enforced the union statute creating the Soviet Union and after a separate treaty of accommodation had been concluded with Germany in 1922.

Ironically, as one of its last acts, the League passed a decision in 1940 which expelled the Soviet Union after the Baltic states had been invaded by the Red Army and forced to join the union.

After World War II, functionalists had no longer the opportunity to confront socialism, whose supporters used the UN Organization as a platform for the articulation of their international theories. Representatives of socialist member states vocalized criticism against colonialism, supported anti-colonial liberation movements and tried to turn the UNO into a forum in which demands for the rights of the so-called Third World could be articulated. As an international theory, socialism became a vehicle for anti-colonialism and was thus warmly received in the newly emerging post-colonial states of Africa and South and Southeast Asia on the eve of and early after their independence.

But, in contradiction to the tradition of internationalism, governments in the newly independent states of Africa and South and Southeast Asia used socialism as an ideology in support of the newly established state institutions over which they had been entrusted to rule. Thus, in these cases, socialism became an instrument for the legitimization of new nation-states which, in fact, were drawn on the institutions that the colonial governments had created. Consequently, the widening appreciation of socialism during the 1950s, 1960s and 1970s did not support the socialist quest for world organization under a revolutionary regime. Instead, most of the governments of the newly independent states did not formally join the socialist camp but the movement of non-aligned states founded in 1955. Therefore, although the governments of the non-aligned states could be expected to support the Soviet Union and its direct allies on crucial issues in the UN, socialists did not fulfil their pledge to restructure the international system.

Nevertheless, in the context of the Cold War, the socialist challenge was taken up by realists in lieu of functionalists. After Kennan and Kaplan, much of the realist theory-making had a direct or indirect anti-socialist sting even though anti-socialism had not belonged to the initial equipment of realist international theory. For one, Carr received much criticism in post-World War II times for having been too soft on socialism.[3]

National Socialism was a radical variant of fascism as the anti-socialist, anti-liberal and anti-democratic ideology to which various European governments as well as non-government movements subscribed during the 1920s, 1930s and early 1940s. In this capacity, Nazism was also the most radical denial of core socialist and functionalist perceptions and assumptions about the international system as well as a challenge of the realist convictions which took root in the western democracies.[4]

Outside Europe, core elements of fascism were traceable in Japanese militarism during the 1930s and early 1940s and – possibly in emulation of German and Japanese precedents – in the Indian subcontinent, Burma and the Indonesian archipelago during World War II.[5] The basic tenet of Nazi international theory was thus a violent rejection of existing international theories. Nazi international theorists, as well as Hitler himself, were eclectics; they picked, usually randomly, bits from existing theories, mixed them and employed them in their struggle against realism. The principal element of Nazi international theory was a radical variant of nationalism as the quest for the unity of the nation as the population of a state.

National Socialism emerged from nineteenth-century biologism. It included the racist belief that certain genetic groups (whereby races and species were usually not distinguished) should display certain physical, psychological and social features of high durability which were held to be inheritable and to shape an individual's body, mind and social behaviour in ways which the individual could not alter.[6] Nazis also availed themselves of evolutionism, compared genetic groups, their bodily physiques, social habits and cultures across the globe and devised ranking schemes of purportedly more or less 'advanced' groups.[7] In combination with racism, evolutionism supported measures of expansion and conquest by allegedly 'superior races' of allegedly 'inferior races'.

Nazism was thus informed by the belief that a nation was or ought to be a genetic group, that it belonged to a compound of closely related genetic groups and that there were hierarchies of allegedly 'superior' and allegedly 'inferior' genetic groups.

Thus, according to Nazism, the unity of a nation was seen as definable in terms of its genetic homogeneity, and each nation was supposed to occupy its purportedly inalterable rank in a worldwide hierarchy.

National Socialism thus proffered the combination of three revisionist ideologies: first, expansionism as the demand that the boundaries of an existing state should be extended to include what was taken to be the entire nation as its population group; secondly, colonialism as a programme for the installation of the government by members of one nation over nations made up from allegedly 'inferior' races; and, thirdly, militant anti-semitism as the justification for the use of military force to destroy, through acts of mass murder, Jews as a group who allegedly jeopardized the genetic homogeneity of a nation.

All three revisionist ideologies had existed in various parts of Europe and elsewhere in the world at times during and after the nineteenth century, but only the Nazis combined all three and turned them into guidelines for government decision-making. Nazis attacked socialists for splitting the nation into classes and heating up class struggles. They blamed functional-ists for having brought about the decline of German influence in the world after World War I, and they accused realists of obstructing the resurrection of Germany to its status as a world power. Because only the latter attack was of practical significance while Nazis held power in Germany, Nazism was primarily a challenger of realism.

Nazi international theory remained confined to the propagation of reactionary strategies. Nazi theorists did not bother to create their own perception of the international system but continued to operate within the framework of biologism. They continued to regard the international system as one single global entity, although they devised strategies to divide the world into three continental blocks.[8] They followed early twentieth-century German criticisms of balance-of-power politics, which they denounced as sinister manipulations, and pledged to strike against the realist concerns for the maintenance of the balance of power.[9]

These reactionary and negative strategies were flawed because they lacked implementability and therefore placed

Nazi politicians in a squeeze: they were forced to search for allies in order to accomplish their revisionist goals, but their choice of allies was seriously limited.[10] After Germany's departure from the League of Nations in 1933, Hitler's government was isolated in Europe, although Mussolini provided diplomatic support. Outside Europe, there was only Japan, but Nazi racism stood against a fully fledged military alliance between Germany and Japan.[11]

Although Japanese militarism, like Nazism, was informed by racist and evolutionist creeds (which were partly borrowed from Germany),[12] the government and the armed forces of Japan displayed little interest in rapprochement with Germany even after Japan had left the League of Nations and faced isolation. In 1933 and 1934 Japanese diplomats had little confidence that Hitler's government would stay in power.[13] The Japanese government was concerned about Hitler's demand for the restitution to German control of the areas in the South Pacific which had been under German colonial rule up to the end of World War I and had been transferred to Japanese control by a League of Nations mandate.

Moreover, the Japanese navy planning staff warned of the strategic danger that rapprochement with Germany would cool down relations with the USA. The Japanese army at that time saw no reason for a military alliance with Germany as the German armed forces were unable to assist the army in its colonial war in China. But, as time went on, Hitler was persuaded to exempt Japan from his racist prejudice and agree to some form of joint agreement, and the initially private initiative of Major General Hiroshi Oshima (1886–1975), who came to Berlin in 1934 to sound the terrain for a military alliance, lured the Japanese army into the belief that a German–Japanese partnership would divert British forces from Asia to Europe and allow the Japanese army to win its war in China.

Such was the thin ice on which the Anti-Comintern Pact was concluded in 1936 as a minimal compromise for the (admitted) political and the (secretly agreed) military cooperation against the Soviet Union. Later supplemented by the strategic Three Powers Pact of September 1940 with Italy to which further countries acceded during World War II, the German–Japanese rapprochement never entailed joint military planning, which was best documented by the failure of the German side to inform its Japanese partners about the conclusion of the Hitler–Stalin Pact of August 1939,[14] but it did entice strategists on the German side to define their long-term goals: to divide the world into a Euro-African block under German rule, an Asian-Pacific block under Japanese rule and an isolated American block.

All that was essentially political map-making without reference to international theory. Nazis remained unaware of the fact that their strategic plan to establish three continental blocks could not possibly be carried out through land warfare in the main, as Hitler thought, but would have required the deployment of substantive naval forces which were not available in Germany. This was so because the Allies used their naval supremacy to force the German armed forces into a naval combat or to give up. As the first choice was impossible, the second outcome was predictable. Nazis, like fascists, were doers, not thinkers. Therefore, their challenge against realism was serious and dangerous not because of any coherence of their international theory but because of their determination to commit themselves and allow others to follow suit in actions that were recognizably unjust and blatantly immoral.

RIVALS OF FUNCTIONALISM AND REALISM: WORLD SYSTEMS THEORIES

Rival theories of functionalism and realism first appeared outside Europe and North America. Their intellectual background was anti-colonialism. Towards the end of the 1950s, mainly Francophone African intellectuals began to urge a new self-confidence of Africans and turned against the cultural impoverishment that European colonial rule had brought about.[15] They also attacked non-traditional indigenous élites who were willing to collaborate and enhance the Europeanization of African cultures in return for their admission to privileged positions in the professions and in government. Their movement was interconnected with the civil rights movement in the USA and in the Caribbean.[16] It produced an ideology of resistance but no fully fledged international theory.

Generating an international theory from a point of view that did not centre upon Europe and North America was left to economists working under the aegis of the UN Economic Commission on Latin America in the early 1960s. Although the 1960s were a period in which high growth rates were projected for Latin America, these scholars tried to determine factors of underdevelopment in their region. They identified the core factor in what they termed structural dependence. They derived this concept from Lenin's theory of world revolution and elaborated it into a dualism of the international division of labour between the capital-accumulating centres and the resource-providing peripheries.

They argued that this international division of labour belonged to the properties of the existing global international system and that it led to the structural dependence of the peripheries on the centres. In the case of Latin America, the structural dependence was taken to have begun with Columbus's voyages. Development thus came to be identified as the process of the reduction of structural dependence in the international system.[17]

Although this so-called *dependencia* theory was initially conceived only for Latin America, it was possible to apply it to other parts of the world and, eventually, to extend it into a form of world systems theory.[18] This came into existence in two variants. One focused on economic, social and political issues, the other on military ones. The first variant is represented in the work of Immanuel Wallerstein (1930–) who began his research in political sociology with work on decolonization in Africa.[19] He then developed his own perception of the international system which he defined as a global system with a division of labour between centres and peripheries. He described two variants of the system which he categorized as world empires and world economies and studied the evolution of world economies from the end of the fifteenth century.

Wallerstein's theory exists in the dual format of a description of the history of the system and of scattered metatheoretical reflections.[20] In these reflections, Wallerstein disclosed that he had conceived the theory as a protest against mainstream social sciences, which was to say that he wished to take issue with functionalists and realists. His pointed opposition to conventional social science approaches allowed him to question a number of assumptions which functionalists and realists would commonly make. Among these assumptions was the functionalist belief that the global international system was a self-sustaining entity with a boundary-maintaining capability of its own.

Wallerstein also produced evidence which disproved the realist assumption that states were paramount actors in the international system. Instead, Wallerstein insisted that economic, social and political changes could entail changes of systemic structures which could transform the international system and the actors in it from the inside and establish temporal as well as spatial boundaries within which an international system existed as a historical phenomenon.

Summing up a discussion of systemic change in the twentieth century which he conceptualized as a power struggle between status-quo oriented and anti-systemic movements, Wallerstein concluded:

> The elements of real power are scattered in many loci. The state-machineries are an important such locus, but far from the only one. We have no quantitative measures of power, but I would guess that state-machineries account for less than half of the world-economy's real power concentrations, and if anything I suspect this estimate is high, not low. Power lies in control of economic institutions. Power lies in the control of veto-structures that have the power to disrupt. Power lies in the control of cultural institutions. Power lies in the [anti-systemic] movements themselves.[21]

One might add that the power of 'state-machineries' would have been even lower in previous centuries. In order to lend more argumentative weight to this onslaught on long-cherished realist convictions, Wallerstein went on to argue that the international system was a transient phenomenon:

> All complex phenomena have their rules, their constraints, their trends or vectors, that is, their structures. Any real

structure (as opposed to imagined structures) has its particularities, due to its genesis, its life history, and its environment, hence has a history which is central to its mode of functioning. The more complex the structure, the more crucial its history. The problem is not to state this as some metaphysical truth, but to manipulate this truth in our study of any real complex phenomenon. My mode of handling this is to conceive the social world as a succession and coexistence of multiple large-scale, long-term entities I call historical systems which have three defining characteristics. They are relatively autonomous, that is, they function primarily in terms of the consequences of processes internal to them. They have time-boundaries, that is, they begin and they end. They have space-boundaries, which, however, can change in the course of their life-history.[22]

Wallerstein's work came too late to receive a critique from functionalists. Realists, however, ignored it perhaps because Wallerstein wrote as a sociologist and not as a political scientist. Nevertheless, his work did receive much attention among social scientists and historians and triggered further research by other scholars.[23] Attempts have been made to apply Wallerstein's approach to older periods and mathematize the centre–periphery relations.[24]

The second variant was more conventional. Its originator, George Modelski (1926–), a political scientist, studied the history of the global international system but took an approach which differed from Wallerstein's in core respects. Modelski was guided by Mahan's realist convictions and confined himself to the analysis of the impact of maritime warfare on the transformation of the international system. He tried to measure a ruler's or government's military potential and political power to conduct international relations across the globe in terms of blue-water naval capability and tried to count the number of available ocean-going vessels at different times and places. To that end he perused secondary literature for available numbers of such ships and constructed chronological tables of leading powers and their main contenders, again beginning late in the fifteenth century.

Modelski believed that a still existing phenomenon called 'the global political system' was 'born (or constructed) about the year 1500' and that 'four states have in turn played a dominant role' in it: Portugal, the Netherlands, Britain and the United States. Portugal and the Netherlands represent one 'long cycle' of about one hundred years each, Britain was paramount in two of them, while the United States dominates the current cycle, a domination which, Modelski believed, would last until 2030. Furthermore, he maintained that each cycle evolved through a similar process, representing an identical sequence of 'basic' events, and argued that, prior to 1500, there were no long cycles of that kind because there was no global world power.

His 'global political system' is held to have been, 'since 1500, a structure whose characteristic medium is the ocean, its vector, the oceanic ship, and its specialized military resource, sea power'. Observations which Modelski described as empirical are taken to show that, within each 'long cycle', the 'world power' was sided by a 'challenger', contesting global world leadership by means of 'global war'. Modelski identified the major challengers as Spain in the first, Britain in the second, France in the third, Germany in the fourth and the Soviet Union in the fifth cycle.[25] Given the absence of evidence adduced from primary sources, it is difficult to assess what Modelski might have wished to consider as empirical in his observations. At least his prediction concerning the future behaviour of the fifth cycle cannot be termed empirical, partly for logical reasons but also because it rests, erroneously as everyone now knows, on no more than the speculative assumption that the fifth cycle would behave like its four predecessors.

Modelski's theory came along as a heroic attempt to award a temporal dimension to the East–West conflict between the USA and the Soviet Union at the time of the Cold War. He rightly deplored the allocation of substantive resources to the activities that he categorized as global warfare in the light of the transience of the relative positions of leaders and challengers in these struggles and their ultimate senselessness. However, this attack on realist convictions was far from convincing in its own right, because realists could argue that the conflicts between rivals for global leadership, whenever they seemed to have occurred, were not due to some innate lust for war in either of the contending parties but because the parties were simply there and either tried to preserve the balance of power or were committed to the goal of its destruction.[26]

Modelski's theory has been elaborated in recent years as subsequent authors have extended the timeframe of the theory backwards to the Middle Ages and have taken into consideration land warfare.[27] Modelski's concept of global warfare as a clash of leading powers and main contenders has been grafted onto studies on specific issues, such as US–Japan relations.[28] But the reception of Modelski's theory has lagged far behind that of Wallerstein's.

NEO-FUNCTIONALISM AND NEO-INSTITUTIONALISM AS VARIANTS OF FUNCTIONALISM

After World War II, functionalists recast their attention from the global to the regional level. The wartime carnage brought back on to the agenda older schemes for regional integration in Europe and the North Atlantic although, under Cold War conditions, European models of regional integration remained dominant. During the 1950s and 1960s, these neo-functionalist scholars in the USA, among them Karl Wolfgang Deutsch (1912–1992), Amitai Etzioni (1929–), Ernest B. Haas (1924–) and Joseph Nye (1937–), devoted themselves to the study of ongoing regional integration processes at the three levels of transatlantic communication, the establishment of regional institutions in Western Europe, East Africa and Latin America and the unification of sovereign states.[29]

The purpose of these studies was to determine the general conditions of success and failure of regional integration processes and to assess the amount of political support deemed necessary for the operation of such military alliances as the North Atlantic Treaty Organization (NATO). Entrenched in the functionalist tradition, neo-functionalist students of regional integration processes took what they identified as nation-states as the starting points of these processes and regarded these states as political systems with a boundary-maintaining capability of their own. As neo-functionalists pitched the nation-states against institutions of regional integration, they had to conceptualize regional integration as processes of the destruction of existing nation-states. Consequently, they saw their foremost task to be devising bureaucratic strategies of luring purportedly unwilling governments of nation-states and their electorates into regional integration processes. These strategies were modelled upon the European experience.

In the 1950s, the prospects for success of regional integration processes leading to the creation of regional institutions above nation-states seemed promising. Hence, neo-functionalists delved in technical details and recommended a myriad of tactical measures which could put into operation what they described as 'spillover effects'. These effects were to enhance an automatism by which cross-national cooperation among governments would, even against the will of those operating and supporting them, generate a need for institutions in charge of matters related to the cooperation. These institutions would then promote regional integration in their own interest. Hence, the recognizability of such 'spillover effects' emerged as the single most important criterion for the measurement of success in regional integration processes.[30]

When, against the theoretical expectation, few 'spillover effects' materialized during the 1960s and early 1970s, theorists quickly cast overboard their initial optimism and began to specify the reasons for what they perceived as failures of regional integration processes. Vis-à-vis Latin America and East Africa, these projections turned into self-fulfilling prophecies when they began to impact on political decision-makers. In Latin America, existing regional institutions became inactive or folded due to political bickering among governments over the absence of 'spillover effects', the shakiness of government institutions and the established vested interest of ruling élites.[31] In East Africa, the East African Community suffered from inertia, became inactive and was eventually dissolved because of disagreement among the participating governments of Kenya, Tanzania and Uganda over the measurement of relative gains and losses and because the European colonial governments had bequeathed to the governments of the newly independent states the dual task of developing regional and state institutions simultaneously.[32]

In 1975 neo-functionalists came to the conclusion that regional integration theory was 'obsolescent',[33] and before long it vanished from the scene. But the bureaucratic mechanism of the 'spillover effects' has taken root in the minds of practitioners. Major reforms of the European regional institutions, such as the Single European Act of 1987, the Maastricht Treaty of 1992 and the decision in 1998 to introduce the euro as a second currency were all justified as means to create 'spillover effects', to enlarge the competence of regional institutions and to advance regional integration in Europe with their help.[34]

In the 1980s, theorists operating in the functionalist tradition returned to the study of the international system and investigated non-state actors, international organizations, institutions and regimes.[35] These so-called neo-liberal institutionalists opposed the realist assumption that the international system was anarchic; pointed towards the growing network of organizations and institutions above the sovereign nation-state; and drew attention to the fact that the effectiveness of decisions made by governments of sovereign nation-states was increasingly being curtailed by the activities of non-government organizations (NGOs), multinational corporations (MNCs) and other non-state actors.[36]

These theorists sharply opposed the realist dogma that states were the only actors of significance in the international system, and predicted that states were on the retreat against non-state actors.[37] Their view was further advanced into the constructivist supposition that the international system has a self-organizing capability and may create its own rules autonomously.[38]

NEO-REALISM AS A VARIANT OF REALISM

War and the state in their interconnectedness with the international system remained at the core of realist interest.[39] During the 1950s, 1960s and 1970s, realists conducted a number of large-scale empirical research projects on the beginning and the correlates of war.[40] These projects were conducted for the purpose of confirming essentials of realist theory, namely that states were the sole actors of significance in the international system, that the international system was anarchic and that, in one way or another, war was the result of breakdown of some sort of balance of power. It was left to Kenneth Waltz (1924–) to cast these convictions into an ahistorical systematic general international theory, which was published in 1979 and which remained the only realist synthesis of international theory throughout the 1980s.[41]

Waltz was more concerned than previous realists about change in systems, although these concerns came into play only when he tried to argue against systems change and in favour of systemic stability:

> Anarchic systems are transformed only by changes in organizing principle and by consequential changes in the number of their principal parties. To say that an international-political system is stable means two things: first, that it remains anarchic; second, that no consequential variation takes place in the number of principal parties that constitute the system. 'Consequential' variations in number are changes of number that lead to different expectations about the effect of structure on units. The stability of the system, so long as it remains anarchic, is then closely linked with the fate of its principal members. The close link is established by the relations of changes in number of great powers to the transformation of the system.[42]

Waltz's first proposition that, in perceived anarchic systems, systemic stability is maintained as long as anarchy prevails, is a simple extension of the systems theoretical definition of open systems as self-help organisms, without much explanatory value in itself. Waltz's second proposition is informed by realist balance-of-power theory and the biologistic conviction that the international system demands active support for its stability.

Against this background Waltz created a mysticism of numbers:

> Systems of two have qualities distinct from systems of three or more. What is the defining difference? The answer is found in the behavior required of parties in self-help (i.e. anarchic) systems: namely, balancing. Balancing is differently done in multi- and bipolar systems . . . Where two powers contend, imbalances can be righted only by their internal

efforts. With more than two, shifts in alignment provide an additional means of adjustment, adding flexibility to the system.[43]

The argument rests on the ancient scales model of the balance of power and reads like a recast in metatheoretical diction of the point which Waltz had previously raised in support of his controversial Cold War thesis about the 'stability of the bipolar world'.[44] In essence, the argument had consisted of two points: (1) that the bipolar system does not require joint efforts for the maintenance of systemic stability, whereas, in a multipolar system, the interacting units have to combine their respective efforts through alliances in order to accomplish stability; and (2) bipolarity is preferable over multipolarity because alliance-making subjects the stability of the system to the contingencies and vicissitudes of partial decision-making processes within the governments of the units in the system.

However, the argument runs contrary to one core assumption on which systems theory has been based. For systems theory has ascribed the stability of systems to boundary-maintaining capabilities and, consequently, if bipolarity does not require joint efforts for the maintenance of its stability, it merely coordinates two separate entities and does not qualify as a system. Therefore, what Waltz advocated with his mysticism of numbers was, as it were, the suggestion to measure weights without scales.

The context of functionalism and realism in the twentieth century exemplified the interconnectedness of theory and practice, even though the division of labour between theorists and practitioners had never before been clearer. The challengers against functionalism and realism were predominantly practitioners: Nazis never bothered to elaborate a coherent international theory, and socialists did hardly more than canonize Lenin's work. The rivals to functionalists and realists were predominantly academic theorists and so were those who proposed variants. Nevertheless, some theorists were willing to make their work applicable for practitioners, and some practitioners did not shy away from theorizing.[45]

Surprisingly, much of the context of functionalism and realism was theory drawn on history. Many theorists went to history for empirical data, usually related to Europe and commonly from times since the fifteenth century. However, with the exception of the *fin de siècle* realist students of the history of the balance of power, theorists did not dig down to primary sources, but relied on the work done by historians.

Further Reading

ANTHOLOGIES

Forsyth, M. G., H. M. A. Keens-Soper and P. Savigear, eds, *The Theory of International Relations: Selected Texts from Gentili to Treitschke* (London, 1970); the editors print originals and translations from widely known works by Gentili, Grotius, Vattel, Rousseau, Kant, Brougham, Gentz, Cobden and Heinrich von Treitschke

Luard, Evan, ed., *Basic Texts in International Relations* (London, 1992); a random selection of policy-related texts, some with relevance to theory, mainly from the nineteenth and twentieth centuries; introduction and brief comments by the editor

Viotti, Paul R. and Mark V. Kauppi, ed., *International Relations Theory: Realism, Pluralism, Globalism* (London, New York, 1987); a narrow selection of theory-related texts from ancient Greek times to the twentieth century, with an emphasis on the twentieth century; introduction, comments and extensive bibliography by the editors; now somewhat dated

Wright, Moorhead, ed., *Theory and Practice of the Balance of Power 1486–1914* (London, Totowa, NJ, 1975); a skilful selection of key texts dealing with assessments of power in international relations, mainly from the seventeenth, eighteenth and nineteenth centuries; introduction, brief comments and short bibliography by the editor

HISTORIES OF INTERNATIONAL THEORY

Brown, Chris, *International Relations Theory: New Normative Approaches* (New York, London, 1992); combines a valuable sketch of the history with a penetrating analysis of recent developments of international theories

Clark, Ian and Iver B. Neumann, eds, *Classical Theories of International Relations* (Basingstoke, London, 1996); a collection of masterly essays on well-known authors, namely Hobbes, Grotius, Kant, Vitoria, Rousseau, Smith, Burke, Hegel, Gentz and Vattel; focus on the authors

Griffiths, Martin, *Fifty Key Thinkers in International Relations* (London, New York, 1999); provides brief biographies and summaries of the work of a variety of mainly twentieth-century theorists of international relations, grouping them into the categories of realism, liberalism, radical/critical theory, theory of international society, international organization, postmodernism, gender and international relations, historical sociology theories of the state as well as theories of nations, without any indication of the criteria for selection

Hinsley, Francis Harry, *Power and the Pursuit of Peace: Theory and Practice in the History of Relations between States* (Cambridge, 1963); an authoritative survey of key international theories, combined with a brief account of the history of international relations in Europe, mainly during the nineteenth and twentieth centuries

Knutsen, Torbjorn, L., *A History of International Relations Theory*, 2nd edn (Manchester, New York, 1997; first published 1992); covers the medieval and modern 'West'; more an annotated list of works on various aspects of international relations than a history

Neumann, Iver B. and Ole Waever, eds, *The Future of International Relations* (London, New York, 1997); this collection of well-informed essays reports on the work of Kenneth Waltz, John Vincent, Robert Keohane and Robert Gilpin, but focuses on the work of Hayward Alker, Bertrand Badie, James Der Derian, Jean Bethke Elshtain, Nicholas Onuf, Robert Walker and Alexander Wendt

Thompson, Kenneth W., *Schools of Thought in International Relations: Interpreters, Issues, and Morality* (Baton Rouge, London, 1996); despite its subtitle a personal account of scholars whose work has contributed to the study of international relations during the twentieth century; emphasis on North America

References

INTRODUCTION

1 Francesco Guicciardini, 'Storia d'Italia', *Opere*, ed. Vittorio di Caprariis (Milan, Naples, 1961), p. 374. The English translation follows Sidney Alexander's with some alterations. Alexander's translation has been edited by: Moorhead Wright, ed., *Theory and Practice of the Balance of Power 1486–1914* (London, Totowa, NJ, 1975), p. 9.

2 Alberico Gentili, *De jure belli libri tres*, vol. II [Hanau, 1598], (Hanau, 1612), p. 65. The English translation follows John C. Rolfe's, printed in Wright, ed., *Theory*, pp. 13–14, with some alterations.

3 Ludwig Martin Kahle, *La balance de l'Europe considerée comme la règle de la paix et de la guerre* (Berlin, Göttingen, 1744), pp. 39–40.

4 Georg Schwarzenberger, *Power Politics: An Introduction to the Study of International Relations* (London, 1941), p. 125 (4th edn, London, 1964).

5 For twentieth-century definitions of power see Bertrand Russell, *Power: A New Social Analysis* (London, 1938), p. 25; Dennis H. Wrong, *Power: Its Forms, Bases, and Uses*, reissue (Oxford, 1988), p. 2 (first published Oxford, 1979).

6 In the context of this book, explanatory theories will be grouped under descriptive theories. This has been done because, in international relations, theories by necessity take into account long processes and depend on descriptive statements about the world. On the debate on explanation in the history of international relations see Harald Kleinschmidt, 'How and to What End Do We Study the History of International Relations?', *Rekishi Jinrui (History and Anthropology)*, xxv (1997), pp. 3–21.

7 See Paul R. Viotti and Mark V. Kauppi, *International Relations Theory: Realism, Pluralism, Globalism* (London, New York, 1987), p. 1. For a wider definition see Kalevi Jaako Holsti, *International Politics*, 6th edn (Englewood Cliffs, 1992), p. 10.

8 Mary Douglas, *Natural Symbols*, new edn (London, New York, 1996), pp. 54–68 (first published London, New York, 1970), suggested similar but not identical categories.

9 See Jeremy M. Black, *Maps and History: Constructing Images of the Past* (New Haven, London, 1997).

ONE · RELIGIOUS UNIVERSALISM IMPOSED

1 Augustine, *De Civitate Dei*, cap XVI/17 (Turnhout, 1955) p. 521. Still in the early fifteenth century, Pierre d'Ailly, *Ymago mundi*, cap. V, ed. Edmond Buron, vol. 1 (Paris, 1930), p. 188, held the opinion that the

ecumene was permeable and that it was possible to walk through it in 1,570 days.

2 See Adso of Montier-en-Der, *Epistola Adsonis Monachi ad Gerbergam Reginam de ortv et tempore Antichristi*, ed. Daniel Verhelst (Turnhout, 1976), pp. 25–8.

3 On the concept of universal rule in the Middle Ages see Othmar Hageneder, 'Weltherrschaft im Mittelalter', *Mitteilungen des Instituts für Österreichische Geschichtsforschung*, XLIII (1985), pp. 257–78.

4 The best early description of the *ecumene*, and one that became a standard reference text throughout the Middle Ages, is by Paulus Orosius, *Historiarum adversum paganos libri VII*, cap. I/2, ed. Carl Zangemeister (Vienna, 1886), pp. 9–40 (reprinted New York, 1966).

5 See on the *mappaemundi*: Jörn-Geerd Arentzen, *Imago mundi cartographica* (Munich, 1984); Anna Dorothee von den Brincken, *Fines Terrae* (Hanover, 1992); Patrick Gautier Dalché, *Géographie et culture: La représentation de l'espace du Ve au XIIe siècle* (Aldershot, 1997); J. B. Harley and David Woodward, eds, *The History of Cartography*, vol. 1 (Chicago, London, 1987); Hartmut Kugler and E. Michael, eds, *Ein Weltbild vor Columbus: Die Ebstorfer Weltkarte* (Weinheim, 1991); William Graham Lister Randles, *De la terre plate au globe terrestre* (Paris, 1980); Rudolf Simek, *Altnordische Kosmographie* (Berlin, New York, 1990); David Woodward, 'Reality, Symbolism, Time, and Space in Medieval World Maps', *Annals of the Association of American Geographers*, LXXV (1985), pp. 510–21.

6 For the medieval literature on paradise see Klaus H. Börner, *Auf der Suche nach dem irdischen Paradies* (Frankfurt, 1984); Reinhold R. Grimm, *Paradisus coelestis: Paradisus terrestris. Zur Auslegungsgeschichte des Paradieses im Abendland bis um 1200* (Munich, 1977).

7 On the medieval theories of the *translatio imperii* see Werner Goez, *Translatio imperii. Ein Beitrag zur Geschichte des Geschichtsdenkens und der politischen Theorie im Mittelalter und in der frühen Neuzeit* (Tübingen, 1958).

8 Beda, *Opera de temporibus*, ed. Charles William Jones (Cambridge, MA, 1943).

9 On millenarian creeds and early medieval concepts of time see Richard Kenneth Emmerson, *Antichrist in the Middle Ages* (Seattle, 1981); Daniel F. Callahan, 'Ademar of Chabannes, Millennial Fears and the Development of Western Anti-Judaism', *Journal of Ecclesiastical History*, XLVI (1995), pp. 19–35; Johannes Fried, 'Endzeiterwartung um die Jahrtausendwende', *Deutsches Archiv für Erforschung des Mittelalters*, XLV (1989), pp. 381–473; Henri Focillon, *L'an Mil* (Paris, 1952); Robert B.C. Huygens, 'Un témoin de la crainte de l'an 1000: La lettre sur les Hongrois', *Latomus*, XV (1956), pp. 225–38; Robert Konrad, *De ortu et tempore Antichristi. Antichristvorstellungen und Geschichtsbild des Abtes Adso von Montier-en-Der* (Kallmünz, 1964); Bernard McGinn, *Visions of the End* (New York, 1979); McGinn, 'Awaiting the End. Research in Medieval Apocalypticism', *Mediaevalia et humanistica*, n.s. XI (1982), pp. 263–89; Horst Dieter Rauh, *Das Bild des Antichrist im Mittelalter*, 2nd edn (Münster, 1978); Hildegard L. C. Tristram, *Sex aetates mundi. Die*

Weltzeitalter bei den Angelsachsen und den Iren (Heidelberg, 1985); Daniel Verhelst, 'La préhistoire des conceptions d'Adson concernant l'Antichrist', *Recherches de théologie ancienne et médiévale*, XL (1973), pp. 52–103.

10 On early medieval methods of time measurement see Gustav Bilfinger, *Die mittelalterlichen Horen und die modernen Stunden* (Stuttgart, 1892; reprint Vacluz, 1997); Gerhard Dohrn-van Rossum, *Geschichte der Stunde* (Munich, Vienna, 1992; English version: Chicago, London, 1997).

11 On medieval experiences of terror see Claude Carozzi and Hélène Taviani Carozzi, *La fin des temps*. *Terreurs et prophéties au Moyen Age* (Paris, 1982); Claude Carozzi, *Weltuntergang und Seelenheil* (Frankfurt, 1996); August Nitschke, 'Die ungleichen Tiere der Sonne', *Festschrift für Wilhelm Messerer zum 60. Geburtstag* (Cologne, 1980), pp. 21–45.

12 On medieval concepts of groups see Ulrich Meyer, *Soziales Handeln im Zeichen des 'Hauses'* (Göttingen, 1998); Otto Gerhard Oexle, 'Gruppen in der Gesellschaft', *Frühmittelalterliche Studien*, XXVIII (1994), pp. 410–23; Oexle, 'Soziale Gruppen in der Ständegesellschaft. Lebensformen des Mittelalters und ihre historischen Wirkungen', *Die Repräsentation der Gruppen*, ed. Otto Gerhard Oexle and Andrea von Hülsen-Esch (Göttingen, 1998), pp. 9–44.

13 The late-seventh-century list of place-names known as the 'Tribal Hidage' lists, side by side, names of places whose formation suggests that the settlements were established by kin groups, neighbourhood groups, groups which were established through a kind of contract between a leader and a band of retainers, and groups whose members accepted for themselves as binding some political tradition and structure of government. See Wendy Davies and Hayo Vierck, 'The Contexts of Tribal Hidage', *Frühmittelalterliche Studien*, VIII (1974), pp. 230–4.

14 For a recent reassessment of early medieval cults of saints see Robert Folz, *Les saints rois du Moyen Age en Occident* (Brussels, 1984); Folz, *Les saintes reines du Moyen Age en Occident* (Brussels, 1992); Susan J. Ridyard, *The Royal Saints of Anglo-Saxon England* (Cambridge, 1988), pp. 243–52.

15 Raban Maur, 'De universo', cap. XVI/2, J.-P. Migne, ed., *Patrologiae cursus completus. Series Latina*, vol. CXI (Paris, 1852), col. 437.

16 Cf. Johannes Fried, '*Gens* und *regnum*. Wahrnehmungs- und Deutungskategorien politischen Wandels im früheren Mittelalter', *Sozialer Wandel im Mittelalter*, ed. Jürgen Miethke and Klaus Schreiner (Sigmaringen, 1994), pp. 73–104; Rolf Hachmann, *Die Goten und Skandinavien* (Berlin, 1970), pp. 279–389; Reinhard Wenskus, *Sächsischer Stammesadel und fränkischer Reichsadel* (Göttingen, 1976).

17 Bishop Gregory of Tours, the late-sixth-century historiographer of the Frankish kingdom, claimed that there was some kind of recognition of the authority of the King of the Franks by the emperors in Byzantium and that King Clovis established his capital at Paris; see Gregory of Tours, *Libri Historiarum Decem*, cap. II/38, ed. Bruno Krusch and Wilhelm Levison (Hanover, 1951), pp. 88–9.

18 On Byzantine–Western relations in the early Middle Ages see Evangelos Chrysos, 'Byzantine Diplomacy AD 300–800', *Byzantine Diplomacy*, ed. John Shepard and S. Franklin (Aldershot, 1992), pp. 25–39; Chrysos,

'Perceptions of the International Community of States during the
Middle Ages', *Ethnogenese und Überlieferung*, ed. Karl Brunner and
Brigitte Merta (Vienna, 1994), pp. 392–407; Karl Hauck, 'Von einer spä-
tantiken Randkultur zum karolingischen Europa', *Frühmittelalterliche
Studien*, I (1967), pp. 3–93; Michael McCormick, 'Clovis at Tours:
Byzantine Public Ritual and the Origins of Medieval Ruler Symbolism',
Das Reich und die Barbaren, ed. Evangelos Chrysos and Alexander
Schwarcz (Vienna, 1989), pp. 155–80.

19 Edited by Andreas Thiel, *Epistolae Romanorum Pontificum Genuinae*, vol. I
(Braunsberg, 1868), pp. 349–58, at pp. 350–1.

20 On the reception of Pope Gelasius's letter see Hartmut Hoffman, 'Die
zwei Schwerter', *Deutsches Archiv für Erforschung des Mittelalters* xx
(1964), pp. 78–114; Lotte Knabe, *Die gelasianische Zweigewaltentheorie bis
zum Ende des Investiturstreits* (Berlin, 1936; reprint, Vaduz, 1965).

21 St Augustine, *De civitate Dei*, cap. XIX/7–13, pp. 671–80. Cf. Augustine,
Quaestionum in Heptateuchum libri VII, cap. VI/10 (Turnhout, 1958),
pp. 318–19.

22 On Augustine's philosophy of peace see Harald Fuchs, *Augustin und der
antike Friedensgedanke* (Berlin, 1926; reprint, Berlin, Zurich, 1965). Louis
J. Swift, 'Augustine on War and Killing. Another View', *Harvard
Theological Review*, LXVI (1973), pp. 369–83.

23 On the meaning of the word *historia* see Laetitia Boehm, 'Der wis-
senschaftstheoretische Ort der historia im früheren Mittelalter',
Speculum historiale (Festschrift für Johannes Spörl), ed. Boehm, Clemens
Bauer and Max Müller (Freiburg, Munich, 1965), pp. 663–93; Boehm,
Geschichtsdenken, Bildungsgeschichte, Wissenschaftsorganisation, ed. Gert
Melville, Rainer A. Müller and Winfried Müller (Berlin, 1996); František
Graus, *Lebendige Vergangenheit. Überlieferung im Mittelalter und die
Vorstellungen vom Mittelalter* (Cologne, Vienna, 1975); Franz Josef
Schmale, *Funktion und Formen mittelalterlicher Geschichtsschreibung*
(Darmstadt, 1985).

24 Eusebius of Caesarea, *Chronicon*, J.-P. Migne, ed., *Patrologiae cursus completus, Series Graeca*, vol. XIX (Paris, 1857), col. 383; Orosius, *Historiae*,
cap. I/1, pp. 3–8.

25 On Orosius see Hans-Werner Goetz, *Die Geschichtstheologie des Orosius*
(Darmstadt, 1980).

26 Bede, *Historia ecclesiastica gentis Anglorum*, cap. v/24, ed. Bertram
Colgrave, R.A.B. Mynors (Oxford, 1969), p. 566. Bede provided a defini-
tion of history similar to that given by Isidore of Seville, *Etymologiae*, cap.
I/41, ed. W. M. Lindsay (Oxford, 1911).

27 On Bede's historiography see Walter Goffart, *Narrators of Barbarian
History* (Princeton, 1988), pp. 235–328; Antonia Gransden, 'Bede's
Reputation as an Historian in Medieval England', *Journal of Ecclesiastical
History*, XXXII (1981), pp. 397–425; Glenn Olsen, 'Bede as Historian',
Journal of Ecclesiastical History, XXXIII (1982), pp. 519–30; Roger Ray,
'Bede's *Vera lex historiae*', *Speculum*, LV (1980), pp. 1–21.

28 Likewise, Isidore of Seville, Jordanes and Gregory of Tours could take
the view that the theatre of their histories was the territory of the Roman
Empire when they wrote their histories of the Visigoths, Ostrogoths and

Franks in the sixth century. See Isidore of Seville, 'Historia Gothorvm, Wandalorvm, Sveborvm ad AD DCXXIV', ed. Theodor Mommsen, *Monumenta Germaniae Historica, Auctores antiquissimi*, vol. XI (Berlin, 1894), pp. 241–303; Jordanes, 'De origine actibvsqve Getarvm', ed. Theodor Mommsen, *Iordanis Romana et Getica* (Berlin, 1882), pp. 53–138; Gregory, *Historiae*.

29 On these aspects of Bede's work see Charles William Jones, *Saints' Lives and Chronicles in Early England* (Ithaca, 1947), pp. 31–50; Jones, *Bede, the Schools and the Computus* (Aldershot, 1994).

30 Cassiodore, *Variarvm libri XII*, cap. XI/1, ed. Åke J. Fridh (Turnhout, 1973), p. 424.

31 On early medieval genealogies see David N. Dumville, *Histories and Pseudo-histories of the Insular Middle Ages* (Aldershot, 1990); Karl Hauck, 'Lebensnormen und Kultmythen in germanischen Stammes- und Herrschergenealogien', *Saeculum*, VI (1955), pp. 186–223; Georg Scheibelreiter, 'Zur Typologie und Kritik genealogischer Quellen', *Archivum*, XXXVII (1992), pp. 1–26.

32 See on the early medieval *memoria* and the organization of early medieval proprietary churches: Otto Gerhard Oexle, 'Memoria und Memorialüberlieferung im früheren Mittelalter', *Frühmittelalterliche Studien*, X (1976), pp. 70–95; David Rollason, 'The Shrines of Saints in Later Anglo-Saxon England', *The Anglo-Saxon Church. Papers on History, Architecture and Archaeology in Honour of Dr Harold McCarter Taylor*, ed. L. A. S. Butler and R. K. Morris (London, 1986), pp. 32–43; Karl Schmid, *Gebetsgedenken und adliges Selbstverständnis im Mittelalter* (Sigmaringen, 1983).

33 Dhuoda, *Manuel pour mon fils* [841–3], cap. III/1, ed. Pierre Riché (Paris, 1975), p. 136. Cf. Raban Maur, 'Liber de reuerentia filiorum erga patres et erga reges' [834], *Monumenta Germaniae Historica, Epistolae Karolini aevi*, vol. III, ed. Ernst Dümmler *et al.* (Hanover, 1898–9), pp. 403–5.

34 *Widsith*, ed. Kemp Malone (Copenhagen, 1962), pp. 23–7.

35 For Scandinavian analogues see Margaret Schlauch, 'Widsith, Vithförull, and Some Other Analogues', *Publications of the Modern Language Association of America*, XLVI (1931), pp. 969–87.

36 See Heinrich Beck *et al.*, (Art.) 'Handel', *Reallexikon der Germanischen Altertumskunde*, 2nd ed., vol XIII (Berlin, 1999), pp. 497–593; Gert Hatz, *Handel und Verkehr zwischen dem Deutschen Reich und Schweden in der späten Wikingerzeit* (Lund, 1974); Richard Hodges and Brian Hobley, eds, *The Rebirth of Towns in the West AD 700–1050* (London, 1988); Stéphane Lebecq, *Marchands et navigateurs frisons du haut Moyen Age*, 2 vols (Lille, 1983); Carsten Müller-Boysen, *Kaufmannsschutz und Handelsrecht im frühmittelalterlichen Nordeuropa* (Neumünster, 1990); Adriaan Verhulst, *Rural and Urban Aspects of Early Medieval North-West Europe* (Aldershot, 1992).

37 Adam of Bremen, *Gesta Hammaburgensis ecclesiae pontificum*, cap. I/60, ed. Bernhard Schmeidler (Hanover, 1917), p. 58; Rimbert, *Vita Anskarii*, caps 19, 20, ed. Georg Waitz (Hanover, 1884), pp. 39–46.

38 The seventh-century chronicles which were attributed in the sixteenth century to Fredegar, 'Chronicon', cap. IV/48, IV/68, ed. Bruno Krusch,

Fredegarii et aliorum Chronica. Vitae Sanctorum (Hanover, 1888), pp. 144–5, 154–5, contain a report on a merchant named Samo who became a ruler among Slavs and died around AD 660. The report makes it clear that, while Samo acted on his own, the King of the Franks demanded compensation for murdered merchants during wars between himself and Slavs. This would imply that some merchants did in fact receive protection from rulers. See Wolfgang H. Fritze, *Untersuchungen zur frühslavischen und frühfränkischen Geschichte*, PhD. Diss. (University of Marburg, 1951; reprint, Bern, Frankfurt, 1993). On migrant producers see Egil Bakka, 'On the Beginning of Salin's Style I in England', *Universitetet i Bergen Årbok* (1958), pp. 1–83; Sonia Chadwick Hawkes and Marc Pollard, 'Gold Bracteates from Sixth-Century Graves in Kent', *Frühmittelalterliche Studien*, xv (1981), pp. 317–70.

39 The best recent summary of these events is in Johannes Fried, *Der Weg in die Geschichte: Die Ursprünge Deutschlands bis 1024* (Berlin, 1994), pp. 244–332.

40 *Annales regni Francorum*, ed. Friedrich Kurze (Hanover, 1895), pp. 136–7.

TWO · UNIVERSALISM CONTESTED AND SECULARIZED

1 The basic texts are in Ernst Sackur, ed., *Sybillinische Texte und Forschungen* (Halle, 1891; reprint ed. Raoul Manselli, Turin, 1976); *Le livre de Sibile de Philippe de Thaon*, ed. H. Shields (London, 1979).

2 *Blickling Homilies*, xi, ed. R. Morris (Oxford, 1874–80), pp. 117–19.

3 The number given in the text as 3,000 years is usually understood as an error for 6,000.

4 Robert B. C. Huygens, 'Un témoin de la crainte de l'an 1000. La lettre sur les Hongrois', *Latomus*, xv (1956), pp. 229–31.

5 Byrhtferth, 'De sexta etate', Byrhtferth, *Manual*, ed. S. J. Crawford (Oxford, 1929), pp. 238–40.

6 Ademar of Chabannes, *Chronique*, cap. III/46–7, ed. Jules Chavanon (Paris, 1897), pp. 168–71. Similarly: Abbo of Fleury, 'Liber apologeticus', J.-P. Migne, ed., *Patrologiae cursus completus. Series Latina*, vol. cxxxix (Paris, 1880), cols 471–2.

7 Benzo of Alba, 'De Christo dixit regnum quoque stemata scripsit', Benzo, *Panegyricus*, cap. I/15, ed. Georg Heinrich Pertz, *Monumenta Germaniae Historica, Scriptores*, vol. xi (Hanover, 1854), p. 605. On the early history of the crusading idea see Carl Erdmann, *Die Entstehung des Kreuzzugsgedankens* (Stuttgart, 1935; reprint, Stuttgart, 1955).

8 On high and late medieval concepts of time see Q. F. Beemelmans, 'Zeit und Ewigkeit nach Thomas von Aquin', *Beiträge zur Geschichte der Philosophie des Mittelalters*, xvii (1914), pp. 1–64; Arno Borst, *Computus, Zeit und Zahl in der Geschichte Europas* (Berlin, 1990); Carlo Maria Cipolla, *Clocks and Culture 1300–1700* (London, 1967); Richard Dales, 'Time and Eternity in the Thirteenth Century', *Journal of the History of Ideas*, xlix (1981), pp. 27–45; Pierre Maurice Marie Duhem, 'Le temps et le mouvement selon les scholastiques', *Revue de philosophie*, xxiii (1913), pp. 453–78; xxiv/1 (1914), pp. 5–15, 136–49, 225–41, 361–80, 470–88; xxiv/2 (1914), pp. 104–51; Gillian R. Evans, 'Time and Eternity:

Boethian and Augustinian Sources of the Thought of the Late Eleventh and Early Twelfth Centuries', *Classical Folia*, XXXI (1977), pp. 105–18; David Saul Landes, *Revolution in Time. Clocks and the Making of the Modern World* (Cambridge, MA, London, 1984); Jacques Le Goff, 'Temps de l'Eglise et temps du marchand', *Annales*, XV (1960), pp. 417–33, reprinted in Le Goff, *Pour un autre Moyen Age* (Paris, 1977), pp. 46–65; Le Goff, 'Le temps du travail dans la "crise" du XIVe siècle', *Le Moyen Age*, LXIX (1963), pp. 597–615; Anneliese Maier, 'Die Subjektivierung der Zeit in der scholastischen Philosophie', *Philosophia naturalis*, I (1950), pp. 361–98; Maier, 'Scholastische Diskussionen über die Wesensbestimmung der Zeit', *Scholastik*, XXVI (1951), pp. 520–56; Augustin Mansion, 'La théorie aristotélienne du temps chez les péripatéciens médiévaux', *Revue néoscolastique de philosophie*, XXXVI (1934), pp. 275–307; J. D. North, 'Monasticism and the First Mechanical Clocks', *The Study of Time*, ed. Julius Thomas Fraser and N. Lawrence (New York, Berlin, 1972), pp. 381–98; Michael Walter, 'Kirchenmusik und Zeitrechnung im Mittelalter', *Mediävistik*, V (1992), pp. 169–86; Ernst Zinner, *Aus der Frühzeit der Räderuhr* (Munich, Düsseldorf, 1954).

9 Otto of Freising, *Historia de duabus civitatibus*, cap. II/51, ed. Adolf Hofmeister (Hanover, 1912), pp. 128–9.

10 See David Parsons, ed., *Tenth-Century Studies* (Chichester, 1975).

11 A good case has been reported from Saxony by Altfrid, 'Vita Liudgeri', ed. Georg Heinrich Pertz, *Monumenta Germaniae Historica, Scriptores*, vol. II (Hanover, 1829), p. 406. On this kin group see Karl Schmid, 'Die "Liudgeriden". Erscheinung und Problematik einer Adelsfamilie', *Geschichtsschreibung und geistiges Leben: Festschrift für Heinz Löwe*, ed. Karl Hauck and Hubert Mordek (Cologne, Vienna, 1978), pp. 71–101.

12 See Georges Duby, *Hommes et structures du Moyen Age* (The Hague, Paris, 1973); Hagen Keller, *Adelsherrschaft und städtische Gesellschaft in Oberitalien. 9.–12. Jahrhundert* (Tübingen, 1979).

13 See Hans Patze, ed., *Der deutsche Territorialstaat im 14. Jahrhundert* (Sigmaringen, 1970); Patze, ed., *Die Burgen im deutschen Sprachraum* (Sigmaringen, 1976); Ernst Pitz, *Europäisches Städtewesen und Bürgertum* (Darmstadt, 1991); Dietmar Willoweit, *Rechtsgrundlagen der Territorialherrschaft* (Cologne, Vienna, 1975).

14 The demand was made explicit through the use of the metaphor of the body politic which became popular in the twelfth century. The metaphor suggested that polities were coherent entities with a hierarchically stratified population under a recognizable uniform government. See John of Salisbury, *Policraticus*, cap. V/6, VI/1-21, ed. C. J. Webb (Cambridge, 1909), vol. I, pp. 298–307, vol. II, pp. 2–62 (reprint, New York, 1979). On the history of the use of the metaphor see Tilman Struve, *Die Entwicklung der organologischen Staatsauffassung im Mittelalter* (Stuttgart, 1978); Michael Wilks, *The Problem of Sovereignty in the Later Middle Ages* (Cambridge, 1964); Wilks, ed., *The World of John of Salisbury* (Oxford, 1984).

15 Aristotle, *Politics*, 1275a, 23.

16 See the statutes of Freiburg 1120 and Worms 1190, ed. Friedrich Keutgen, *Urkunden zur städtischen Verfassungsgeschichte* (Berlin, 1901), pp. 109, 117–18 (reprint, Aalen, 1965).

17 See the statute of Cologne 1396, ed. W. Stein, 'Verbundbrief', *Akten zur Geschichte der Verfassung und Verwaltung der Stadt Köln im 14. und 15. Jahrhundert* (Bonn, 1893), pp. 187–98 (reprint, Bonn, 1993).

18 Aristotle, *Politics*, 1254a.

19 On Engelbert: George Bingham Fowler, *Intellectual Interests of Engelbert of Admont* (New York, 1947; reprint, New York, 1967); Marlies Hamm, 'Engelbert von Admont als Staatstheoretiker', *Studien und Mitteilungen zur Geschichte des Benediktinerordens und seiner Zweige*, LXXV (1974), pp. 343–495; Andreas Posch, *Die staats-und kirchenpolitische Stellung Engelberts von Admont* (Paderborn, 1920).

20 Engelbert of Admont, 'De ortu, progressu et fine regnorum et praecipue regni seu imperii Romani', cap. 2, ed. Melchior Goldast, *Politica imperialia* (Frankfurt, 1614), p. 755.

21 See on the covenant theory: Yves Marie-Joseph Congar, 'Quod omnes tangit, ab omnibus tractari et approbari debet', *Die geschichtlichen Grundlagen der modernen Volksvertretung*, ed. Heinz Rausch, vol. 1 (Darmstadt, 1980), pp. 115–82, first published in *Revue du droit français et étranger* 36 (1958), pp. 210–59; Antonio Marongiu, 'Das Prinzip der Demokratie und der Zustimmung (Quod omnes tangit, ab omnibus approbari debet)', Rausch, *Grundlagen*, vol. 1, pp. 183–211, first published in *Studia Gratiana post octava saecularia*, VIII (1962), pp. 555–75; Jürgen Miethke, 'Politisches Denken in der Krise der Zeit', *Institutionen und Geschichte. Theoretische Aspekte und mittelalterliche Befunde*, ed. Gert Melville (Cologne, Vienna, 1992), pp. 157–86; Gaines Post, 'A Romano-Canonical Maxim "Quod omnes tangit" in Bracton', *Traditio*, IV (1946), pp. 197–251; Post, 'A Roman Legal Theory of Consent. *Quod omnes tangit* in Medieval Representation', *Wisconsin Law Review* (1950), pp. 66–78; Wolfgang Stürner, *Peccatum und Potestas. Der Sündenfall und die Entstehung der herrschaftlichen Gewalt im mittelalterlichen Staatsdenken* (Sigmaringen, 1986).

22 See on Bartolus: Jürgen Miethke, 'Politisches Denken und monarchische Theorie. Das Kaisertum als supranationale Institution im späteren Mittelalter', *Ansätze und Diskontinuität deutscher Nationsbildung im Mittelalter*, ed. Joachim Ehlers (Sigmaringen, 1989), pp. 121–44; Cecil Nathan Sidney Woolf, *Bartolus of Sassoferato. His Position in the History of Medieval Political Thought* (Cambridge, 1913).

23 Bartolus of Sassoferato, 'Commentarium ad Digestas novum', ad dig. 49/15, 22–4, Bartolus, *Opera*, vol. VI (Venice, 1570–71), fols 227–8.

24 Aristotle, *Nichomachean Ethics*, 1129a, 32–1129b,1.

25 Dante Alighieri, 'De monarchia', cap. I/2–3, ed. Bruno Nardi, Dante, *Opere minori*, vol. II, (Milan, Naples, 1979), pp. 328–30.

26 Marsilius of Padua, *Defensor pacis*, cap. I/15, I/16, ed. Richard Scholz, vol. 1 (Hanover, 1932), pp. 84–112.

27 John Quidort of Paris, *De potestate regali et papali*, cap. I, ed. Fritz Bleienstein (Stuttgart, 1969), pp. 71–5.

28 St Augustine, *De civitate Dei*, cap. XIX/7–12 (Turnhout, 1955), pp. 671–8; 'Decretalia', pars II, causa XXIII, qu. I, cap. 3–7, ed. Aemilius Ludovicus Richter, *Corpus iuris canonici*, part II, *Decretalium collectiones* (Leipzig, 1881), pp. 892–93; Thomas Aquinas, 'Summa theologiae', cap.

II/2, qu. 40, ar 1–4, ed. Roberto Busa, *Sancti Thomae Aquinatis Opera omnia*, vol. II (Stuttgart, 1980), pp. 579–80.

29 See on Aquinas's theory of just war Joan D. Tooke, *The Just War in Aquinas and Grotius* (London, 1965).

30 See Kelly Robert DeVries, *Medieval Military Technology* (Peterborough, Ont., Lewiston, NY, 1992); DeVries, *Infantry Warfare in the Early Fourteenth Century* (Woodbridge, 1996).

31 For a fresh look at trade across the tricontinental *ecumene* in the thirteenth and fourteenth centuries: Janet Lippman Abu-Lughod, *Before European Hegemony. The World System AD 1250–1350* (New York, Oxford, 1989).

32 For one, Francesco Balducci Pegolotti, *La pratica della mercatura*, ed. Allan Evans (Cambridge, MA, 1936; reprint, New York, 1970), a mid-fourteenth-century merchant, provided rules of how to do business in general terms and even specified travel routes for his fellow merchants.

33 Giovanni de Piano Carpini, 'History of the Mongols', ed. A. van den Wyngaert, *Sinica Franciscana*, vol. I (Quaracchi, 1929); William of Rubruck, *The Journey of William of Rubruck to the Eastern Parts of the World*, ed. William W. Rockhill (London, 1900); 'Directorium ad faciendum passagium transmarinum', ed. C. Raymond Beazley, *American Historical Review*, XII (1907), pp. 813–57, XIII (1908), pp. 79–115; Christopher Dawson, *Mission to Asia* (Toronto, Buffalo, London, 1980).

34 See Wilks, *Problem of Sovereignty*.

35 Gregory VII, 'Dictatus Papae', ed. Erich Caspar, *Das Register Gregors VII*, vol. I, nr 55a (Berlin, 1920), pp. 202–8.

36 On the history of this title: Jürgen Petersohn, 'Rom und der Reichstitel Sacrum romanum imperium', *Sitzungsberichte der Wissenschaftlichen Gesellschaft an der Johann-Wolfgang-Goethe-Universität Frankfurt*, XXXII/4 (1994), pp. 75–101.

37 See Dieter Berg, *England und der Kontinent* (Bochum, 1987), pp. 475–98.

38 See Gerhard Dilcher, *Bürgerrecht und Stadtverfassung im europäischen Mittelalter* (Cologne, Weimar, Vienna, 1996).

39 See Paul-Joachim Heinig, *Reichsstädte, Freie Städte und Königtum 1389–1450* (Wiesbaden, 1983).

40 *Die Urkunden der Deutschen Könige und Kaiser*, vol. IV: *Die Urkunden Konrads II.*, ed. Harry Bresslau, 2nd edn (Berlin, 1957), p. XXVI.

41 See Werner Ohnsorge, *Ostrom und der Westen* (Darmstadt, 1983).

42 Gregory VII, 'Ad universos Christianos', J.-P. Migne, ed., *Patrologiae cursus completus. Series Latina*, vol. CXLVIII (Paris, 1853), cols 451–3.

43 See Michael A. Köhler, *Allianzen und Verträge zwischen fränkischen und islamischen Herrschern im Vorderen Orient* (Berlin, New York, 1991); Jonathan Riley-Smith, *What Were the Crusades?* (London, 1977).

44 William of Malmesbury, *Gesta regum Anglorum*, ed. William Stubbs, vol. II (London, 1889), p. 417 (reprint, Vaduz, 1964).

45 On late medieval imperial policy see Sabine Wefers, *Das politische System Kaiser Sigismunds* (Stuttgart, 1989); Paul-Joachim Heinig, *Kaiser Friedrich III. (1440–1493). Hof, Regierung und Politik*, 3 vols (Cologne, Weimar, Vienna, 1997).

THREE · THE GLOBALIZATION OF SECULAR UNIVERSALISM

1 *Mandeville's Travels. Edited from Ms. Cotton Tiberius C. XVI in the British Museum* by P. Hamelius (London, 1923; reprint, Vaduz, 1960).

2 Conveniently accessible in Kenneth Nebenzahl, *Atlas of Columbus and the Great Discoveries* (Chicago, New York, San Francisco, 1990), p. 13.

3 Marco Polo, *The Book of Ser Marco Polo, the Venetian, Concerning the Kingdoms and Marvels of the East*, ed. Henry Yule, 2 vols, 3rd edn (London, 1929); *Notes and Addenda* by Henri Cordier (London, 1920). For a recent review of the sources see Folker E. Reichert, *Begegnungen mit China. Die Entdeckung Ostasiens im Mittelalter* (Sigmaringen, 1992).

4 See Hubert Daunicht, *Der Osten nach der Erdkarte al-Huwarismis. Beiträge zur historischen Geographie und Geschichte Asiens* (Bonn, 1966); Gerald Randall Tibbetts, *Arab Navigation in the Indian Ocean before the Coming of the Portuguese* (London, 1971; reprint, London, 1981); Tibbetts, *A Study of the Arab Texts Containing Material on South-East Asia* (Leiden, 1979).

5 See Günter Hamann, 'Der Eintritt der südlichen Hemisphäre in die europäische Geschichte', *Sitzungsberichte der Österreichischen Akademie der Wissenschaften*, Philosophisch-Historische Klasse, CCLX (1968), pp. 11–465.

6 For a recent study of these debates see Anna-Dorothee von den Brincken, *Fines Terrae* (Hanover, 1992); Jeffrey Burton Russell, *Inventing the Flat Earth, Columbus and Modern Historians* (New York, Westport, London, 1991).

7 See Hermann Wagner, 'Die Rekonstruktion der Toscanelli-Karte vom J[ahr] 1474 und die Pseudo-Facsimilia des Behaim-Globus vom J[ahr] 1492', *Nachrichten der Königlichen Gesellschaft der Wissenschaften zu Göttingen*, Philosophisch-Historische Klasse (1894), pp. 208–312.

8 For the historical context of these deliberations see John H. Parry, 'Asia-in-the-West', *Terrae incognitae*, VIII (1976), pp. 549–71; Folker E. Reichert, 'Columbus und Marco Polo – Asien in Amerika', *Zeitschrift für historische Forschung*, XV (1988), pp. 1–63; Reichert, 'Zipangu; Japans Entdeckung im Mittelalter', *Japan und Europa 1543–1929*, ed. Doris Ledderose-Croissant and Lothar Ledderose (Berlin, 1993), pp. 24–37.

9 Letter by Hieronymus Müntzer to King John II of Portugal, ed. Henri Harrisse, *The Discovery of North America* (London, Paris, 1892), pp. 393–5 (reprint, Amsterdam, 1961).

10 See Henry E. J. Stanley, ed., *The Three Voyages of Vasco da Gama and His Viceroyality* (London, 1869; reprint, New York, 1963), p. 152.

11 See *The Voyages of Cadamosto and Other Documents on Western Africa in the Second Half of the Fifteenth Century*, ed. G. R. Crone (London, 1937), pp. 19–23.

12 See Günter Georg Kinzel, *Die rechtliche Begründung der frühen portugiesischen Landnahmen an der westafrikanischen Küste zur Zeit Heinrich des Seefahrers* (Göttingen, 1976).

13 See Peter Edward Russell, 'White Kings or Black Kings', *Medieval and Renaissance Studies in Honour of Brian Tate* (Oxford, 1986), pp. 151–63; reprinted in Russell, *Portugal, Spain and the African Atlantic, 1343–1490* (Aldershot, 1995), XVI.

14 See Carl Erdmann, 'Der Kreuzzugsgedanke in Portugal', *Historische Zeitschrift*, CXLI (1929), pp. 23–53.

15 For the contexts see Ulrich Knefelkamp, *Die Suche nach dem Reich des Priesterkönigs Johannes* (Gelsenkirchen, 1986); Taddesse Tamrat, *Church and State in Ethiopia 1270–1527* (Oxford, 1972), pp. 248–67.

16 Stanley, *Voyages of Vasco da Gama*.

17 E.g. the Catalan *mappamundi*, c. 1450, printed in Peter Whitfield, *The Image of the World*, 2nd edn (London, 1997), p. 27.

18 Treaty of Alcaçovas, 4 September 1479, ed. Antonio de la Torre and Luis Suarez Fernandez, *Documentos referentes a las relaciones con Portugal durante el reinado de los reyes católicos*, vol. I (Valladolid, 1958), pp. 245–9.

19 For a recent summary of the expedition see Paolo Emilio Taviani, *Columbus. The Great Adventure* (New York, 1991).

20 See Antonio Muro Oreon, 'Cristobal Colón. El original de la capitulación de 1492 y sus copias contemporaneas', *Anuario de estudios americanos*, VII (1950), pp. 511–13; Manuel Giménez Fernandez, 'Nuevas consideraciones sobre la historia y el sentido de las letras alejandrinas de 1493 referentes a las Indias', *Anuario de estudios americanos*, I (1944), pp. 174, 212, 232.

21 Tordesillas treaty of 7 June 1494, printed in *Fontes historiae iuris gentium*, vol. II, ed. Wilhelm Georg Grewe (Berlin, New York, 1988), pp. 110–11.

22 On the making of the Tordesillas treaty and its implications see *El tratado de Tordesillas y su proyección*, 2 vols (Valladolid, 1973).

23 On the use of this theory in the sixteenth century see Anthony Pagden, *The Fall of Natural Man*, paperback edn (Cambridge, 1986), pp. 27–56.

24 Aristotle, *Politics*, 1254b.

25 John Major, *In secvndvm librum sententiarvm* (Paris, 1519), fol. CLXXXVIIr.

26 Pope Alexander VI, Bull 'Inter cetera' (3 May 1493), ed. Josef Metzler, *America Pontificia primi seculi evangelizationis 1493–1592*, vol. I (Vatican City, 1991), p. 73.

27 On the debate see Jörg Fisch, Die europäische Expansion und das Völkerrecht (Stuttgart, 1984); Lewis Hanke, *All Mankind is One. A Study of the Disputation between Bartolomé de Las Casas and Juan Ginés de Sepúlveda on the Religious and Intellectual Capacity of the American Indians* (DeKalb, 1974), pp. 73–107.

28 Bartolomé de Las Casas, *In Defense of the Indians*, ed. Stafford Poole (DeKalb, 1974), especially pp. 54–70, 262–6, 326–39.

29 Pope Paul III, Bull 'Veritas ipsa' (2 June 1537), ed. Metzler, *America Pontificia*, vol. I, pp. 365–6.

30 On the history of papal claims to control islands in the ocean before Alexander VI see Luis Weckmann, *Las bulas alejandrinas de 1493 y la teoría política del papado medieval* (Mexico City, 1949), pp. 37–228.

31 Tomasso de Vio, Cardinal Cajetan, ed., *Sancti Thomae Aquinatis doctoris angelica opera omnia cum commentariis Thomae de Vio Caetani*, vol. IX (Rome, 1897), pp. 94–5.

32 Francisco de Vitoria, 'De Indis sive de iure belli Hispanorum in barbaros relectio posterior', ed. Walter Schätzle, *Klassiker des Völkerrechts*, vol. II (Tübingen, 1952), pp. 118–75.

33 Alberico Gentili, *De jure belli libri tres*, cap. VII [Hanau, 1598], (Hanau, 1612); ed. John C. Rolfe (Oxford, London, 1933), pp. 53–159.

34 See on the emergence of the concept of international law: Gezina Hermina Johanna van der Molen, *Alberico Gentili and the Development of International Law*, 2nd edn (Leiden, 1968; first published, Amsterdam, 1937); Ernst Reibstein, *Johannes Althusius als Fortsetzer der Schule von Salamanca* (Karlsruhe, 1955).

35 On the correspondence see Arnold Esch, 'Enea Silvio Piccolomini als Papst Pius II', *Lebenslehren und Weltentwürfe im Übergang vom Mittelalter zur Neuzeit*, ed. Hartmut Boockmann, Bernd Moeller and Karl Stackmann (Göttingen, 1989), pp. 119–21; F. Gaeta, 'Sulla "Lettera a Maometto" di Pio II', *Bollettino dell' Istituto storico italiano per il medio evo*, LXXVII (1965), pp. 127–32; Hans Pfeffermann, *Die Zusammenarbeit der Renaissancepäpste mit den Türken* (Winterthur, 1946), pp. 77–81.

36 Afonso d'Albuquerque, *The Commentaries of the Great Afonso Dalboquerque, Second Viceroy of India*, ed. Walter de Gray Birch, vol. III (London, 1870), pp. 124–8.

37 Francisco Alvarez, *The Prester John of the Indies. A True Relation of the Lands of the Prester John. Being the Narrative of the Portuguese Embassy to Ethiopia in 1520*, 2 vols, ed. Charles F. Beckingham and G.W.B. Huntingford (Cambridge, 1961).

38 On George of Podiebrad see Frederick Gotthold Heyman, *George of Bohemia* (Princeton, 1965). On similar proposals connected with the crusading idea see Francis Harry Hinsley, *Power and the Pursuit of Peace: Theory and Practice in the History of Relations between States* (Cambridge, 1963), pp. 14–16; Otto Gerhard Oexle, 'Utopisches Denken im Mittelalter. Pierre Dubois', *Historische Zeitschrift*, CCIV (1977), pp. 293–339.

39 George of Podiebrad, *The Universal Peace Organization of King George of Bohemia. A Fifteenth-Century Plan for World Peace* (New York, London, 1972).

40 Explicit reference to the coincidence of his birth with the Turkish advance on the Balkans was made by Emperor Maximilian I in the biography which he authorized to be written about himself. See Maximilian I, *Weisskunig* (Vienna, 1775), p. 54 (reprint, Weinheim, 1985).

41 See *Arte intorno al 1492. Hispania–Austria. I Re Cattolici, Massimiliano I e gli inizi della Casa d'Austria in Spagna* (Milan, 1992).

42 Jakob Mennel, *Der 'Habsburger Kalender' (Urfassung)*, ed. Wolfgang Irtenkauf (Göppingen, 1979). Mennel, *Fürstliche Chronik Kaiser Maximilians Geuburtspiegel*. Vienna, Austrian National Library, Ms. Cod. Palat. Vind. 3072--77. Mennel, *Der Zaiger*. Vienna, Austrian National Library, Ms. Cod. Palat. Vind. 7892.

43 Martin Waldseemüller, *Cosmographiae Introductio* (Strasbourg, 1507; reprint ed. Franz Ritter von Wieser, Strasbourg, 1907; another reprint, Amsterdam, New York, 1968). The author dedicated this work, in which recent discoveries in the American continent were recorded, to Maximilian I.

44 The letter by Hieronymus Müntzer to King John II of Portugal, 14 July 1493 (in Harrisse, *Discovery*), was commissioned by Maximilian. Cf. the letter by King Manuel I of Portugal, to Emperor Maximilian I, 26 August

1499. See on the correspondence: Alfred Kohler, 'Maximilan I. und das Reich der "1500 Inseln"', *Österreich und die Neue Welt*, ed. Elisabeth Zeilinger (Vienna, 1993), pp. 5–6.

45 See Franz Schestag, 'Kaiser Maximilian I. Triumph', *Jahrbuch der Kunsthistorischen Sammlungen des Allerhöchsten Kaiserhauses* 1 (1883), pp. 154–81. The miniatures for the triumph are included in Franz Winzinger, ed., *Die Miniaturen zum Triumphzug*, 2 vols (Graz, 1972–3). A description is provided by S. Appelbaum, *The Triumph of Maximilian I* (New York, 1964). The *Ehrenpforte* has been edited by Eduard Chmelarz in a supplement to the *Jahrbuch der Kunsthistorischen Sammlungen des Allerhöchsten Kaiserhauses*, vol. 4 (1885–6; reprint, Graz, 1972) and by Peter Smith, *Maximilian's Triumphal Arch* (New York, 1972).

FOUR · THE ETHICS OF SELF-CONSTRAINT

1 On this form of military organization see Fritz Redlich, *The German Military Enterpriser and His Work Force* (Wiesbaden, 1964).

2 This number was given by Zacharias Lochner, *Zwey Büchlein der gerechneten Schlachtordnung* (Ingolstadt, 1557).

3 See Beate Hentschel, 'Zur Genese einer optimistischen Anthropologie in der Renaissance oder die Wiederentdeckung des menschlichen Körpers', *Gepeinigt, begehrt, vergessen. Symbolik und Sozialbezug des Körpers im späten Mittelalter und in der frühen Neuzeit*, ed. Klaus Schreiner and Norbert Schnitzler (Munich, 1992), pp. 85–105; Franz-Joachim Verspohl, 'Entdeckung der Schönheit des Körpers', *Erfindung des Menschen*, ed. Richard van Dülmen (Vienna, Cologne, Weimar, 1998), pp. 139–58.

4 Giovanni Pico della Mirandola, 'Oratio de hominis dignitate, Pico, *Opera omnia* (Basle, 1557), pp. 315–19 (reprint, Hildesheim, New York, 1969; another edn by Gerd von der Gönna, Stuttgart, 1997), pp. 42–8.

5 See e.g. Antonio del Pollaiuolo, *The Battle of the Nude Men*, 1475; Berlin, Staatliche Museen Preußischer Kulturbesitz, Kupferstichkabinett; Michelangelo, *The Battle of Cascina*, 1505, Holkham Hall, Holkham, Wells, Norfolk; Hans Holbein, the Younger, *Lansquenets' Battle*, c. 1530, Basle, Öffentliche Kunstsammlung.

6 Jean Molinet, *Chroniques*, ed. J.-A. Buchon, vol. 2 (Paris, 1828), pp. 207–8; Vincenzo Quirini, *Relazione del Dec. 1507*, ed. Eugenio Alberi, *Le relazioni degli ambasciatori Veneti al Senato*, ser. I, vol. VI (Florence, 1862), p. 24.

7 On Lipsius see Eco O. G. Haitsma Mulier, 'Neostoicisme en het vroegmoderne Europa', *Theoretische geschiedenis*, V (1978), pp. 69–82; M.E.H. Nicolette Mout, 'In het schip. Justus Lipsius en de Nederlandse opstand tot 1591', *Bestuurdes en geleerden*, ed. S. Groenveld (Amsterdam, 1985), pp. 55–64; Gerhard Oestreich, *Neostoicism and the Early Modern State*, ed. Brigitta Oestreich and Helmut G. Koenigsberger (Cambridge, 1982); Oestreich, *Antiker Geist und moderner Staat bei Justus Lipsius* (Göttingen, 1989); Petrus Hermannus Schrijvers, 'Justus Lipsius. Over standvastigheid bij algemene rampspoed', *Lampas*, XVI (1983), pp. 107–28.

8 Justus Lipsius, *Politicorum sive de doctrina civilis libri sex* (Leiden, 1589), English version, *Six Bookes of Politickes or Civil Doctrine*, ed. W. Jones (London, 1594), p. 128 (reprint, Amsterdam, New York, 1970 – spelling and punctuation have been modernized).

9 Niccolò Machiavelli, 'Il principe' (1513), cap. 17, 18, Machiavelli, *Opere*, vol. I (Verona, 1968), pp. 51–6; Giovanni Botero, *Della ragion di stato* (Venice, 1589), English version, *The Reason of State and the Creation of Cities* (New Haven, 1956).

10 Justus Lipsius, *De constancia libri duo* (Antwerp, 1584), English version, *Two Bookes of Constancie*, ed. John Stradling (London, 1595), p. 98; modern English version ed. R. Kirk and C. M. Hall (New Brunswick, 1939 – spelling and punctuation have been modernized).

11 Lipsius, *Constancie*, p. 79.

12 *Ibid.*, pp. 77–9.

13 *Ibid.*, pp. 95–6.

14 For earlier-sixteenth-century allusions to contractualism see Marius Salamonius, *De principatu libri septem* (Rome, 1544), p. 38; Francisco de Vitoria, 'Relectio de potestate civili' (1528), Vitoria, *Relectiones morales* (Frankfurt, 1696), p. 5. On the history of contractualism see Peter Blickle, 'Kommunalismus, Parlamentarismus, Republikanismus', *Historische Zeitschrift*, CCXLII (1986), pp. 529–56; Blickle, 'Kommunalismus. Begriffsbildung in heuristischer Absicht', *Landgemeinde und Stadtgemeinde in Mitteleuropa*, ed. Blickle (Munich, 1991), pp. 5–38; Willem P. Blokmans, 'Du contrat féodal à la souveraineté du peuple', *Assemblee di stati e istituzioni rappresentative nella storia del pensiero politico moderno* (Rimini, 1983), pp. 135–50; John Wiedhofft Gough, *The Social Contract*, 2nd edn (Oxford, 1957, first published 1938; reprint, Westport, 1978); Werner Näf, 'Herrschaftsverträge und die Lehre vom Herrschaftsvertrag', *Schweizer Beiträge zur Allgemeinen Geschichte*, VII (1949), pp. 26–52; Gerhard Oestreich, 'Die Idee des religiösen Bundes und die Lehre vom Staatsvertrag', *Zur Geschichte und Problematik der Demokratie. Festgabe für Hans Herzfeld* (Berlin, 1958), pp. 11–32, reprinted in *Die Entstehung des modernen souveränen Staates*, ed. Hanns Hubert Hofmann (Cologne, Berlin, 1967), pp. 137–51.

15 Juan de Mariana, *De rege et regis institutione libri III*, cap. I/1 (Toledo, 1599), pp. 21–2 (reprint, Aalen, 1969).

16 Francisco Suarez, *De legibus (III 1-16): de civili potestate*, III/ii, 4–6, ed. L. Perena and V. Abril (Coimbra, 1612; Madrid, 1975), pp. 24–7.

17 Richard Hooker, *Of the Lawes of Ecclesiasticall Politie. Eyght Bookes* (London, 1594), pp. 70–3 (reprint, Amsterdam, New York, 1971).

18 Johannes Althusius (praes.), Hugo Pelletarius (resp.), Disputatio politica de regno recte instituendo et administrando (Herborn, 1602), theses 6–56; Althusius, *Politica methodice digesta*, caps I/2, I/7, IX/12, XIX/12 (Herborn, 1603), reprint ed. Carl Joachim Friedrich (Cambridge, 1932), pp. 15, 16, 90, 161 (other reprints: New York, 1979; Aalen, 1981).

19 See on the history of consocialism: Hans Daalder, 'Consocialism, Center and Periphery in the Netherlands', *Mobilization, Centre–Periphery Structures and Nation-Building*, ed. P. Toresvik (Bergen, 1981),

pp. 181–240; Arend Lijphart, 'Consociational Democracy', *World Politics*, XXI (1968/9), pp. 207–11; Kenneth Douglas McRae, ed., *Consociational Democracy* (Toronto, 1972).

20 See on Aristotelianism: Horst Dreitzel, *Protestantischer Aristotelismus und absoluter Staat* (Wiesbaden, 1970); Dreitzel, 'Der Aristotelismus in der politischen Philosophie Deutschlands im 17. Jahrhundert', *Aristotelismus und Renaissance. In memoriam Charles B. Schmitt*, ed. E. Kessler, C. H. Lohr and W. Sparn (Wiesbaden, 1988), pp. 163–92.

21 Printed in Ernst Heinrich Kossman and A. F. Mellink, ed., *Texts Concerning the Revolt of the Netherlands* (Cambridge, 1974), pp. 165–73.

22 On early modern republicanism see Helmut Georg Koenigsberger, *Estates and Revolutions* (Ithaca, 1971); Koenigsberger, ed., *Republiken und Republikanismus im Europa der Frühen Neuzeit* (Munich, Vienna, 1988).

23 Lipsius, *Politickes*, pp. 187–207; Lipsius, *De militia Romana* (Antwerp, 1595–6); Lipsius, *Poliorceticon* (Antwerp, 1596).

24 St Augustine, *Quaestionum in Heptateuchum libri VII*, cap. VI/10 (Turnhout, 1958), pp. 318–19; Augustine, *De civitate Dei*, XIX (Turnhout, 1955), pp. 657–99.

25 Lipsius, *Politickes*, pp. 130–1.

26 *Ibid.*, p. 133.

27 *Ibid.*, p. 152.

28 *Ibid.*, pp. 152–60.

29 Flavius Vegetius Renatus, *De re militari*, cap. I/15, ed. Alf Önnerfors (Stuttgart, 1995).

30 Francesco Patrizi, *De paralleli militari*, 2 vols (Rome, 1594–5).

31 Lipsius, *Politickes*, p. 133.

32 In the seventeenth century, this word together with the word repose denoted the balance of power. See Gottfried Wilhelm Leibniz, 'Bedencken Welchergestalt securitas publica interna et externa und status praesens im Reich iezigen Umständen nach auf festen Fuss zu stellen' (1670), Leibniz, *Politische Schriften*, 3rd edn, vol. I (Berlin, 1983), p. 138.

33 Lipsius, *Constancie*, p. 79.

34 On the printing history of Lipsius's work see Heinz Dollinger, 'Kurfürst Maximilian von Bayern und Justus Lipsius', *Archiv für Kulturgeschichte*, XLVI (1964), p. 236; Ferdinand van der Haeghen, *Bibliographie Lipsienne*, 3 vols (Ghent, 1886–8); Gerhard Oestreich, 'Der römische Stoizismus und die oranische Heeresreform', *Historische Zeitschrift* CLXXVI (1953), p. 23; Oestreich, *Antiker Geist*, pp. 213–19.

35 Jean Bodin, *Les six livres de la République*, cap. I/8 (Paris, 1576), pp. 212–19; reprint ed. Christiane Frémont, Marie-Dominique Couzinet and Alain Rochais, vol. I (Paris, 1986).

36 On these laws see Arlette Jouanna, 'Die Debatte über die absolute Gewalt im Frankreich der Religionskriege', *Der Absolutismus – ein Mythos?*, ed. Ronald G. Asch and Heinz Duchhardt (Cologne, Weimar, Vienna, 1996), pp. 57–78.

37 On the Oranian reforms see Werner Hahlweg, *Das Heerwesen der Oranier und die Antike* (Berlin, 1941; reprint, Osnabrück, 1987); Hahlweg, ed.,

Die Heeresreform der Oranier. Das Kriegsbuch des Grafen Johann von Nassau-Siegen (Wiesbaden, 1973); Frieder Hepp, *Religion und Herrschaft in der Kurpfalz um 1600* (Heidelberg, 1993), pp. 234–50; Jacob de Gheyn, *Wapenhandelinghe van roers, musquetten ende spiessen*, ed. Johannes Bas Kist (Lochem, 1982; reprint, The Hague, 1607); Harald Kleinschmidt, *Tyrocinium militare* (Stuttgart, 1989), pp. 96–149; Rolf Naumann, *Das kursächsische Defensionswerk* (Leipzig, 1916); Helmut Schnitter, *Volk und Landesverteidigung* (Berlin, 1977); Schnitter, *Absolutismus und Heer* (Berlin, 1987), pp. 68–86, 127–34; Winfried Schulze, *Landesdefension und Staatsbildung* (Vienna, Cologne, Graz, 1973); Karl Wolf, *Aufbau eines Volksheeres in den Gebieten der Wetterauer Grafenkorrespondenz zur Zeit der Grafen Johann des Ältern und Johann des Mittlern zu Nassau* (Wiesbaden, 1937); Jan Willem Wijn, Het krijgswezen in den tijd van Prins Maurits PhD Diss. (Utrecht, 1934).

38 Aelianus Tacticus, *De instruendis aciebus*, Editio princeps 1487, ed. Hermann Köchly and Wilhem Rüstow, *Griechische Kriegsschriftsteller*, vol. II (Leipzig, 1855), pp. 201–471. A French version appeared (Paris, 1616). An English version was edited by John Bingham, *The Tacticks of Aelian* (London, 1616; reprint, Amsterdam, New York, 1968); *Das Strategikon des Maurikios*, ed. George T. Dennis (Vienna, 1981).

39 Molinet, *Chroniques*, pp. 207–8.

40 Willibald Pirckheimer, *Bellum Suitense sive Helveticum* cap. II/1 (Zurich, 1737), pp. 16–19; new edn by K. Rück (Munich, 1895).

41 On the lansquenets' mode of fighting see Peter Burschel, *Söldner in Nordwestdeutschland* (Göttingen, 1994); Kleinschmidt, *Tyrocinium*, pp. 43–70; Martin Nell, *Die Landsknechte* (Berlin,1914; reprint, Vaduz, 1965); Ernst Schubert, *Fahrendes Volk im Mittelalter* (Bielefeld, 1995), pp. 324–34, 415–27.

42 On the English trained bands see Charles Grieg Cruickshank, *Elizabeth's Army*, 2nd edn (London, Oxford, 1966); Ann Curry, *The Hundred Years War* (Basingstoke, London, 1993); John Rigby Hale, *Renaissance War Studies* (London, 1983); Robert Hardy, *The Longbow* (Cambridge, 1976).

43 Edward III, Writ (1 June 1363), ed. Thomas Rymer, *Foedera*, vol. III/2 (The Hague, 1740), p. 79.

44 John Smythe, *Instructions, Observations and Orders Mylitarie* (London, 1595), pp. 5, 9, 22–3.

45 Robert Dudley, Earl of Leicester, 'Leicester's Disciplinary Code', ed. Cruickshank, *Elizabeth's Army*, p. 298.

46 See Jérémé Billon, *Les principes de l'art militaire* (Lyon, 1613); Adam van Breen, *De naussauische wapen-handelinge van schilt, spies, parrier ende targe* (The Hague, 1618); Jakob de Gheyn, *Wapenhan-delinghe van roers, musketen ende spiessen* (The Hague, 1607); Pierre Isselbourg, *Künstliche Waffenhandlung der Musqueten und Piquen oder langen Spiessen* (Nuremberg, 1620); Louys de Mongomery, Seigneur de Courbuson, *La milice françoise* (Paris, 1610); *Scola militaris exercitationis* (Cologne, 1619); Johann Jakobi von Wallhausen, *Kriegskunst zu Fuß* (Oppenheim, 1615).

1 Jan Amos Comenius, 'Didactica magna' (written in 1627), *Opera didactica omnia* (Amsterdam, 1657), cap. V/15; René Descartes, 'The Passions of the Soul' (1649), *The Philosophical Writings*, vol. 1 (Cambridge, 1985), pp. 539–40. Cf. Thomas Hobbes, *Leviathan* (London, 1651), p. 1; new edn by Richard Tuck (Cambridge, 1996), p. 9; Anthony Ashley Cooper, Earl of Shaftesbury, *Characteristics of Men*, vol. 1, *Sensus communis* (London, 1723); re-ed. Shaftesbury, *The Standard Edition* (Stuttgart, 1992), pp. 40–4, 48, 74–6.

2 Carl von Linné, *Systema naturae* (Halle, 1740), pp. 42–9.

3 On Grotius see Hedley Bull, Benedict Kingsbury and Adam Roberts, eds, *Hugo Grotius and International Relations* (Oxford, New York, 1990); Peter Haggenmacher, *Grotius et la doctrine de la guerre juste* (Paris, 1964; new edn, Paris, 1983).

4 Hugo Grotius, *De jure belli ac pacis libri tres* (Paris, 1625), reprint of Amsterdam edn, 1646 (Washington, DC, 1913), p. 575.

5 Hugo Grotius, *Mare liberum. Sive De iure quod Batavis competit ad Indicana commercia* (written 1604–5) (Leiden, 1618), pp. 15, 61–4; reprint ed. James Brown Scott, Grotius, *The Freedom of the Seas. Or the Right Which Belongs to the Dutch to Take Part in the East Indian Trade* (New York, 1916), pp. 24–5, 87–91. The essay was originally chapter XII of Grotius's work *De iure praedae* which was written for the Dutch East India Company. Grotius left this work behind in manuscript and it became known through the edition by Henricus Gerardus Hamaker (The Hague, 1868).

6 Thomas Hobbes, *De Cive. The English Version Entitled in the First Edition Philosophicall Rudiments Concerning Government and Society* [London, 1651], ed. Howard Warrender (Oxford, 1983), pp. 170–1; Samuel von Pufendorf, *De jure naturae et gentium libri octo* (Amsterdam, 1688; reprint, Oxford, London, 1934), pp. 714–15. On this aspect of Hobbes's international theory see Donald W. Hanson, 'Thomas Hobbes's "Highway to Peace"', *International Organization*, XXXVIII (1984), pp. 329–54; Stanley Hoffmann, 'Rousseau on War and Peace', Hoffmann, *The State of War* (London, 1965), p. 61; Michael C. Williams, 'Hobbes and International Relations', *International Organization*, L (1996), pp. 213–36.

7 Christian Wolff, *Jus gentium methodo scientifica pertractatum* (Halle, 1759); reprint ed. Marcel Thomann (Hildesheim, New York, 1972), pp. 763–4; Emer[ich] de Vattel, *Le droit des gens. Ou principes de la loi naturelle appliqués à la conduite et aux affairs des nations et souverains* (London, 1758), original, vol. 1, pp. 9–10; reprint ed. Charles G. Fenwick (Washington, DC, 1916; reprint Geneva, 1983); Carl Theodor von Dalberg, Elector of Mainz, *Von Erhaltung der Staatsverfassungen* (Erfurt, 1795), pp. 6–7.

8 Lorenzo de' Medici, Letter to Giovanni Lanfredini, his envoy in Rome (17 October 1489), *Scritti scelti di Lorenzo de' Medici*, ed. Emilio Bigi (Turin, 1955), pp. 667–70; translation by John Warrington printed in Moorhead Wright, ed., *Theory and Practice of the Balance of Power 1486–1914* (London, Totowa, NJ, 1975), pp. 4–7.

9 Francesco Guicciardini, 'Storia d'Italia', *Opere*, ed. Vittorio de Caprariis (Milan, Naples, 1961), p. 374. See also Guicciardini, 'Lorenzo il

Magnifico', *Scritti politici e ricordi*, ed. R. Palmarocchi (Bari, 1933), pp. 223–8; Geoffray Fenton, ed., *The Historie of Guicciardin* (London, 1579), p. VI.

10 Francis Bacon, 'Notes for a Speech Considering a War with Spain' (1623/1624), ed. Wright, *Theory*, pp. 27–31; spelling and punctuation have been modernized by Harald Kleinschmidt.

11 Francis Bacon, 'Of Empire', Bacon, *A Harmony of Essays*, ed. Edward Arber (London, 1871), pp. 301–3 (reprint New York, 1966); spelling and punctuation have been modernized as above.

12 Fenton, *Historie*, p.VI.

13 On seventeenth- and eighteenth-century mechanicism see Arno Baruzzi, *Mensch und Maschine. Das Denken sub specie machinae* (Munich, 1973); Karl Wolfgang Deutsch, 'Mechanism, Organism and Society: Some Models in Natural and Social Science', *Philosophy of Science*, XVIII (1951), pp. 230–52; Sigfried Giedion, *Mechanization Takes Command* (Oxford, 1948); Heikki Kirkinen, *Les origines de la conception moderne de l'homme machine* (Helsinki, 1960); Johannes Kunisch, 'Das "Puppenwerk" der stehenden Heere', *Zeitschrift für historische Forschung*, XVII (1990), pp. 49–83; M. Landau, 'On the Use of Metaphor in Political Analysis', *Social Research*, XXVIII (1961), pp. 331–43; Klaus Maurice and Otto Mayr, eds, *Die Welt als Uhr* (Munich, Berlin, 1980); Mayr, *Authority, Liberty and Automatic Machinery in Early Modern Europe* (Baltimore, London, 1986); Ahlrich Meyer, 'Mechanische und organische Metaphorik politischer Philosophie', *Archiv für Begriffsgeschichte*, XIII (1969), pp. 128–47; Dietmar Peil, *Untersuchungen zur Staats- und Herrschaftsmetaphorik in literarischen Zeugnissen von der Antike bis zur Gegenwart* (Munich, 1983), pp. 489–595, 835; Wolfgang Röd, *Geometrischer Geist und Naturrecht* (Munich, 1970) (Abhandlungen der Bayerischen Akademie der Wissenschaften, Philosophisch-Historische Klasse. N. F. 70); Carl Schmitt, 'Der Staat als Mechanismus bei Hobbes und Descartes', *Archiv für Rechts- und Sozialphilosophie*, XXX (1936/7), pp. 622–32; Schmitt, *The Leviathan in the State Theory of Thomas Hobbes*, ed. George Schwab (Westport, London, 1996); Stefan Smid, 'Recht und Staat als Maschine', *Der Staat* XXVII (1988), pp. 325–50; Barbara Stollberg-Rilinger, *Der Staat als Maschine* (Berlin, 1986), pp. 101–201; Aram Vartanian, *La Mettrie's L'homme machine* (Princeton, 1960), pp. 57–94.

14 Christoph Besold, *Dissertatio politico-juridica de foederum jure* (Strasbourg, 1622), p. 12; Grotius, *De jure*, p. 52; Samuel von Pufendorf (praes.), Daniel Christiernin (resp.), 'De systematibus civitatum', Pufendorf, ed., *Dissertationes academicae selectiores* (Frankfurt, 1678), p. 228; Johann Erdmann Schmidt (praes.), Cratus Wilhelm von Schell (resp.), *De civitatis origine civitatvmqve systematibus exemplo Reipvblicae Batavorvum illvstratis*, Phil. Diss. (University of Jena, 1745); Ernst Carl Wieland (praes.), Gottlob Friedrich Schmerbauch (resp.), *De systemate civitatvm*, Phil. Diss. (University of Leipzig, 1777).

15 Henry St John Viscount Bolingbroke, 'Letters on the Study and Use of History' (1735), *Works*, ed. David Mallet, vol. II (London, 1754), pp. 369–70; reprint ed. Bernhard Fabian (Hildesheim, 1968).

16 Arnold Hermann Ludwig Heeren, 'Der Deutsche Bund in seinen Verhältnissen zu dem Europäischen Staatenverein', Heeren, *Historische Werke*, 4th edn, vol. II (Göttingen, 1821), pp. 427, 429.

17 Jean-Jacques Rousseau, 'Extrait d'un projet de paix perpétuelle de M. Abbé de Saint-Pierre' (1756), Rousseau, *The Political Writings*, ed. C. E. Vaughan, vol. I (Cambridge, 1915), pp. 370–1 (reprint, Oxford, 1962).

18 Emeric de Crucé, *The New Cineas* (1623), ed. C. F. Farrell and E. R. Farrell (New York, London, 1972), pp. 46, 49; Maximilien de Béthune de Sully, *Sully's Grand Design of Henry IV* (1607), ed. David Ogg (London, 1921), pp. 25–6. Both authors included their thoughts on the balance of power and on international relations in revisionist proposals for perpetual peace and suggested that stability could be accomplished through the formation of roughly equal-sized Christian polities in Europe.

19 Jonathan Swift, 'The Conduct of the Allies', Swift, *Political Tracts 1711–1713*, ed. Herbert Davis (Oxford, 1973), p. 7.

20 *Ibid.*, p. 64.

21 Wright, *Theory*, pp. 50–1.

22 Treaty of Peace and Friendship between Great Britain and Spain, signed at Utrecht, 13 July 1713, Art. II, ed. Clive Parry, *Consolidated Treaties Series*, vol. XXVIII (Dobbs Ferry, 1969), p. 299.

23 *Natural Reflections upon the Present Debates about Peace and War* (London, 1712), pp. 61–2.

24 Alexander Pope, 'Poems on Several Occasions' (1717), Pope, *Poetical Works*, ed. Herbert Davis (London, 1966), p. 678.

25 Ludwig Martin Kahle, *La balance de l'Europe considerée comme la règle de la paix et de la guerre* (Berlin, Göttingen, 1744), pp. 14–17, 67–70; Bolingbroke, 'Letters', pp. 74–8; Bolingbroke, *The Idea of a Patriot King*, ed. S. W. Jackman (Indianapolis, New York, Kansas City, 1965), pp. 74–8; David Hume, 'Of the Balance of Power' (1752), Hume, *Essays Moral, Political, and Literary*, ed. T. H. Green, T. H. Grose, vol. I (London, 1882), pp. 348–56; (reprint, Aalen, 1964). See also Jacob Friedrich von Bielfeld, *Institutions politiques* (The Hague, 1760), pp. 87–8; Johann Friedrich Kayser (praes.), Eberhard Georg Wittich (resp.), 'Dissertatio ivris gentivm et pvblici de tvendo aeqvilibrio Evropae' (Giessen, 1723); Georg Ludwig Erasmus von Huldenberg, *De Aequilibrio alioqve legali juris gentium arbitrio* (Helmstedt, 1748); Johann Jacob Lehmann, *Trutina vulgo Evropae norma belli pacisqve hactenus a svmmis imperantibus habita* (Jena, 1716); Johann Christoph Muhrbeck (praes.), Karl Friedrich von Bering (resp.), 'Dissertatio de bilance gentium'; (Greifswald, 1772); Antoine Pecquet, *L'esprit des maximes politiques* (Paris, 1757), p. 15; Johann Jacob Schmauss, *Historie der Balance von Europa* (Leipzig, 1741).

26 Kahle, *Balance*, pp. 155–6; author's translation.

27 *Ibid.*, pp. 144–5; author's translation.

28 On the mechanistic concept of the personality of the state see Gotthardt Frühsorge, *Der politische Körper. Zum Begriff des Politischen im 17. Jahrhundert und in den Romanen Christian Weises* (Stuttgart, 1974); W. Zuber, 'Die Staatsperson Pufendorfs im Lichte der neueren Staatslehre', *Archiv für öffentliches Recht*, XXX (1939), pp. 33–70.

29 On seventeenth- and eighteenth-century theories of the state see Frederick Smith Carney, *The Associational Theory of Johannes Althusius*, PhD Diss., (University of Chicago, 1960); Salvador Castellote Cubells, *Die Anthropologie des Suarez* (Freiburg, Munich, 1962); Horst Dreitzel, *Protestantischer Aristotelismus und absoluter Staat* (Wiesbaden, 1970); Francesco Ercole, *Da Bartolo all' Althusio. Saggi sulla storia del pensiero pubblicistico del Rinascimento Italiano* (Florence, 1932); Carl Joachim Friedrich, *Johannes Althusius und sein Werk im Rahmen der Entwicklung der Theorie von der Politik* (Berlin, 1975); Martin van Gelderen, *The Political Thought of the Dutch Revolt* (Cambridge, 1992); Otto von Gierke, *Johannes Althusius und die Entwicklung der naturrechtlichen Staatstheorien*, 3rd edn (Breslau, 1913; first published Breslau, 1880; reprint, Aalen, 1981); Ottfried Höffe, 'Zur vertragstheoretischen Begründung politischer Gerechtigkeit. Hobbes, Kant und Rawls im Vergleich', *Ethik und Politik* (Frankfurt, 1979), pp. 195–226; Preston King, *The Ideology of Order. A Comparative Analysis of Jean Bodin and Thomas Hobbes* (London, 1974); Werner Krawietz, 'Kontraktualismus oder Konsozialismus? Grundlagen und Grenzen des Gemeinschaftsdenkens in der politischen Theorie des Johannes Althusius', *Politische Theorie des Johannes Althusius*, ed. Karl-Wilhelm Dahm, Werner Krawietz and Dieter Wyduckel (Berlin, 1988), pp. 391–423; Leonhard Krieger, *The Politics of Discretion. Pufendorf and the Acceptance of Natural Law* (Chicago, London, 1965); Friedrich Merzbacher, 'Der homo politicus symbioticus und das ius symbioticum bei Johannes Althusius', *Recht und Staat. Festschrift für Günther Küchenhoff zum 65. Geburtstag*, ed. H. Hablitzel and M. Wollenschläger (Berlin, 1972), pp. 107–14; Richard Saage, *Vertragsdenken und Utopie* (Frankfurt, 1989); Carl Siedschlag, 'Machtstaat und Machtstaatsgedanke in den politischen Lehren des Johannes Althusius und des Justus Lipsius', *Politische Theorie*, pp. 313–32; Peter Jochen Winters, *Die 'Politik' des Althusius und ihre zeitgenössischen Quellen* (Freiburg, 1963).
30 Kahle, *Balance*, pp. 106–7, 109–11, 113–14.
31 Among other critics: Christian Friedrich Stisser, *Freymuthige und bescheidene Erinnerungen wider des berühmten Göttingischen Professors, Herrn Doctor Kahle, Abhandlung von der Balance Europens als der vornehmsten Richtschnur des Krieges und Friedens* (Leipzig, 1745), pp. 28–9; Stisser, *Fortsetzung . . .* (Leipzig, 1756), pp. 127–8. Supporters, among others: Hume, 'Of Balance'.
32 Johann Heinrich Gottlob Justi, *Die Chimäre des Gleichgewichts von Europa* (Altona, 1758); *Betrachtungen über das Gleichgewicht von Europa* (1741), p. 9 (microfiche edn Flugschriftensammlung Gustav Freytag, nr 6203); Gottlob August Tittel, *Erläuterungen der theoretischen und praktischen Philosophie* (Frankfurt, 1786), pp. 200–2, 204 (reprint, Brussels, 1973).
33 Here understood as handbooks containing data about states as territorial polities. See for the methodology of statistics: Gottfried Achenwall, *Vorbereitung zur Staatswissenschaft der heutigen fürnehmsten Europäischen Reiche und Staaten* (Göttingen, 1748); Anton Friedrich Büsching, *Vorbereitung zur gründlichen und nützlichen Kenntnis der geographischen Beschaffenheit und Staatsverfassungen* (Hamburg, Vienna, 1758; 4th edn 1768); Johann Christoph Gatterer, *Ideal einer allgemeinen Weltstatistik*

(Göttingen, 1773); August Ferdinand Lüder, *Einleitung in die Staatenkunde* (Leipzig, 1792); Lüder, *Kritische Geschichte der Statistik* (Göttingen, 1817); Johann Georg Meusel, *Lehrbuch der Statistik* (Leipzig, 1792; 2nd edn 1794, 3rd edn 1804, 4th edn 1817); Julius August Renner, *Lehrbuch der Staatskunde der vornehmsten europäischen Staaten* (Braunschweig, 1786); August Ludwig von Schlözer, *Theorie der Statistik* (Göttingen, 1804).

34 Pecquet, *L'esprit*, pp. 191–206.

35 Explicitly demanded by Bielfeld, *Institutions*, pp. 94–5.

36 John Lind, *Letters Concerning the Present State of Poland* (London, 1773), pp. 58–9, 181–7. On the mixed reactions in public opinion in France and Britain on the first partition see Jean Fabre, *Stanislaus-August Poniatowski et l'Europe des Lumières* (Paris, 1952); David Bayne Horn, *British Public Opinion and the First Partition of Poland* (Edinburgh, London, 1945).

37 Nicolaus Hieronymus Gundling, 'Erörterung der Frage, ob wegen der anwachsenden Macht der Nachbarn man den Degen entblössen könne', *Gundlingiana*, part 5 (Halle, 1716; separate printing, Leipzig, 1757), pp. 3, 5, 24; Gundling, *Ausführlicher Discours über den ietzigen Zustand der Europäischen Staaten* (Frankfurt, Leipzig, 1734), part II, p. 47. Similar arguments were suggested in *Réflexions touchant l'équilibre* (1741), pp. 10–15; David Georg Strube, 'Eine Prüfung der ans Licht getretenen Réflexions touchant d'équilibre', Strube, *Nebenstunden*, vol. II (Hanover, 1747), pp. 281–4.

38 *Staats-Betrachtungen über gegenwärtigen Preußischen Krieg in Teutschland in wie fern solcher das allgemeine Europäische, vornehmlich aber das besondere Teutsche Interesse betrift* (Vienna, 1761). *Mit Anmerkungen wieder aufgelegt* (Berlin, 1761); edited without the '*Anmerkungen*' by Johannes Kunisch, *Das Mirakel des Hauses Brandenburg* (Munich, Vienna, 1978), pp. 102–41.

39 Vattel, *Droit des gens*, pp. 39–40 (original), p. 251 (English version).

40 *Ibid.*, pp. 41–3 (original), pp. 241–52 (English version).

41 Francis Hutcheson, *A System of Moral Philosophy*, vol. II (London, 1755), p. 216.

42 Johann Peter Süßmilch, *Die göttliche Ordnung in den Veränderungen des menschlichen Geschlechts, aus der Geburt, dem Tode und der Fortpflanzung desselben erwiesen*, vol. I, 3rd edn (Berlin, 1765), pp. 396–7; reprint ed. Jürgen Cromm (Göttingen, 1988).

43 Johann Heinrich Gottlob von Justi, *Grundsätze der Policeywissenschaft* (Göttingen, 1782), pp. 76–85 (reprint, Frankfurt, 1969).

44 Johann Heinrich Gottlob von Justi, *Der Grundriß einer guten Regierung* (Frankfurt, Leipzig, 1759), pp. 74–85; Dalberg, *Erhaltung*, pp. 6–7.

45 Jean-Jacques Rousseau, 'Le contrat social' (1762), *The Political Writings*, ed. C. E. Vaughan, vol. I (Cambridge, 1915), pp. 454–8 (reprint, Oxford, 1962); English version, ed. J. H. Brumfitt and John C. Hall, *The Social Contract and Discourses* (London, Melbourne, 1973), pp. 192–3.

46 François Quesnay, 'Maximes générales', *Oeuvres*, ed. E. Daire (Paris, 1846), p. 81 (reprint, Osnabrück, 1966).

47 Justi, *Policeywissenschaft*, pp. 76–85; Süßmilch, *Göttliche Ordnung*, vol. I, pp. 311–420.

48 On the history of peacemaking procedures see Jörg Fisch, *Krieg und Frieden im Friedensvertrag* (Stuttgart, 1979); Robert F. Randle, *The Origins of Peace: A Study of Peacemaking and the Structure of Peace Settlements* (New York, London, 1973); Francis Stephen Ruddy, *International Law in the Enlightenment: The Background of Emmerich de Vattel's* Le Droit des Gens (Dobbs Ferry, 1975), pp. 259–80.

49 Charles Irenée Castel Abbé de Saint-Pierre, *Project pour rendre la paix perpétuelle en Europe* (Utrecht, 1713), p. 37; reprint ed. Simone Goyard-Fabre (Paris, 1986); author's translation.

50 *Ibid.*, p. 38; author's translation.

51 *Ibid.*, p. 37; author's translation.

52 *Ibid.*, p. 40; author's translation.

53 Rousseau, 'Extrait', pp. 370–1. For a reassessment of the position of Rousseau in the history of international theory see Michael C. Williams, 'Rousseau, Realism and *Realpolitik*', *Millennium*, xviii (1989), pp. 185–203.

54 Immanuel Kant, 'Zum ewigen Frieden' (1795), Kant, *Werke in zwölf Bänden*, ed. Wilhelm Weischedel, vol. xi (Frankfurt, 1968), pp. 193–251; English version in Kant, *Political Writings*, 2nd edn, ed. Hans Reiss (Cambridge, 1991), pp. 93–130. On Kant's international theory: Charles Covell, *Kant and the Law of Peace* (London, 1998), pp. 68–100; Andrew J. Hurrell, 'Kant and the Kantian Paradigm in International Relations', *Review of International Studies*, xvi (1990), pp. 183–205.

55 Jeremy M. Black, *Why Wars Happen* (London, 1998).

56 Wenzel Anton Kaunitz-Rietberg, 'Vortrag vom 27. Juni 1755', *Archiv für österreichische Geschichte*, xlviii (1872), pp. 19–38.

57 Kahle, *Balance*, pp. 98–9.

58 See Heinz Duchhardt, ed., *Zwischenstaatliche Friedenswahrung in Mittelalter und Früher Neuzeit* (Cologne, Vienna, 1991); Duchhardt, *Balance of Power und Pentarchie* (Paderborn, Munich, Vienna, Zurich, 1997), pp. 7–94.

59 Jean Bodin, *Les six livres de la République*, vol. ii (Paris, 1576), pp. 899–1006; reprint ed. Christiane Frémont, Marie-Dominique Couzinet and Alain Rochais (Paris, 1986); Bogislaus von Chemnitz [i.e. Hippolitus a Lapide], *Dissertatio de ratione status in imperio nostro Romano-Germanico* (Freistadt, 1647), pp. 25, 40, 50.

60 Johann Jacob Moser, *Von der Landeshoheit derer teutschen Reichsstände überhaupt* (Frankfurt, Leipzig, 1773), pp. 16–17 (reprint, Osnabrück, 1968).

61 Johann Stephan Pütter, *Beyträge zur näheren Erläuterung und richtigen Bestimmung einiger Lehren des teutschen Staats- und Fürstenrechts*, part I (Göttingen, 1777), pp. 30–2.

62 Gottfried Wilhelm Leibniz, ed., *Codex juris gentium diplomaticus* (Hanover, 1693–1700; another edn Wolfenbüttel, 1747); Jean DuMont, ed., *Corps universel diplomatique du droit des gens* (Amsterdam, 1726–39); Georg Friedrich von Martens, ed., *Recueil des principaux traités d'alliance, de paix, de trêve, de neutralité, de commerce, de limites, d'échange, etc.*, 7 vols (Göttingen, 1791–1801), 2nd edn, 8 vols (Göttingen, 1817–35; reprint, New York, 1967); Martens, ed., *Nouveau recueil*, 17 vols (Göttingen, 1817–42); Martens, ed., *Nouveau supplémens*, ed. Friedrich Wilhelm

August Murhard, 3 vols (Göttingen, 1839–42); Martens, ed., *Nouveau recueil général de traités*, ed. F.W.A. Murhard (Göttingen, 1843–79). The Westphalia treaties themselves were circulated in more than 28 known editions all of which had a total print run of between 14,000 and 42,000 copies. See Konrad Repgen, 'Der Westfälische Friede und die zeitgenössische Öffentlichkeit', *Westfalen*, LXXV (1997), pp. 37–8.

63 Kayser, *Ivs gentivm*, pp. 40–1; author's translation.

64 On the influence of the public press on international relations in the eighteenth century see Jeremy M. Black, 'The Press, Party and Foreign Policy in the Reign of George I', *Publishing History*, XIII (1983), pp. 23–40; Andreas Gestrich, *Absolutismus und Öffentlichkeit* (Göttingen, 1994).

65 Kahle, *Balance*, pp. 87–8.

66 Wenzel Anton Kaunitz-Rietberg, 'Denkschriften', *Archiv für Österreichische Geschichte*, XLVIII (1872), pp. 75–7; author's translation.

67 On Kaunitz's policy concepts see Lothar Schilling, *Kaunitz und das Renversement des alliances* (Berlin, 1994).

68 Such was the criticism among others by François Marie Arouet de Voltaire (Art.), 'Guerre', Voltaire, *Dictionnaire philosophique*, vol. 3 (Paris, 1764), Voltaire, *Oeuvres complètes*, ed. Louis Moland, vol. XIX (Paris, 1879), pp. 318–22 (reprint, Vaduz, 1967).

69 Adam Smith, *An Inquiry into the Nature and Causes of the Wealth of Nations*, vol. II (London, 1776), pp. 689–90, 701–2, 706–8; reprint ed. R. H. Campbell, A. S. Skinner and W. B. Todd (Oxford, 1976).

70 On military drill see Joel Cornette, *Le roi de guerre* (Paris, 1993), pp. 50–6; Harald Kleinschmidt, *Tyrocinium militare* (Stuttgart, 1989), pp. 196–270; Günther Lottes, 'Zähmung des Menschen durch Drill und Dressur', *Erfindung des Menschen. Schöpfungsträume und Körperbilder. 1500–2000*, ed. Richard van Dülmen (Cologne, Weimar, Vienna, 1998), pp. 221–40; John A. Lynn, *Giant of the Grand Siècle. The French Army 1610–1715* (Cambridge, 1997), pp. 397–414; John A. Houlding, *Fit for Service* (Oxford, 1981); William H. McNeill, *Keeping together in Time. Dance and Drill in Human History* (Cambridge, MA, London, 1995); J. A. de Moor, 'Experience and Experiment. Some Reflections upon the Military Developments in 16th and 17th Century Western Europe', *Exercise of Arms*, ed. Marco van Hoeven (Leiden, 1997), pp. 17–32; Geoffrey Parker, *The Military Revolution* (Cambridge, 1988; 2nd edn, Cambridge, 1996).

71 This was the phrase used by Frederick II in his political testament of 1752, ed. Richard Dietrich, *Politische Testamente der Hohenzollern* (Munich, 1981), p. 229. Eighteenth-century drill manuals were usually printed by command of territorial rulers and councils of urban communities.

72 *Exercir-Reglement für die Königlich Preußische Infanterie* (Berlin, 1743), §§ II/2, 7 (reprint, Osnabrück, 1976); author's translation.

73 *Exercir-Reglement für die Churfürstlich sächßische Infanterie* (Dresden, 1776), § IV/2, 13; author's translation.

74 Frederick, *Testament*, p. 229.

75 Julius Bernhard von Rohr, *Ceremoniel-Wissenschaft der Privat-Personen* (Berlin, 1782), p. 184; reprint ed. Gotthardt Frühsorge (Weinheim, 1990); author's translation.

1 For a quick and late reference see *Grosses vollständiges Universal-Lexicon*, vol. xiv (Leipzig, Halle, 1735), col. 224 (reprint, Graz, 1995).

2 Thomas Burnet, *Sacred Theory of the Earth*, 2nd edn (London, 1691), pp. 240–1; (first published London, 1681); reprint ed. Basil Willey (Carbondale, 1965).

3 Robert Hooke, *The Posthumous Works*, ed. R. Waller (London, 1705), pp. 299, 333 (reprint, London, 1971); Giovanni Battista Vico, *Principij di una scienza nouva*, 3rd edn (Naples, 1744), table facing p. 37 (reprint, Tokyo, 1989).

4 Matthew Hale, *The Primitive Origination of Mankind* (London, 1677), p. 201.

5 Georges Louis Le Clerc, Comte de Buffon, *Les époques de la nature*, Buffon, *Oeuvres complètes*, vols ix, x (Paris, 1778).

6 On the backward extension of the age of the world see Paolo Rossi, *The Dark Abyss of Time* (Chicago, London, 1985); Martin John Spencer Rudwick, *The Meaning of Fossils*, 2nd edn (Chicago, London, 1985; 1st edn, London, 1972); Donald J. Wilcox, *The Measure of Times Past. Pre-Newtonian Chronologies and the Rhetoric of Relative Time* (Chicago, London, 1987).

7 Carl von Linné, *Systema naturae*, 12th edn (1766).

8 Johann Gottfried Herder, *Ideen zur Philosophie der Geschichte der Menschheit* (1784–91), Herder, *Sämmtliche Werke*, ed. Bernhard Suphan, vol. xiv (Berlin, 1909), titles of Book 1, Chapter 3 and of Book 2, Chapter 1.

9 James Hutton, *Theory of the Earth*, vol. i (Edinburgh, 1795), p. 301; first published in *Transactions of the Royal Society of Edinburgh* (1788), pp. 209–304; reprint ed. Victor A. Eyles and George W. White, *Hutton's System of the Earth. 1785, Theory of the Earth. 1788, Observations on Granite. 1794* (Darien, CT, 1979), p. 125.

10 Herder, *Ideen*, Book xv, cap. 4, pp. 235–6; author's translation.

11 Johann Gottfried Herder, *Briefe zu Beförderung der Humanität* [1793–7], Herder, *Sämmtliche Werke*, ed. Suphan, vol. xviii (Berlin, 1883), p. 56.

12 Jeremy Bentham, 'Plan for an Universal and Perpetual Peace', Bentham, *The Works*, ed. John Bowring, vol. ii (London, 1838), pp. 543–50 (reprint, New York, 1962).

13 Bentham, 'Plan', p. 546; August Ludwig von Schlözer, *Vorstellung seiner Universal-Historie* (Göttingen, Gotha, 1772), pp. 14–15, 18; reprint, Horst Walter Blanke and Dirk Fleischer, ed., *Theoretiker der deutschen Aufklärungshistorie*, vol. i (Stuttgart, 1990), pp. 669–70.

14 Henry Peter Lord Brougham and Vaux, 'Balance of Power', *The Works*, vol. i (London, Glasgow, 1857), pp. 3–50 (this essay was first published anonymously in the *Edinburgh Review*, i [1803], pp. 345–81); Arnold Herman Ludwig Heeren, 'Der Deutsche Bund in seinen Verhältnissen zu dem Europäischen Staatenverein', *Historische Werke*, 4th edn, vol. ii (Göttingen, 1821), pp. 427–9; Karl Heinrich Ludwig Pölitz, *Die Staatswissenschaft im Lichte unserer Zeit*, 2nd edn, vol. v (Leipzig, 1828), p. 57; Johann Battista Fallati, 'Die Genesis der Völkergesellschaft',

Zeitschrift für die gesamte Staatswissenschaft, I (1844), pp. 160–89, 260–328, 558–608; Montague Bernard, *Four Lectures on Subjects Connected with Diplomacy* (London, 1868), pp. 95–6; Friedrich von Bernhardi, *Deutschland und der nächste Krieg*, 2nd edn (Stuttgart, Berlin, 1912), pp. 117–19; Hans Delbrück, 'Deutschlands Stellung in der Weltpolitik', Delbrück, *Vor und nach dem Weltkrieg. Politische und historische Aufsätze 1902–25* (Berlin, 1926), p. 13.

15 This is a phrase used by Talcott Parsons, *The Social System* (New York, 1951), pp. 481–2, 487.

16 On nineteenth-century biologism see Meyer H. Abrams, 'Coleridge's Mechanical Fancy and Organic Imagination', *The Mirror and the Lamp* (New York, 1976), pp. 167–77; Ernst-Wolfgang Böckenförde, 'Der Staat als Organismus', Böckenförde, *Recht, Staat, Freiheit* (Frankfurt, 1991), pp. 263–72; John William Coker, *Organismic Theories of the State* (New York, 1910); Karl Wolfgang Deutsch, 'Mechanism, Organism and Society: Some Models in Natural and Social Science', *Philosophy of Science*, XVIII (1951), pp. 230–52; Karl M. Figlio, 'The Metaphor of Organization', *History of Science*, XIV (1976), pp. 17–53; Erich Kaufmann, 'Über den Begriff des Organismus in der Staatslehre des 19. Jahrhunderts', Kaufmann, *Rechtsidee und Recht* (Göttingen, 1960), pp. 46–66; Albert Theodor van Krieken, *Über die sogenannten organischen Staatstheorien* (Leipzig, 1873); M. Landau, 'On the Use of Metaphor in Political Analysis', *Social Research*, XXVIII (1961), pp. 331–43; Gunter Mann, 'Medizinisch-biologische Ideen und Modelle in der Gesellschaftslehre des 19. Jahrhunderts', *Medizinhistorisches Journal*, IV (1969), pp. 1–23; Mann, ed., *Biologismus im 19. Jahrhundert* (Stuttgart, 1973); Ahlrich Meyer, 'Mechanische und organische Metaphorik politischer Philosophie', *Archiv für Begriffsgeschichte*, XIII (1969), pp. 159–63.

17 Johann Gottlieb Fichte, 'Beitrag zur Berichtigung der Urteile des Publikums über die Französische Revolution [(Danzig, 1793)]', Fichte, *Schriften zur Französischen Revolution* (Leipzig, 1988), pp. 93–4; author's translation.

18 Johann Gottlieb Fichte, *Die Grundzüge des gegenwärtigen Zeitalters* (Berlin, 1806), Fichte, *Werke 1801–1806*, ed. Reinhard Lauth and Hans Gliwitzki (Stuttgart, 1991), p. 357; English version in Moorhead Wright, ed., *Theory and Practice of the Balance of Power 1486–1914* (London, Totowa, NJ, 1975), pp. 89–90.

19 August Hermann Ludwig Heeren, 'Versuch einer historischen Entwickelung der Entstehung und des Wachsthums des Brittischen Colonial-Interesse', *Historische Werke*, vol. I (Göttingen, 1821), p. 259; author's translation.

20 Brougham, 'Balance of Power', pp. 12–13; the original is in *Edinburgh Review*, I (1803), pp. 353–4.

21 Friedrich von Gentz, *Fragmente aus der neuesten Geschichte des politischen Gleichgewichts in Europa*, 2nd edn (St Petersburg, 1806), pp. XXIV, 1 (reprint, Osnabrück, 1967); author's translation.

22 *Ibid.*, p. 16; author's translation.

23 Gentz, *Fragmente*, p. 21, explicated his theoretical statement with a reference to the partitions of Poland of 1772, 1793 and 1795 which, in his

view, had been brought about by the alliance of Austria, Prussia and Russia for the purpose of destroying one actor in the system. Gentz observed correctly that this had been contrary to the principles of eighteenth-century balance-of-power rules. On the Vienna Congress see Charles Kingsley Webster, *The Foreign Policy of Castlereagh* (London, 1925); Webster, *The Art and Practice of Diplomacy* (New York, 1962).

24 Karl August Freiherr von Hardenberg [Remarks on the Formation of His Plan for a Constitution, 3 Sept. 1814], dispatched to Metternich, ed. Klaus Müller, *Quellen zur Geschichte des Wiener Kongresses* (Darmstadt, 1986), p. 338; author's translation.

25 Charles-Maurice de Talleyrand-Périgord, *Mémoires*, ed. le Duc de Broglie, vol. II (Paris, 1891), p. 534; author's translation.

26 Karl Theodor Freiherr von Hacke [On the Prussian Proposal on the Principles of a German Constitution, 30 Sept. 1814], ed. Müller, *Quellen*, p. 346; author's translation.

27 The Vienna Congress had a so-called Statistical Commission: Hardenberg [Plan for the Future Shape of Europe], ed. Müller, *Quellen*, pp. 33–59; Talleyrand, *Mémoires*, p. 100. For the older use see Arthur Young, *Political Arithmetic* (London, 1774; reprint, New York, 1967; another reprint, Orpingdon, 1970).

28 Wilhelm von Humboldt, 'Denkschrift über die deutsche Verfassung' (Dec. 1813), Humboldt, *Politische Denkschriften*, ed. Bruno Gebhardt, vol. II (Berlin, 1903), pp. 97–8.

29 Brougham, 'Balance of Power', pp. 2–3 (*Edinburgh Review*, I [1803], p. 346).

30 See, among many, Johann Caspar Bluntschli (Art.), 'Gleichgewicht', *Staatswörterbuch*, 2nd edn, vol. II (Zurich, 1871), p. 81.

31 Leopold von Ranke, 'Die grossen Mächte' [1832], ed. Theodor Schieder, Ranke, *Die grossen Mächte. Politisches Gespräch* (Göttingen, 1963), pp. 3–43.

32 Wilhelm Butte, *Ideen über das politische Gleichgewicht von Europa mit besonderer Rücksicht auf die jetzigen Zeitverhältnisse* (Leipzig, 1814); Gould Francis Leckie, *An Historical Research into the Nature of the Balance of Power in Europe* (London, 1817); Goldmann, *Die europäische Pentarchie* (Leipzig, 1839), p. 21; *Das gestörte Gleichgewicht Europas* (Berlin, 1855); Joseph Maria Ritter von Aresin-Fatton, *Das europäische Gleichgewicht* (Vienna, 1859), pp. 11–13; Constantin Frantz, *Untersuchungen über das europäische Gleichgewicht* (Berlin, 1859), pp. 385–94; *Das europäische Gleichgewicht der Zukunft* (Berlin, 1859), pp. 20–1.

33 Richard Cobden, 'The Balance of Power' (1836), Cobden, *Political Writings*, vol. I (London, New York, 1867), p. 269.

34 See Michael Donelan, ed., *The Reason of States* (London, Boston, Sydney, 1978); Harold Chalconer Dowdell, 'The Word "State"', *Law Quarterly Review*, XXXIX (1923), pp. 98–125; Paul-Ludwig Weinacht, *Staat. Studien zur Begriffsgeschichte des Wortes von den Anfängen bis ins 19. Jahrhundert* (Berlin, 1968).

35 An unequivocal reference to the new meaning occurred in an early work by Georg Wilhelm Friedrich Hegel on the constitution of Germany, apparently written in 1802: Hegel, *Frühe Schriften* (Frankfurt, 1971), p. 461.

36 Georg Jellinek, *Allgemeine Staatslehre*, [Berlin, 1900], 7th reprint of 3rd edn (Bad Homburg vor der Höhe, 1960), pp. 394–434.

37 See Helmut Berding, ed., *Nationales Bewußtsein und kollektive Identität* (Frankfurt, 1994); Alfred Cobban, *Nation-State and National Self-Determination*, rev. edn (London, 1969), pp. 23–56 (1st edn, Chicago, 1944); Joachim Ehlers, 'Mittelalterliche Voraussetzungen für nationale Identität in der Neuzeit', *Nationale und kulturelle Identität*, ed. Bernhard Giesen (Frankfurt, 1991), pp. 77–99; Eric John Hobsbawm, *Nations and Nationalism since 1780* (Cambridge, 1990); Franz Walter Müller, 'Zur Geschichte des Wortes und Begriffes "nation" im französischen Schrifttum des Mittelalters bis zur Mitte des 15. Jahrhunderts', *Romanische Forschungen*, LVIII/IX (1947), pp. 247–321; Alfred Schröker, *Die deutsche Nation. Beobachtungen zur politischen Propaganda des ausgehenden 15. Jahrhunderts* (Lübeck, 1974).

38 Wilhelm Rüstow, *Die Grenzen der Staaten* (Zurich, 1868), pp. 1–5; August von Bulmerincq, *Praxis, Theorie und Codification des Völkerrechts* (Leipzig, 1874), pp. 48–9.

39 Johann Gottlieb Fichte, *Reden an die deutsche Nation* (Berlin, 1808), *Werke*, ed. Immanuel Hermann Fichte, vol. VII (Berlin, 1846), pp. 264–79 (reprint, Berlin, 1971).

40 Georg Wilhelm Friedrich Hegel, *Philosophie des Rechts. Die Vorlesung von 1819/20 in einer Nachschrift*, ed. Dieter Henrich (Frankfurt, 1983), pp. 208, 225–6, 280–91.

41 On Clausewitz's theory of war see Raymond Aron, *Penser la guerre. Clausewitz*, 2 vols (Paris, 1976); Azar Gat, *The Origins of Military Thought: From the Enlightenment to Clausewitz* (Oxford, 1989); Jehuda L. Wallach, *The Dogma of the Battle of Annihilation* (Westport, London, 1986).

42 Carl von Clausewitz, *Vom Kriege* (Berlin, 1832; new edn, Berlin, 1980), pp. 199–200.

43 Jacques Antoine Hippolyte de Guibert, *Essai sur la tactique* (Paris, 1772), p. 55.

44 David Dundas, *Principles of Military Movements* (London, 1788), p. 41.

45 *Ordonnance du Roi pour regler l'exercice de ses troupes d'infanterie* (Paris, 1776); *Reglement concernant l'exercice et les manoeuvres de l'infanterie* (Paris, 1791).

46 Fallati, 'Genesis'.

47 Robert von Mohl, 'Die Pflege der internationalen Gemeinschaft als Aufgabe des Völkerrechtes', Mohl, *Staatsrecht, Völkerrecht und Politik*, vol. I (Tübingen, 1860), pp. 579–636; James Lorimer, 'Le problème final du droit international', *Revue du droit international et de législation comparée*, IX (1877), pp. 161–206. For evolutionist paradigms in anthropology see Lewis Henry Morgan, *Ancient Society* (New York, 1877; reprint, Tucson, 1985); Edward Burnett Tyler, *Anthropology* (New York, London, 1926), pp. 401–40.

48 On the demand for public access to legal documents in the eighteenth century see Andreas Würgler, *Unruhen und Öffentlichkeit. Städtische und ländliche Protestbewegungen im 18. Jahrhundert* (Tübingen, 1995).

49 See Harold Nicolson, *The Congress of Vienna* (London, 1970), pp. 182–200 (first published 1946).

50 James Mackintosh, Address to the House of Commons, 27 April
1814, ed. James Joll, *Britain and Europe* (London, 1961), pp. 66–7. Cf.
George Canning, Address to the House of Commons, 12 Dec. 1826,
Speeches of the Right Honourable George Canning, vol. 6 (London, 1836),
pp. 109–10.

SEVEN · FUNCTIONALISM

1 For a general survey of functionalism see Mark Abrahamson,
Functionalism (Englewood Cliffs, 1978); A. J. R. Groom and Paul Taylor,
Functionalism (London, 1975). The concept of liberalism is notoriously
difficult to define. See Charles Covell, *Kant, Liberalism and the Pursuit of
Justice in the International Order* (Münster, Hamburg, 1994); Dieter
Langewiesche, *Deutscher Liberalismus* (Frankfurt, 1986); Theodor
Schieder, 'Das Verhältnis von politischer und gesellschaftlicher
Verfassung und die Krise des bürgerlichen Liberalismus', *Historische
Zeitschrift*, CLXXVII (1954), pp. 49–74; James Weinstein, *The Corporate
Ideal in the Liberal State 1900–1918* (Boston, 1968).

2 See Alan James, *Sovereign Statehood. The Basis of International Society*
(London, 1986); against: Hermann J. Blanke, *Föderalismus und
Integrationsgewalt* (Berlin, 1991); Michael Burgess and Alain-G. Gagnon,
eds, *Comparative Federalism and Federation* (Toronto, Buffalo, 1993);
Ernst Deuerlein, *Föderalismus* (Munich, 1972); Godehard Josef Ebers,
Die Lehre vom Staatenbunde (Breslau, 1910); Helmut Quaritsch, *Staat und
Souveränität* (Frankfurt, 1970); Quaritsch, *Souveränität* (Berlin, 1986);
K. C. Weare, *Federal Government* (Oxford, 1963).

3 Christoph Besold, *Dissertatio politico-juridica de foederum jure* (Strasbourg,
1622); Ludolf Hugo, *Dissertatio de statu regionum Germaniae* [1661]
(Helmstedt, 1708); Johann Stephan Pütter, *Beyträge zur näheren
Erläuterung und richtigen Bestimmung einiger Lehren des teutschen Staats-
und Fürstenrechts*, part 1 (Göttingen, 1777), pp. 30–2. Further sources
have been discussed by Burgess and Gagnon, *Federalism*; Otto von
Gierke, *Johannes Althusius und die Entwicklung der naturrechtlichen
Staatstheorien*, 3rd edn (Breslau, 1913), pp. 25–6 (first published Breslau,
1880; reprint, Aalen, 1981).

4 John Austin, *The Province of Jurisprudence Determined*, ed. Herbert Lionel
Adolphus Hart (London, 1954), pp. 239–52 (first published London,
1832).

5 Paul Laband, *Das Staatsrecht des Deutschen Reiches*, [Tübingen, 1876] 4th
edn (Tübingen, Leipzig, 1901), pp. 53–4. The opposite position, namely
that there was no material difference between a federation and a confederation and that, consequently, sovereignty would in any case reside with
the member states had been argued already in the seventeenth century by
Samuel von Pufendorf, *De jure naturae et gentium*, cap. VII/5,17; VII/6,1
(Amsterdam, 1688; reprint, Oxford, London, 1934), pp. 715–17, 722,
and was taken up in the nineteenth century by John Caldwell Calhoun,
'A Discourse on the Constitution and Government of the United States'
(*c.* 1849), Calhoun, *A Disquisition of Government and A Discourse on the
Constitution and Government of the United States*, ed. Richard Crallé (New

York, 1968), pp. 120–1, in the USA, and by Max von Seydel, 'Der Bundesstaatsbegriff', *Zeitschrift für die gesamte Staatswissenschaft*, XXVIII (1872), pp. 198, 208, in Bavaria.

6 Laband, *Staatsrecht*, pp. 52–3; author's translation.

7 *Ibid.*, p. 57; author's translation.

8 Heinrich Rosin, 'Grundzüge einer allgemeinen Staatslehre nach den politischen Reden und Schriftstücken des Fürsten Bismarck', *Annalen des Deutschen Reichs für Gesetzgebung, Verwaltung und Statistik* (1898), pp. 81–126; Heinrich Triepel, 'Die Kompetenz des Bundesstaats und die geschriebene Verfassung', *Staatsrechtliche Abhandlungen. Festgabe für Paul Laband* (Tübingen, 1908), pp. 247–335; Philipp Zorn, 'Neue Beiträge zur Lehre vom Bundesstaat', *Annalen des Deutschen Reichs für Gesetzgebung, Verwaltung und Statistik* (1884), pp. 453–83; Eugène Borel, *Sur la souveraineté et l'état fédératif* (Bern, 1886); Louis Erasme LeFur, *Etat fédéral et confédération d'états* (Paris, 1896); James Lorimer, *The Institutes of the Law of Nations*, vol. I (Edinburgh, 1883), pp. 194–203. See on applications of federalism in colonial affairs: Donald Rothchild, ed., *Politics of Integration* (Nairobi, 1968); Bruce W. Hodgkins *et al.*, *Federalism in Canada and Australia* (Orchard Park, NY, 1989).

9 Albert Schäffle, *Bau und Leben des socialen Körpers*, vol. IV/2 (Tübingen, 1881), pp. 216–19. Cf. Heinrich Ahrens, *Die Philosophie des Rechts. Die organische Staatslehre auf philosophisch-anthropologischer Grundlage* (Vienna, 1850); Herbert Spencer, *Principles of Sociology*, vol. I (New York, London, 1910), pp. 449–53.

10 See George Catlin, *The Science and Method of Politics* (London, 1927), pp. 181–3; Charles Pentland, *International Theory and European Integration* (London, 1973), pp. 64–99; Trevor Taylor, *Approaches and Theories in International Relations* (London, 1978), p. 239.

11 Schäffle, *Bau*, pp. 217–18.

12 *Ibid.*, p. 219; author's translation.

13 Constantin Frantz, *Der Föderalismus als das leitende Princip für die sociale, staatliche und internationale Organisation* (Mainz, 1879), pp. 316, 402, reprint (Aalen, 1962).

14 Max Scheler, *Der Genius des Krieges und der Deutsche Krieg* (Leipzig, 1915), pp. 370–3; re-ed. in Scheler, *Politisch-pädagogische Schriften*, ed. Manfred S. Frings (Berlin, Munich, 1982); Georg Simmel, 'Deutschlands innere Wandlung' (Nov. 1914), Simmel, *Der Krieg und die geistigen Entscheidungen* (Munich, Leipzig, 1917), pp. 7–29.

15 Otto Hintze, 'Imperialismus und Weltpolitik', *Die deutsche Freiheit* (1917), p. 117; author's translation.

16 Otto Hintze, 'Imperialismus und Weltpolitik' (1907), Hintze, *Staat und Verfassung*, ed. Fritz Hartung (Leipzig, 1941), p. 459; author's translation.

17 Hintze, 'Imperialismus' (1917), p. 118.

18 Kaiser Wilhelm II put on record this concept of 'world politics' in his public address of 18 January 1896 on the occasion of the 25th anniversary of the foundation of the German Empire.

19 See Max Huber, 'Beiträge zur Kenntnis der soziologischen Grundlagen des Völkerrechts und der Staatengesellschaft', *Jahrbuch des öffentlichen Rechts*, IV (1910), p. 70.

20 See on liberal internationalism; Cornelia Navori, 'The Great Illusion Revisited. The International Theory of Norman Angell', *Review of International Studies* XV (1989), pp. 341–58. Louis Bisceglia, *Norman Angell and the Liberal Internationalism in Britain 1931–1939* (New York, 1982); John Donald Bruce Miller, *Norman Angell and the Futility of War. Peace and the Public Mind* (London, 1986).

21 Norman Angell, *The Great Illusion* (London, 1910); Hans Wehberg, *Die internationale Friedensbewegung* (Mönchengladbach, 1911).

22 Henry Noel Brailsford, *The War of Steel and Gold*, 10th edn (London, 1918), pp. 28–9 (first published 1914); David Jayne Hill, *World Organization as Affected by the Nature of the Modern State* (New York, 1911), pp. 131–2; Huber, 'Beiträge', pp. 56–134; Huber, 'Die Gleichheit der Staaten', *Rechtswissenschaftliche Beiträge: Festgabe des Auslandes zu Joseph Kohlers 60. Geburtstag*, ed. Fritz Berolzheimer (Stuttgart, 1909), pp. 88–108.

23 Lassa Francis Lawrence Oppenheim, *International Law*, vol. I, 4th edn, ed. Arnold D. McNair (London, 1928), p. 99.

24 Hans Wehberg, 'Ideen und Projekte betr[effend] die Vereinigten Staaten von Europa in den letzten 100 Jahren', *Die Friedens-Warte*, LI (1941), pp. 11–82; new edn, ed. Frank Boldt and Karl Holl (Bremen, 1984).

25 Oppenheim, *International Law*, p. 99.

26 *Ibid.*, pp. 100–1, 361.

27 Walther Schücking, 'Die Organisation der Welt', *Staatsrechtliche Abhandlungen. Festgabe für Paul Laband* (Tübingen, 1908), pp. 594–5.

28 Huber, 'Beiträge', pp. 61, 68.

29 'Convention for the Formation of a Universal Postal Union', 1 June 1878, ed. Wilhelm Georg Grewe, *Fontes historiae juris gentium*, vol. III/1 (Berlin, New York, 1992), pp. 538–45.

30 Schücking, 'Organisation', pp. 594–5. On internationalism see Karl Bünzli, *Der Beitrag der Schweiz zum Zustandekommen universeller Kodifikation des Völkerrechts* (Zurich, 1984); Hedley Bull, 'The Emergence of a Universal International Society', Hedley Bull and Watson Adams, eds, *The Expansion of International Society* (New York, 1984), pp. 117–26; Bull, 'The Grotian Conception of International Society', *Diplomatic Investigations*, ed. Herbert Butterfield and Martin Wight (Cambridge, MA, 1966), pp. 51–73; Madeleine Heeren, 'Modernisierung, Außenpolitik und Integration im Jahrhundert des Internationalismus', *Historische Mitteilungen, herausgegeben im Auftrag der Ranke-Gesellschaft*, VII/1 (1994), pp. 1–43; Akira Iriye, *Cultural Internationalism and World Order* (Baltimore, 1997); Francis Stewart Leland Lyons, *Internationalism in Europe 1815–1914* (Leiden, 1963).

31 Huber, 'Beiträge', p. 85; Schücking, 'Organisation', pp. 594, 610–11.

32 Huber, 'Beiträge', pp. 94–5.

33 Quoted from Hans-Jürgen Schlochauer, *Die Idee des ewigen Friedens* (Bonn, 1953), p. 136.

34 See Alfred Hermann Fried, *Handbuch der Friedensbewegung* (Vienna, Leipzig, 1905); Fried, *Die Haager Conferenz, ihre Bedeutung und ihre Ergebnisse* (Berlin, 1900); Fried, *Die zweite Haager Konferenz, ihre Arbeiten, ihre Ergebnisse und ihre Bedeutung* (Leipzig, 1908); James Brown

Scott, *The Hague Peace Conferences of 1899 and 1907* (Baltimore, 1909). On the preparations for the conferences see Jost Dülffer, *Regeln gegen den Krieg? Die Haager Friedenskonferenzen 1899 und 1907 in der internationalen Politik* (Berlin, Frankfurt, Vienna, 1981); Jean Freymond, 'Diplomatie multilaterale et négociation informelle', *Relations internationales*, XL (1984), pp. 403–12; Verdiana Grossi, *Le pacifisme européen 1889–1914* (Brussels, 1994).

35 It was speculated early on that the Muraviev memorandum had been inspired by financial difficulties of the Russian government. See Emile Joseph Dillon, *The Eclipse of Russia* (London, Toronto, 1918), pp. 274, 277–8.

36 For its published pronouncements on international organization at the end of World War I see Hermann Grauert, 'Zur Geschichte des Weltfriedens und der Idee einer Liga der Nationen', *Historisches Jahrbuch*, XXXIX (1920), pp. 115–243; Christian Louis Lange and August Schon, *Histoire de l'Internationalisme*, 3 vols (Oslo, 1919–54); Jakob ter Meulen, *Der Gedanke der internationalen Organisation*, 2 vols in 3 parts (The Hague, 1929–40) (vol. I was first published as a Zurich doctoral dissertation in 1917); Albert Frederick Pollard, *The League of Nations in History* (London, New York, 1918); Walther Schücking, *Der Bund der Völker* (Leipzig, 1918); Veit Valentin, *Geschichte des Völkerbundsgedankens in Deutschland* (Berlin, 1920); Elizabeth York [i.e. Lottie Elizabeth Bracher], *Leagues of Nations* (New York, 1919).

37 See David Playfair Heatley, *Diplomacy and the Study of International Relations* (Oxford, 1919). On the history of the discipline see Michael Banks, 'The Evolution of International Relations Theory', Banks, ed., *Conflict in World Society* (Brighton, 1984), pp. 3–21; Ernst-Otto Czempiel, 'Die Entwicklung der Lehre von den internationalen Beziehungen', *Politische Vierteljahresschrift*, VI (1965), pp. 270–90; Klaus-Jürgen Gantzel, *Kolonialrechtswissenschaft, Kriegsursachenforschung, Internationale Angelegenheiten. Materialien zur Geschichte des Instituts für Internationale Angelegenheiten der Universität Hamburg 1923–1983 im Widerstreit der Interessen* (Baden-Baden, 1983); Kalevi Jeako Holsti, 'The Study of International Politics During the Cold War', *Review of International Studies* XXIV, special issue (1998), pp. 17–46. Randolph C. Kent and Gunnar P. Nielsson, eds, *The Study and Teaching of International Relations* (London, New York, 1980); Gene M. Lyons, 'The Study of International Relations in Great Britain', *World Politics*, XXXVIII (1986), pp. 626–45; Reinhard Meyers, *Die Lehre von den internationalen Beziehungen. Ein entwicklungsgeschichtlicher Überblick* (Königstein, 1981); W. C. Olson and Nicholas Onuf, 'The Growth of a Discipline Reviewed', *International Relations. British and American Perspectives*, ed. Steve Smith (Oxford, 1985), pp. 1–28; Brian Porter, ed. *The Aberystwyth Papers. International Politics 1919–1939* (London, 1972); Volker Rittberger, ed., *Theorien der internationalen Beziehungen* (Opladen, 1990); Steve M. Smith, 'The Development of International Relations Theory', *Teaching Politics*, XIV (1985), pp. 103–23; Steve M. Smith, 'Paradigm Dominance in International Relations. The Development of International Relations as a Social Science', *The Study of International*

Relations, ed. Hugh C. Dyer and Leon Mangasarian (New York, 1989), pp. 3–27; Steve M. Smith and Ken Booth, eds *International Theory Today* (Cambridge, Oxford, 1995); Steve Smith, Ken Booth and Marysia Zalewski, eds, *International Theory. Positivism and Beyond* (Cambridge, 1996); Peter Wilson, 'The Myth of The "First Great Debate"', *Review of International Studies*, special issue (1998), pp. 1–150.

38 Paul Samuel Reinsch, *World Politics at the End of the Nineteenth Century as Influenced by the Oriental Situation* (London, 1900), pp. 3–26.

39 Arthur James Grant, ed., *Introduction to the Study of International Relations* (London, 1916). Other introductions followed quickly: Sidney Woolf, *International Government* (Westminster, 1916); T. J. Lawrence, *The Society of Nations* (New York, 1919); Stephan Haley Allen, *International Relations* (Princeton, 1920); Herbert A. Gibbons, *Introduction to World Politics* (New York, 1922); P. M. Brown, *International Society* (New York, 1923); Raymond L. Buell, *International Relations* (New York, 1925).

40 See on Zimmern: *Thinking of the Twenty Years' Crisis. Inter-war Idealism Reassessed*, ed. David Long and Peter Wilson (Oxford, 1995); D. J. Markwell, 'Sir Alfred Zimmern Fifty Years on', *Review of International Studies*, XII (1986), pp. 277–92.

41 Alfred Zimmern, *Learning and Leadership: A Study of the Needs and Possibilities of International Intellectual Cooperation* (London, 1928); Zimmern, *The League of Nations and the Rule of Law 1918–1935* (London, 1936); Zimmern, *Spiritual Values and World Affairs* (Oxford, 1939).

42 David Mitrany, *The Progress of International Government* (London, 1933); Mitrany, *A Working Peace System*, new ed. Hans J. Morgenthau; Chicago, 1966; first edn London,1943, partly reprinted in *The European Union*, ed. Brent F. Nelsen and Alexander C.-G. Stubb (Boulder, London, 1994), pp. 77–98; Mitrany, 'The Prospect of Integration. Federal or Functional', *Journal of Common Market Studies* IV (1965), pp. 123–34. On Mitrany see Mark F. Imber, 'Re-reading Mitrany. A Pragmatic Assessment of Sovereignty', *Review of International Studies*, x (1984), pp. 103–23; Paul Taylor, 'Functionalism. The Theory of David Mitrany', *International Organization*, ed. Paul Taylor and A.J.R. Groom (London, 1978), pp. 236–52; 'Introduction to David Mitrany', *The Functional Theory of Politics* (London, New York, 1975), pp. ix–xxv.

43 Ludwig von Bertalanffy, 'An Outline of General Systems Theory', *British Journal for the Philosophy of Science*, I (1950), pp. 139–40, 155–7.

44 Bronislaw Malinoswki, 'The Functional Theory', *A Scientific Theory of Culture and Other Essays* (New York, 1960), p. 150; Talcott Parsons, 'Order and Community in the International System', *International Politics and Foreign Policy*, ed. James N. Rosenau (Glencoe, 1961), p. 123.

45 See Gérard Leclerc, *Anthropologie et colonialisme* (Paris, 1972).

46 Among them Talcott Parsons, *The Social System* (New York, 1951); Alfred Reginald Radcliffe-Brown, *Structure and Function in Primitive Society* (London, 1952).

47 On Wilson's foreign policy concepts see Lloyd E. Ambrosius, *Wilsonian Statecraft. Theory and Practice of Liberal Internationalism during World War I* (Wilmington, DE, 1991); Edward Henry Buehrig, *Woodrow Wilson and the Balance of Power* (Bloomington, 1955); Thomas J. Knock, *To End All*

Wars. Woodrow Wilson and the Quest for a New World Order (Oxford, New York, 1992; new edn, Princeton, 1995); Arno J. Mayer, *Political Origins of the New Diplomacy 1917–1918* (New Haven, 1959).

48 Woodrow Wilson, *The Public Papers*, vol. xl/(Princeton, 1982), pp. 535–6; vol. xlv (1984), pp. 534–9, vol liii (1986), pp. 532, 599.

49 William Barry, 'Mr Wilson's Monism', *National Review*, lxxiii (1919), pp. 337–45; Arthur W. Spencer, 'The Organization of International Force', *American Journal of International Law*, ix (1915), p. 66; Tor Hugo Wistrand, 'The Principle of Equilibrium', *American Journal of International Law*, xv (1921), pp. 528–9.

50 Statement by British Colonial Secretary Stanley in 1943, printed in *British Imperial Policy and Decolonization*, ed. A. N. Porter and A. J. Stockwell, vol. i (Basingstoke, 1987), p. 142.

EIGHT · REALISM

1 See on the intellectual history of realism: James E. Dougherty and Robert L. Pfaltzgraff, *Contending Theories of International Relations*, 3rd edn (New York, 1990), p. 81 (first published 1981); Benjamin Frankel, ed., *Roots of Realism* (London, Portland, OR, 1996); Frankel, 'Restating the Realist Case', *Realism. Restatements and Renewal*, ed. Frankel (London, Portland, OR, 1996), pp. ix–xx; Martin Griffiths, *Realism, Idealism and International Politics* (London, New York, 1995; 1st edn, London, New York, 1992); Edward Vose Gulick, *Europe's Classical Balance of Power* (Ithaca, 1955), pp. 3–91; Cynthia Eagle Russett, *The Concept of Equilibrium in American Social Thought* (New Haven, London, 1966); Rosalyn L. Simowitz, *The Logical Consistency and Soundness of the Balance of Power Theory* (Denver, 1982), pp. 1–15; Michael Joseph Smith, *Realist Thought from Weber to Kissinger* (Baton Rouge, London, 1987); Steve Smith, 'The Development of International Relations and as a Social Science', *Millennium*, xvi (1987), pp. 189–206; Roger D. Spegele, *Political Realism in International Theory* (Cambridge, 1996), pp. 22–80; John J. Weltman, *Systems Theory in International Relations* (Boston, 1973), pp. 1–34.

2 There are rival views on the dating of the origins of realism. Robert G. Gilpin, 'The Richness of the Tradition of Political Realism', *International Organization*, xxxviii (1984), p. 290, has traced realism back to Thucydides. Edward Hallett Carr, *The Twenty Years' Crisis 1919–1939* (London, Basingstoke, 1981) pp. 63–5 (first published, London, 1939), thought that realism went back to Machiavelli, whereas Martin Wight, *International Theory. The Three Traditions*, ed. Gabriele Wight and Brian Porter (Leicester, 1991), pp. 16–17, and Hedley Bull, *Anarchical Society* (London, Basingstoke, 1977), pp. 101–26, considered Machiavelli and Hobbes as originators. Stanley Hoffman, *The State of War* (New York, 1965), p. 86, and W. B. Gallie, *Philosophers of Peace and War* (Cambridge, 1978), pp. 18–19, have named Rousseau as the founding father of realism. Scholars who have held these views have not considered realism as a branch of biologism but have regarded it as a theoretical justification of *Realpolitik*. For the debate see Laurie M. Johnson Bagby, 'The Use and

Abuse of Thucydides', *International Organization*, XLVIII (1994),
pp. 131–53; Francis Harry Hinsley, *Power and the Pursuit of Peace: Theory and Practice in the History of Relations between States* (Cambridge, 1963),
pp. 46–61; Michael C. Williams, 'Rousseau, Realism and *Realpolitik*',
Millennium, XVIII (1989), pp. 185–203.

3 Robert Stuart Viscount Castlereagh, 'Principles of the Concert' (1818),
ed. Evan Luard, *Basic Texts in International Relations* (London, 1992),
p. 431.

4 One or the other theorist joined in and confined membership in the
international system to the 'entirety of the Christian and civilized states'
of the world operating on the balance of power as its 'stable though not
unchangeable basis'. See e.g. Karl Heinrich Ludwig Pölitz, *Die
Staatswissenschaften*, vol. v, 2nd edn (Leipzig, 1828), pp. 38–9.

5 Eyre Crowe, 'Memorandum dated 1 Jan. 1907', *British Documents on the
Origins of the War*, vol. VI, ed. Harold Temperley and George Peabody
Gooch (London, 1930), pp. 402–3. See also Edward Grey, 'Minutes of
the Committee of Imperial Defence' (25 May 1911), in *British
Documents*, pp. 782–4.

6 See Karl Jacob, 'Die Chimäre des Gleichgewichts', *Archiv für
Urkundenforschung*, VI (1918), pp. 341–4; A. von Kirchheim, 'Politisches
Gleichgewicht', *Deutsche Revue*, XL/4 (1915), pp. 308–13; Heinrich Otto
Meisner, 'Vom europäischen Gleichgewicht', *Preußische Jahrbücher*,
CLXXVI (1919), pp. 222–45; Ferdinand Jakob Schmidt, 'Das Ethos des
politischen Gleichgewichtsgedankens', *Preußische Jahrbücher*, CLVIII
(1914), pp. 1–15; Alfred Stern, 'Das politische Gleichgewicht', *Archiv für
Politik und Geschichte*, III (1925), pp. 29–37.

7 Mahan argued explicitly against Norman Angell, *The Great Illusion*
(London, 1910).

8 Alfred Thayer Mahan, *Armaments and Arbitration or the Place of Force in
the International Relations of States* (New York, 1912), pp. 15–32.

9 *Ibid.*, p. 131.

10 See J. J. Ruedorffer [i.e. Kurt Riezler], *Grundzüge der Weltpolitik der
Gegenwart* (Stuttgart, Berlin, 1914), pp. 5–39, 183–91.

11 Friedrich Meinecke, *Die Entstehung des Historismus* (Munich, Berlin,
1936); re-ed. Carl Hinrichs, Meinecke, *Werke*, vol. III (Stuttgart, 1965);
English version (London, 1972); Karl Heussi, *Die Krise des Historismus*
(Tübingen, 1932); Ernst Troeltsch, *Der Historismus und seine Überwin-
dung* (Berlin, 1924).

12 Léonce Donnadieu, *Essai sur la théorie d'équilibre* (Paris, 1900); Charles
Dupuis, *Le principe d'équilibre et le Concert Européen de la Paix de Westphalie
à l'Acte d'Algésiras* (Paris, 1909); Gabriel Albert Auguste Hanotaux,
Etudes diplomatiques. La politique de l'équilibre (Paris, 1912); Olof Höijer,
La théorie de l'équilibre et le droit des gens (Paris, 1917); Ernst Kaeber, *Die
Idee des europäischen Gleichgewichts in der publizistischen Literatur vom 16.
bis zur Mitte des 18. Jahrhunderts* (Berlin, 1907; reprint, Hildesheim,
1971); Ernest Nys, 'La théorie de l'équilibre européen', *Revue de droit
international et législation comparée*, XXV (1893), pp. 34–57; Nys, *Les origines du droit international* (Brussels, 1894), pp. 165ff.; Aleksandr
Nikolaevič de Stiglits [Stieglitz], *De l'équilibre politique, du légitimisme et*

du principe des nationalités, vol. I (Paris, 1893). On the historicist approach to international relations see Robert Jervis, 'Systems Theory and Diplomatic History', *Diplomacy*, ed. P. G. Lauren (New York, 1979), pp. 212–44; Robert J. B. Walker, 'History and Structure in the Theory of International Relations', *Millennium*, XVIII (1989), pp. 163–83.

13 Gulick, *Balance of Power*, pp. 184–261. For recent restatements see Paul W. Schroeder, 'Historical Reality vs. Neo-realist Theory', *International Security*, XIX (1994), pp. 108–48; Michael Sheehan, *The Balance of Power* (London, New York, 1996), pp. 1-23.

14 Edwin Montefiore Borchard, 'The United States as a Factor in the Development of International Relations', *The History and Nature of International Relations*, ed. Edmund Aloysius Walsh (New York, 1922), pp. 230–1; Goldsworthy Lowes Dickinson, *The International Anarchy* (London, 1926), pp. 2–23; Paul Scott Mowrer, *Our Foreign Affairs* (New York, 1924), p. 252; Albert Frederick Pollard, 'The Balance of Power', *Journal of the British Institute of International Affairs* II (1923), pp. 51–64.

15 Winston Spencer Churchill, *The World Crisis 1911–1914* (London, 1923), p. 9.

16 *Ibid.*, pp. 5, 188–9.

17 Winston Spencer Churchill, *The Second World War*, vol. II, *The Gathering Storm* (London, 1948), pp. 207–8.

18 Winston Spencer Churchill, *The Sinews of Power. Postwar Speeches* (Boston, 1949), p. 103.

19 Charles Edward Merriam, *History of Sovereignty since Rousseau* (New York, 1900).

20 Quincy Wright, *A Study of War* (Chicago, 1941), pp. 695–6, 698, 2nd edn (Chicago, 1965).

21 Quincy Wright, *The Study of International Relations* (New York, 1955), p. 148.

22 See e.g. 'The Uganda Agreement' (1900), *Laws of the Uganda Protectorate*, ed. Arthur W. Lewey and Charles Mathew (Entebbe, 1937), pp. 1373–85; Donald Rothchild, ed., *Politics of Integration. An East African Documentary* (Nairobi, 1968), pp. 21–2.

23 Wright, *Study of War*. A. F. Kovacs, The Development of the Principle of the Balance of Power from the Treaty of Westphalia to the Congress of Vienna, Ms. Library of the University of Chicago, Wright Papers, 1932. See on Wright: Kenneth W. Thompson, *Schools of Thought in International Relations* (Baton Rouge, London, 1996), pp. 10–26.

24 Quincy Wright, 'International Law and the Balance of Power', *American Journal of International Law*, XXXVII (1943), p. 98.

25 Carl Joachim Friedrich, *Foreign Policy in the Making. The Search for a New Balance of Power* (New York, 1938), p. 138.

26 Nicholas John Spykman, *America's Strategy in World Politics. The United States and the Balance of Power* (New York, 1942), p. 460. Although at the time of the publication of this work the future defeat of the German and the Japanese armed forces was recognizable, Spykman ranked Germany and Japan together with the USA, the United Kingdom, the Soviet Union and China as 'great powers'.

27 On Morgenthau see Christoph Frei, *Hans J. Morgenthau*, 2nd edn (Bern, 1994); Peter Gellman, 'Hans J. Morgenthau and the Legacy of Political Realism', *Review of International Studies*, XIV (1988), pp. 247–66; Robert Jervis, 'Hans Morgenthau, Realism, and the Scientific Study of International Politics', *Social Research*, LXI (1994), pp. 856–76; Jaap W. Nobel, 'Morgenthau's Theory and Practice', *Review of International Studies*, XV (1989), pp. 281–93; Nobel, 'Morgenthau's Struggle with Power', *Review of International Studies*, XXI (1995), pp. 61–85; Smith, Hans Pichler, 'The Godfathers of "Truth". Max Weber and Carl Schmitt in Morgenthau's Theory of Power Politics', *Review of International Studies*, XXIV (1998) pp. 185–200. *Realist Thought*, pp. 134–64; Kenneth W. Thompson and Robert J. Myers, *Truth and Tragedy: A Tribute to Hans Morgenthau* (New Brunswick, 1983); Alfons Söllner, 'German Conservatism in America. Morgenthau's Political Realism', *Telos* LXXII (1987) pp. 161–77; J. Ann Tickner, 'Hans Morgenthau's Principles of Political Realism', *Gender and International Relations*, ed. Rebecca Grant and Kathleen J. Newland (Bloomington, 1991), pp. 27–40, first published in *Millenium* XVII (1988).

28 Hans Joachim Morgenthau, *Politics among Nations*, 5th edn (New York, 1973), pp. 27–39, 167–221, 548–50 (first published 1948).

29 Reinhold Niebuhr, *Moral Man and Immoral Society* (New York, London, 1932), pp. 19, 83ff. On Niebuhr see Thompson, *Schools*, pp. 38–40.

30 Friedrich Meinecke, *Die Idee der Staatsräson* (Munich, Berlin, 1924); re-ed. Walther Hofer, Meinecke, *Werke*, vol. 1 (Stuttgart, 1957), 2nd edn (1960); English version (London, 1957). On Meinecke see *Friedrich Meinecke heute*, ed. Michael Erbe (Berlin, 1981).

31 Erich Marcks, *Englische Machtpolitik*, ed. Willy Andreas (Leipzig, 1940); Hermann Oncken, 'Über die Zusammenhänge zwischen äußerer und innerer Politik', *Vorträge der Gehe-Stiftung*, IX (1918), pp. 119–52. On the neo-Rankean research tradition see Hans-Heinz Krill, *Die Rankerenaissance. Max Lenz und Erich Marcks* (Berlin, 1962).

32 He translated parts of Ranke's work into English. See Theodore Hermann von Laue, *Leopold von Ranke. The Formative Years* (Princeton, 1950).

33 Walther Kienast, 'Die Anfänge des europäischen Staatensystems im späteren Mittelalter', *Historische Zeitschrift*, CLIII (1936), pp. 229–71.

34 On Carr see Hedley Bull, 'The Twenty Years Crisis Thirty Years On', *International Journal*, XXIV (1969), pp. 625–38; Graham Evans, 'E. H. Carr and International Relations', *British Journal of International Studies*, 1 (1975), pp. 77–97; William Thornton Rickert Fox, 'Carr and Political Realism', *Review of International Studies*, XI (1985), pp. 1–16; Paul Howe, 'The Utopian Realism of E. H. Carr', *Review of International Studies*, XX (1994), pp. 277–97; Hans Joachim Morgenthau [rev. art.], 'The Political Science of E. H. Carr', *World Politics*, I (1949), pp. 127–34; Smith, *Realist Thought*, pp. 68–98.

35 Carr, *Twenty Years' Crisis*, pp. 224, 26–7, 11.

36 *Ibid.*, p. 10.

37 Similarly: Georg Schwarzenberger, *Power Politics* (London, 1941), p. 125 (4th edn, 1964).

38 On Fox see Elizabeth C. Hanson, 'William T. R. Fox and the Study of World Politics', *The Evolution of Theory in International Relations. Essays in Honor of William T. R. Fox*, ed. Robert L. Rothstein (Columbia, SC, 1991), pp. 1–20.

39 [George Frost Kennan], 'The Sources of Soviet Conduct', *Foreign Affairs* xxv (1947), pp. 566–82. Similarly in *Foreign Relations of the United States, 1946* (Washington, 1969), pp. 700–707. On Kennan's realism see Smith, *Realist Thought*, pp. 165–91.

40 Henry Alfred Kissinger, *A World Restored* (London, 1957); Kissinger, *Diplomacy* (New York, 1994), pp. 78–102. It was already well known at the time that Kissinger was opposed to Willy Brandt's *Ostpolitik* because he thought it would weaken the Atlantic alliance. See Kissinger, *The White House Years* (Boston, Toronto, 1979), pp. 405–12. See on Kissinger: Robert D. Schulzinger, *Henry Kissinger, Doctor of Diplomacy* (New York, 1991).

41 John Hermann Herz, *Political Realism and Political Idealism* (Chicago, 1951); Herz, 'Power Politics and World Organization', *American Political Science Review*, xxxvi (1942), pp. 1039–52; Herz, 'The Rise and Demise of the Territorial State', *World Politics*, ix (1957), pp. 473–93.

42 John Herz, 'Idealist Internationalism and the Security Dilemma', *World Politics*, ii (1950), p. 157. For a comment see Quincy Wright [rev. art.], 'Realism and Idealism in International Politics', *World Politics*, v (1952), pp. 116–28.

43 Morton A. Kaplan, *Systems and Process in International Politics* (New York, 1957); Kaplan, 'The Systems Approach to International Politics', Kaplan, *Macropolitics* (Chicago, 1969), pp. 209–42; Kaplan, *Towards Professionalism in International Theory* (New York, London, 1979).

44 Raymond Aron, *Peace and War* (Garden City, 1966).

45 Martin Wight, *Power Politics* (London, 1946; reprint, New York, 1978); Martin Wight and Herbert Butterfield, eds, *Diplomatic Investigations* (London, 1966); Martin Wight, *Systems of States*, ed. Hedley Bull (Leicester, 1977); Wight, *International Theory*.

46 On Wight see Chris Brown, *International Relations Theory: New Normative Approaches* (New York, London, 1992), pp. 4–8; Hedley Bull, 'Martin Wight and the Theory of International Relations', Wight, *International Theory*, pp. ix–xxiii (first published *British Journal of International Studies*, ii [1976], pp. 101–16); Barry Buzan, 'From International System to International Society: Structural Realism and Regime Theory Meet the English School', *International Organization*, xlvii (1993), pp. 327–52; Timothy Dunne, *Inventing International Society: A History of the English School* (London, New York, 1998); Roger Epp, 'The English School on the Frontiers of International Relations', *Review of International Studies* xxiv, special issue (1998), pp. 47–63; Sheila Grader, 'The English School of International Relations', *Review of International Studies*, xiv (1988), pp. 29–44; Pierre Hassner, 'Beyond the Three Traditions: The Philosophy of War and Peace in Historical Perspective', *International Affairs*, lxx (1994), pp. 737–56; Robert H. Jackson, 'Martin Wight, International Theory and the Good Life', *Millennium*, xix (1990), pp. 261–72; Roy Jones, 'The English School of International Relations: A Case for Closure', *Review of International*

Studies, VII (1981), pp. 1–22; Brian Porter, 'Patterns of Thought and Practice. Martin Wight's "International Theory"', *The Reason of States*, ed. Michael Donelan (London, 1978), pp. 64–74; Peter Wilson, 'The English School of International Relations', *Review of International Studies*, XV (1989), pp. 49–58; David Yost, 'Political Philosophy and the Theory of International Politics', *International Affairs*, LXX (1994), pp. 263–90.

47 Bull, *Anarchical Society*; Bull, 'Society and Anarchy in International Relations', *Diplomatic Investigations*, ed. Herbert Butterfield and Martin Wight (London, 1966), pp. 35–50; Bull, 'The New Balance of Power in Asia and the Pacific', *Foreign Affairs*, XLIX (1972), pp. 669–81. It is true that, in his later publications, Bull moved away from his realist origins. See Bull, 'Hobbes and International Anarchy', *Social Research*, XLVIII (1981), pp. 717–39; Bull, 'The International Anarchy in the 1980s', *Australian Outlook*, XXXVII (1983), pp. 127–31. On Bull's work see Stanley Hoffmann, 'Hedley Bull and His Contribution to International Relations', *International Affairs*, LXII (1986), pp. 179–95; R. John Vincent, 'Hedley Bull and Order in International Relations', *Millennium*, XVII (1988), pp. 195–214; *Order and Violence. Hedley Bull and International Relations* , ed. R. John Vincent and John Donald Bruce Miller (Oxford 1990).

48 For the debate see Bagby, 'Use and Abuse of Thucydides'; Gilpin, 'The Richness of the Tradition of Political Realism'; Alexander Wendt, 'Anarchy Is What States Make of It', *International Organization*, XLVI (1992), pp. 395–403.

49 Carr, *Twenty Years' Crisis*, p. 231.

50 Criticisms of the positivist bias innate in realism appeared already in the 1950s: Robert Tucker, 'Professor Morgenthau's Theory of Political "Realism"', *American Political Science Review*, XLVI (1952), pp. 214–24; Benno Wassermann, 'The Scientific Pretensions of Professor Morgenthau's Theory of Power Politics', *Australian Outlook*, XIII (1959), pp. 55–70. They were later articulated powerfully by Friedrich August von Hayek, *Law, Legislation and Liberty*, vol. I, *Rules and Order* (Chicago, London, 1973), pp. 16–17. For recent restatements see Richard K. Ashley, 'The Poverty of Neorealism', *International Organization*, XXXVIII (1984), pp. 230–61; Barry Buzan, 'The Timeless Wisdom of Realism?', Steve Smith, Ken Booth and Marysia Zalewski, eds, *International Theory. Positivism and Beyond* (Cambridge, 1996), pp. 47–65; Stanley Hoffmann, 'Notes on the Limits of Realism', *Social Research*, XLVIII (1981), pp. 653–9.

NINE · CHALLENGERS, RIVALS AND VARIANTS: FUNCTIONALISM AND REALISM IN CONTEXT

1 Rudolf Hilferding, *Das Finanzkapital* (Vienna, 1910); Rosa Luxemburg, *Die Akkumulation des Kapitals* (Berlin, 1913); Vladimir Il'ich Lenin, *Imperialism, the Highest* [originally: the Latest] *Stage of Capitalism* (written in 1916); English translation of the original version (London, 1917); English translation of the final version (New York, 1933). See also John Atkinson Hobson, *Imperialism* (London, 1902). Hobson was a left liberal whose views were similar to those of Hilferding.

2 On liberal and socialist theories of imperialism see David Long, *Towards a New Liberal Internationalism: The International Theory of J. A. Hobson* (Cambridge, 1995); Wolfgang Justin Mommsen, *Theories of Imperialism* (Chicago, London, 1979); Hans-Christoph Schröder, *Sozialistische Imperialismusdeutung* (Göttingen, 1973).

3 On the biography of Carr see R. W. Davies, 'Carr, Edward Hallett', *Dictionary of National Biography 1981–1985* (Oxford, 1990), pp. 75–6.

4 See Ernst Nolte, *Der Faschismus in seiner Epoche* (Munich, 1963); Davies, 'Edward Hallett Carr', *Proceedings of The British Academy* LXIX (1983), pp. 473–511.

5 Fascism was used as an ideology by the anti-colonial liberation movements, specifically Subhas Chandra Bose in India, Aung San in Burma and local supporters of the Japanese military in Indonesia. See Johannes H. Voigt, *Indien im Zweiten Weltkrieg* (Munich, 1978); Aung San Suu Kyi, *Aung San of Burma*, 2nd edn (Edinburgh, 1991), pp. 15–16 (first published Brisbane, 1984); Joseph Silverstein, ed., *The Political Legacy of Aung San* (Ithaca, 1993), pp. 19–20 (1st edn 1972); Ken'ichi Gotô, 'Impuls und Erbe der japanischen Militärherrschaft in Indonesien', *Zeitschrift für Geschichtswissenschaft*, XLVII (1999), pp. 109–29.

6 Egon von Eickstedt, *Rassenkunde und Rassengeschichte der Menschheit* (Stuttgart, 1934); Ilse Schwidetzky, *Turaniden-Studien* (Mainz, 1950) (Abhandlungen der Akademie der Wissenschaften und der Literatur Mainz. Mathematisch-Narturwissenschaftliche Klasse. 1950, 9.).

7 Houston Stuart Chamberlain, *Die Grundlagen des neunzehnten Jahrhunderts*, vol. 1 (Munich, 1942), pp. 310–78 (first published 1899); Hans Friedrich Karl Günther, *Rassenkunde des deutschen Volkes* (Munich, 1939; first published 1922).

8 Karl Haushofer, *Weltpolitik von heute* (Berlin, 1934).

9 Gerhart Jentsch, *Das Ende des europäischen Gleichgewichts* (Berlin, 1940); Ulrich P. Scheuner, *Das europäische Gleichgewicht und die britische Seeherrschaft* (Hamburg, 1943).

10 See on Nazi foreign policy concepts: Klaus Hildebrand, *Vom Reich zum Weltreich* (Munich, 1969); Hildebrand, *Das vergangene Reich*, 2nd edn (Stuttgart, 1996); Wolfgang Michalka, ed., *Nationalsozialistische Außenpolitik* (Darmstadt, 1978); Michalka, *Ribbentrop und die deutsche Weltpolitik. 1933–1940* (Munich, 1980).

11 Hitler had committed himself in *Mein Kampf* to derogatory statements about Japan and the Japanese, and these statements were understood to give expression to his unwillingness to agree to cooperation between the German and the Japanese armed forces. See on this aspect of German–Japanese relations: Harald Kleinschmidt, *Württemberg und Japan* (Stuttgart, 1991), pp. 41–57.

12 Hiroyuki Katô, *Der Kampf ums Recht des Stärkeren und seine Entwicklung* (Tokyo, Berlin, 1894), pp. 170–97.

13 See Andreas Hillgruber, 'Die "Hitler-Koalition"', *Vom Staat des Ancien Régime zum modernen Parteienstaat*, ed. Helmut Berding (Munich, Vienna, 1978), pp. 467–83; Harald Kleinschmidt, 'Reassessing the German–Japanese Relationship during the 1920s', *Kokusai seijikeizai kenkyû (International Political Economy)* 11 (1998), pp. 1–13; Gerhard Krebs

and Bernd Martin, eds, *Formierung und Fall der Achse Berlin–Tokyo* (Munich, 1994); Masaki Miyake, 'Japan und die nationalsozialistische Machtergreifung', *Die nationalsozialistische Machtergreifung*, ed. Wolfgang Michalka (Paderborn, 1984), pp. 301–12.

14 For Japanese war plans see Sumio Hatano, '"Wilsonianism" in Wartime Japan and Its Legacy', *Why Global Uniformity?*, ed. Harald Kleinschmidt (Tsukuba, 1995), pp. 261–76.

15 Léopold Sédar Senghor, *Liberté*, vol. III, *Négritude et civilisation de l'universal* (Paris, 1977).

16 Frantz Fanon, *Studies in a Dying Colonialism* (London, 1989).

17 André Gunder Frank, *World Accumulation 1492–1789* (New York, 1978); Frank, *Dependent Accumulation and Underdevelopment* (New York, London, 1978); Frank, 'A Theoretical Introduction to 5000 Years of World System History', *Review* (Binghamton), XIII (1990), pp. 155–248.

18 For a recent survey and discussion see André Gunder Frank and Barry K. Gills, eds, *The World System. Five Hundred Years or Five Thousand?* (London, New York, 1993).

19 Immanuel Wallerstein, *Africa. The Politics of Independence* (New York, 1961).

20 Immanuel Wallerstein, *The Modern Capitalist World-System*, 3 vols (New York, 1974–89); Wallerstein, *Geopolitics and Geoculture* (Cambridge, 1991); Wallerstein, *Unthinking Social Science. The Limits of Nineteenth-Century Paradigms* (Cambridge, 1991).

21 Wallerstein, *Unthinking Social Science*, pp. 35–6; first published in A. Bergesen, ed., *Crises in the World-System* (Beverly Hills, 1983).

22 Wallerstein, *Unthinking Social Science*, pp. 229–30; first published in *European Journal of Operational Research* 30 (1987).

23 For the discussion on historical sociology see *Civilizations and World Systems*, ed. Stephen K. Sanderson (Walnut Creek, CA 1995); *Vision and Method in Historical Sociology*, ed. Theda Skocpol (Cambridge, 1984); Dennis Smith, *The Rise of Historical Sociology* (Cambridge, 1991); Charles Tilly, *Big Structures, Large Processes, Huge Comparisons* (New York, 1984).

24 Janet Lippman Abu-Lughod, *Before European Hegemony* (New York, Oxford, 1989); Salvatore Ciriacono, 'The Venetian Economy and the World Economy of the Seventeenth and Eighteenth Centuries', *The Early-Modern World System in Geographical Perspective*, ed. Hans-Jürgen Nitz (Stuttgart, 1993), pp. 120–35; Frank and Gills, *The World System*; Christopher Chase-Dunn, *Global Formation: Structures of the World-Economy* (Oxford, 1989); Chase-Dunn and Thomas D. Hall, *Rise and Demise. Comparing World Systems* (Boulder, Oxford, 1997).

25 George Modelski, 'The Long Cycle of Global Politics and the Nation State', *Comparative Studies in Society and History*, XX (1978), pp. 214, 217; Modelski, 'The Study of Long Cycles', Modelski, ed., *Exploring Long Cycles* (Boulder, London, 1987), pp. 4, 10; Modelski and William R. Thompson, *Sea Power in Global Politics* (Seattle, 1987).

26 For a review of the theory see Harald Kleinschmidt, 'Historical Method and the History of International Relations', *Das andere Wahrnehmen. August Nitschke zum 65. Geburtstag*, ed. Martin Kintzinger, Wolfgang Stürner and Johannes Zahlten (Cologne, Weimar, Vienna, 1991), pp. 653–70.

27 Karen Rasler and William R. Thompson, *War and State Making. The Shaping of the Global Wars* (New York, 1989); Thompson, 'Dehio, Long Cycles and the Geohistorical Context of Structural Transition', *World Politics*, xxv (1992/3), pp. 127–52.

28 Walter LaFeber, *The Clash* (New York, 1997), p. 256.

29 Karl Wolfgang Deutsch, *Political Community and the North Atlantic Area* (Princeton, 1957); Amitai Etzioni, *Political Unification* (Huntington, NY, 1974); Ernest B. Haas, *The Uniting of Europe* (Stanford, 1958; 2nd edn 1968); Joseph Samuel Nye, Jr., *Pan-Africanism and East African Integration* (Cambridge, MA, 1965). For early reviews of neo-functionalist regional integration theory see Charles Pentland, *International Theory and European Integration* (London, 1973); James Patrick Sewell, *Functionalism and World Politics* (Princeton, 1966).

30 For the debate see Béla Balassa, 'Regional Integration and Trade Liberalization in Latin America', *Journal of Common Market Studies*, x (1971/2), pp. 58–77; Ernst B. Haas and Philippe C. Schmitter, 'Economics and Differential Patterns of Political Integration', *International Organization*, xviii (1964), pp. 705–37; Haas, 'The Uniting of Europe and the Uniting of Latin America', *Journal of Common Market Studies*, v (1966/7), pp. 315–43; Leon N. Lindberg, *The Political Dynamics of European Economic Integration* (Stanford, 1963), p. 6; Philippe C. Schmitter, 'Central American Integration. Spill-Over, Spill-Around or Encapsulation', *Journal of Common Market Studies*, ix (1970/71), pp. 1–48; Miguel S. Wionczek, 'The Rise and Decline of Latin American Economic Integration', *Journal of Common Market Studies*, ix (1970/71), pp. 49–66. Realist scepticism about these arguments was vocalized by Joseph S. Nye, 'Patterns and Catalysts in Regional Integration', *International Organization*, xix (1965), pp. 870–9.

31 Leon N. Lindberg and Stuart A. Scheingold, eds, *Regional Integration. Theory and Research* (Cambridge, MA, 1971).

32 See Stefan Collignon, *Regionale Integration und Entwicklung in Ostafrika* (Hamburg, 1990); Victor Hermann Umbricht, *Multilateral Mediation* (Dordrecht, Boston, London, 1988).

33 Ernest B. Haas, *The Obsolescence of Regional Integration Theory* (Berkeley, 1975); Haas, 'Why Collaborate? Issue Linkage and International Regimes', *World Politics* 32 (1979/80), pp. 357-405; Haas, 'Words that Can Hurt You', *International Regimes*, ed. Stephen D. Krasner (Ithaca, London, 1983), pp. 23–43.

34 For the recent debate on neo-functionalism see Darryl Jarvis, 'Integration Theory Revisited. Haas, Neofunctionalism and the Problematics of European Integration', *Policy, Organisation and Society*, vii (1994), pp. 17–33; Andrew Moravcsik, 'Preferences and Power in the European Community', *Journal of Common Market Studies*, xxxi (1993), pp. 473–524; Jeppe Tranholm-Mikkelsen, 'Neofunctionalism, Obstinate or Obsolete', *Millennium*, xx (1991), pp. 1–22. For surveys of recent regional integration theory and processes see: *Regionalism in World Politics*, ed. Louise Fawcett and Andrew Hurrell (Oxford, 1995); *Varieties of Regional Integration*, ed. Mikiko Iwasaki (Münster, Hamburg, 1995).

35 For the debate see David A. Baldwin, ed., *Neorealism and Neoliberalism* (New York, 1993).

36 Robert O. Keohane, *After Hegemony* (Princeton, 1984); Krasner, *International Regimes*; Susan Strange, *The Retreat of the State* (Cambridge, 1996), pp. 3–87. For a realist response to these theories see Joseph M. Grieco, 'Anarchy and the Limits of Cooperation: A Realist Critique of the Newest Liberal Institutionalism', Baldwin, *Neorealism*, pp. 116–40.

37 See on recent developments in international theory: Hayward R. Alker, *Rediscoveries and Refomulations* (Cambridge, 1996), pp. 394–421; Richard K. Ashley and R.B.J. Walker, 'Reading Dissidence/Writing the Discipline. Crisis and the Question of Sovereignty in International Studies', *International Studies Quarterly*, xxxiv (1990), pp. 367–416; Chris Brown, *International Relations Theory* (New York, London, Toronto, etc., 1992); Yale H. Ferguson and Richard W. Mansbach, *Polities. Authority, Identities and Change* (Columbia, SC, 1996); Richard Ned Lebow and Thomas Risse-Kappen, eds, *International Relations Theory and the End of the Cold War* (New York, 1995); Mark Neufeld, *The Restructuring of International Relations Theory* (Cambridge, 1995); *Regime Theory and International Relations*, ed. Volker Rittberger and Peter Mayer (Oxford, 1993; reprint, Oxford, 1997); Pauline Marie Rosenau, *Post-modernism and the Social Sciences* (Princeton, 1992), pp. 121–4, 168; Steve Smith, Ken Booth and Marysia Zalewski, eds, *International Theory. Positivism and Beyond* (Cambridge, 1996); J. Ann Tickner, *Gender in International Relations* (New York, 1992).

38 Richard K. Ashley, 'The Poverty of Neorealism', *International Organization*, xxxviii (1984), pp. 225–88; Ashley, 'Untying the Sovereign State. A Double Reading of the Anarchy Problématique', *Millennium*, xvii (1988), pp. 227–62; Chris Brown, *International Relations Theory: New Normative Approaches* (New York, London, 1992), pp. 195–228; Seyom Brown, *International Relations in a Changing Global System: Toward a Theory of the World Polity* (Boulder, San Francisco, Oxford, 1992), pp. 131–8; Fawcett and Hurrell, *Regionalism*; Friedrich V. Kratochwil, *Rules, Norms and Decisions* (Cambridge, 1989); Nicholas Greenwood Onuf, *World of Our Making. Rules and Rule in Social Theory and International Relations* (Columbia, SC, 1989), pp. 38–9, explicitly following Kant. Alexander E. Wendt, 'Anarchy Is What States Make of It', *International Organization*, xlvi (1992), pp. 391–425; Wendt, 'Constructing International Politics', *International Security*, xx (1995), pp. 71–81; Rüdiger Wolfrum, ed., *Strengthening the World Order. Universalism vs Regionalism* (Berlin, 1990).

39 Paradigmatic: Kenneth Neal Waltz, *Man, the State and War. A Theoretical Analysis* (New York, 1954).

40 For summaries see Robert Carver North, Ole Rudolph Holsti and Nazli Choucri, 'A Reevaluation of the Research Program of the Stanford Studies in International Conflict and Integration', *Quantitative International Politics*, ed. F. W. Hoole and Dina A. Zinnes (New York, 1976), pp. 435–59; Joel David Singer, ed., *The Correlates of War*, 2 vols (New York, London, 1979); Bruce Bueno de Mesquita, *The War Trap* (New Haven, London, 1981).

41 For the debate on neorealism see Ashley, 'The Poverty of Neorealism'; Baldwin, *Neorealism*; Barry Buzan, 'Rethinking System and Structure', Buzan, Charles Jones and Richard Little, *The Logic of Anarchy* (New York, 1993), pp. 22–8; Dale C. Copeland, 'Neorealism and the Myth of Bipolar Stability', *Realism: Restatements and Renewal*, ed. Benjamin Frankel (London, Portland, OR, 1996), pp. 29–89; Fred Halliday and J. Rosenberg, 'Interview with Ken Waltz', *Review of International Studies*, XXIV (1998), pp. 371–86; Wendt, 'Anarchy Is What States Make of It'.

42 Kenneth Neal Waltz, *Theory of International Politics* (Reading, MA, 1979), pp. 161–2.

43 *Ibid.*, p. 163.

44 Kenneth Neal Waltz, 'The Stability of a Bipolar World', *Daedalus*, XCIII (1964), pp. 881–909.

45 On the gap between realist theory-making and the practical conduct of international relations see Richard W. Mansbach and Yale Ferguson, *The Elusive Quest. Theory and International Politics* (Columbia, SC, 1989).

Index